T0332756

Privacy-preserving Computing

Privacy-preserving computing aims to protect the personal information of users while capitalizing on the possibilities unlocked by big data. This practical introduction for students, researchers, and industry practitioners is the first cohesive and systematic presentation of the field's advances over four decades. The book shows how to use privacy-preserving computing in real-world problems in data analytics and AI, and includes applications in statistics, database queries, and machine learning. The book begins by introducing cryptographic techniques such as secret sharing, homomorphic encryption, and oblivious transfer, and then broadens its focus to more widely applicable techniques such as differential privacy, trusted execution environment, and federated learning. The book ends with privacy-preserving computing in practice in areas like finance, online advertising, and healthcare, and finally offers a vision for the future of the field.

KAI CHEN is Professor at the Department of Computer Science and Engineering of the Hong Kong University of Science and Technology, where he leads the Intelligent Networking and Systems (iSING) Lab and the WeChat-HKUST Joint Lab on Artificial Intelligence Technology. His research interests include data center networking, high-performance networking, machine learning systems, and hardware acceleration.

QIANG YANG is Chief AI Officer at Webank and Professor Emeritus at the Department of Computer Science and Engineering of the Hong Kong University of Science and Technology. He is an AAAI, ACM, and IEEE Fellow and Fellow of the Canadian Royal Society. He has authored books such as *Intelligent Planning*, *Crafting Your Research Future*, *Transfer Learning*, and *Federated Learning*. His research interests include artificial intelligence, machine learning and data mining, automated planning, transfer learning, and federated learning.

Privacy-preserving Computing for Big Data Analytics and AI

KAI CHEN

*Hong Kong University of Science and
Technology*

QIANG YANG

*WeBank and Hong Kong University of
Science and Technology*

CAMBRIDGE
UNIVERSITY PRESS

Shaftesbury Road, Cambridge CB2 8EA, United Kingdom

One Liberty Plaza, 20th Floor, New York, NY 10006, USA

477 Williamstown Road, Port Melbourne, VIC 3207, Australia

314–321, 3rd Floor, Plot 3, Splendor Forum, Jasola District Centre, New Delhi – 110025, India

103 Penang Road, #05–06/07, Visioncrest Commercial, Singapore 238467

Cambridge University Press is part of Cambridge University Press & Assessment,
a department of the University of Cambridge.

We share the University's mission to contribute to society through the pursuit of
education, learning and research at the highest international levels of excellence.

www.cambridge.org
Information on this title: www.cambridge.org/9781009299510

DOI: 10.1017/9781009299534

Originally published in Chinese as "Privacy-Preserving Computing" by Publishing House
of Electronics Industry in 2022

© Kai Chen and Qiang Yang 2022

First published in English by Cambridge University Press & Assessment 2024

English translation © Kai Chen and Qiang Yang 2024

This publication is in copyright. Subject to statutory exception and to the provisions
of relevant collective licensing agreements, no reproduction of any part may take
place without the written permission of Cambridge University Press & Assessment.

A catalogue record for this publication is available from the British Library

ISBN   978-1-009-29951-0   Hardback

Cambridge University Press & Assessment has no responsibility for the persistence
or accuracy of URLs for external or third-party internet websites referred to in this
publication and does not guarantee that any content on such websites is, or will
remain, accurate or appropriate.

Contents

Preface

We are in an era of big data where daily user activities generate huge amounts of data that fuel the advances of data-driven technologies, such as artificial intelligence (AI). However, these data inevitably contain private information of users, the disclosure of which would result in severe consequences. Therefore, how to exploit the knowledge contained within large-scale data without compromising user privacy becomes an important but challenging goal. The term *privacy-preserving computing* thus emerges as a summary of the theoretical and technical advances in pursuit of this goal.

Privacy-preserving computing is a field of rich history and fruitful achievements. Over 40 years ago, the theory of secure multiparty computation, which aims to jointly execute computing tasks while concealing partial inputs, marked the advent of privacy-preserving computing. In recent years, privacy-preserving computing remains an active research topic as we witness the technology of federated learning, enabling joint training of machine learning models without disclosing private data. Over the decades, privacy-preserving computing has grown into an inclusive and fruitful field, comprising secret sharing (SS), garbled circuits (GC), oblivious transfer (OT), differential privacy (DP), homomorphic encryption (HE), trusted execution environment (TEE), and federated learning (FL). In addition, with its applications in real-world tasks (such as database queries, data analytics, and machine learning) and scenarios (such as finance and health care), privacy-preserving computing is also a versatile subject that contributes to social well-being.

Despite the success and advances of privacy-preserving computing, we note that a comprehensive book that systematically describes the field is still absent. In fact, existing advances in privacy-preserving computing are still scattered in journal papers, technical talks, blogs, tutorials, and other publications without a unified and comprehensive taxonomy to summarize them. Consequently, the authors believe that the lack of a unified and systematic introduction hampers the development and application of privacy-preserving computing, as illustrated by the following examples:

- We gave a presentation entitled "Privacy-Preserving Computing: Theory and Efficiency" during a seminar organized by the China Computer Federation (CCF), where the audience mainly consisted of interested professors and students from universities in China. The presentation was a great success, and from the many questions received from the audience, we observed that despite their interests in privacy-preserving computing, their understanding of the topic was still vague and fragmented. Specifically, they were rather unclear about the scope, categorization, and detailed techniques in privacy-preserving computing. Thus, a comprehensive introduction that covers a wide range of privacy-preserving computing techniques would be helpful to students and researchers.
- We often met with organizations who were passionate about privacy-preserving computing but were not equipped with sufficient knowledge. A typical example would be the Hong Kong Science and Technology Park (HKSTP). As hundreds of sci-tech companies are located in HKSTP, it has the motivation to create a better environment for innovative startups. However, corporate data generally contains sensitive information about the companies and is thus not easily accessible. Therefore, we extensively discussed with HKSTP the concepts, techniques, and practical issues of federated learning. We believe that the interests in federated learning and other privacy-preserving computing techniques are general, and that a book that covers practical aspects and case studies of privacy-preserving computing would be helpful to industrial practitioners.

Motivated by our observations, we wrote this book on privacy-preserving computing in an attempt to build a unified taxonomy on privacy-preserving computing and also to guide its practical real-world applications. The whole process of writing the book lasted for over a year and involved the efforts of many students from the HKUST Intelligent Systems and Networking (iSING) Lab. We read and summarized many research papers, including some of our own, trying to introduce the fundamental techniques, case studies, and large-scale platforms of privacy-preserving computing in plain and comprehensible language. We finally envisioned the future directions and challenges of privacy-preserving computing.

To summarize, we hope that with this book on privacy-preserving computing we can build a unified and comprehensive taxonomy and overview of the field. Meanwhile, we are also aware that this book is still far from being an encyclopedia, in that it cannot cover every aspect of privacy-preserving computing. Nonetheless, we still hope that our efforts can mark the first step toward this goal and motivate future researchers to make new contributions.

Summary of Contents

The contents of this book can be divided into three parts:

(i) Encrypted computation (Chapters 2–5). This part of the book aims to introduce cryptographic techniques to achieve privacy-preserving computing, including secret sharing (SS), homomorphic encryption (HE), oblivious transfer (OT), and garbled circuits (GC). These cryptographic techniques serve as foundations of many privacy-preserving computing protocols and applications. In each chapter, we cover basic knowledge about the cryptographic technique and some practical examples of applications.

(ii) Privacy-preserving computation (Chapters 6–8). This part of the book aims to introduce noncryptographic techniques to achieve privacy-preserving computing, including differential privacy (DP), trusted execution environment (TEE), and federated learning (FL). These techniques focus on protecting data privacy in a more diverse range of application scenarios.

(iii) Privacy-preserving computing platforms and case studies (Chapters 9–10). This part of the book aims to show how the introduced techniques are successfully applied in practice and on a large scale. Chapter 9 introduces the federated learning platform, FATE, as well as some platforms for encrypted databases. It also covers the efficiency problem in real-world privacy-preserving computing platforms and potential solutions. Chapter 10 introduces some case studies where privacy-preserving computing techniques are applied, including finance, risk management, online advertising, database queries, health care, and public services.

Acknowledgments

First, we would like to express our gratitude toward a group of outstanding Ph.D. students, researchers, and engineers who have dedicated huge amounts of effort to this book, including (in alphabetical order)

- Di Chai, who contributed to the writing of Chapters 2 and 10.
- Tianjian Chen, who contributed to the writing of Chapter 10.
- Xiaodian Cheng, who contributed to the writing of Chapter 9.
- Kun Guo, who contributed to the writing of Chapter 10.
- Shuihai Hu, who contributed to the writing of Chapter 9.
- Yilun Jin, who contributed to the writing of Chapters 3, 4, 5, 6, and 10.
- Zhenghang Ren, who contributed to the writing of Chapters 4, 5, 7, 8, and 10.
- Han Tian, who contributed to the writing of Chapters 3, 6, and 10.
- Liu Yang, who contributed to the writing of Chapters 2 and 10.
- Junxue Zhang, who contributed to the writing of Chapter 7.

During the preparation of this book, we consulted over 200 related books, articles, and research papers. We would also like to thank the authors of these works for their contributions to the field of privacy-preserving computing.

Finally, we would like to thank our families for their understanding and continued support. Without them, the book would not have been possible.

1

Introduction to Privacy-preserving Computing

Massive data and powerful computing resources have become the primary driving force in the development of big data and artificial intelligence. On one hand, mobile phones, social websites, and various sensors collect people's everyday activities continuously. On the other hand, high-performance computing facilities and efficient machine learning algorithms enable the training of complex models. However, improper usage of sensitive information in machine learning and data analysis may lead to catastrophes. For example, the leakage of personal information may expose individuals to fraud crimes. As a result, developing privacy-preserving theories and systems has become extremely necessary. In this chapter, we introduce the fundamental definitions and theories of privacy-preserving computing to help readers understand the basic concepts, technologies, and solutions of privacy-preserving computing.

1.1 Definition and Background

Nowadays, with the pervasive application of computers, a large amount of data is collected and processed by computers, which poses the following challenges to privacy protection:

- **Increased cost for privacy protection.** Massive, sensitive data such as names, ID numbers, and property information is stored in various forms of computer devices and accessed, updated, and transferred frequently. Its sheer scale and complex and volatile application scenarios greatly increase privacy protection costs compared with those of gathering only a small amount of information by statistical agencies in the early days.
- **Increased difficulty in privacy protection.** On one hand, private data can be stored in various locations such as personal mobile devices and data centers. Therefore, privacy protection schemes need to deal with privacy

1

protection issues under different devices or hosting modes. On the other hand, the risk of computer intrusion and sensitive data theft cannot be eliminated due to the prevalence of computing devices and the sophistication of attacking techniques. The diversity and complexity of modern devices increase the difficulty of privacy protection compared with processing with pen and paper manually in the early days.

- **Increased damage caused by privacy leakage.** The pervasion and abuse of sensitive data greatly increase the damage caused by privacy leakage. For example, disclosed ID numbers can be used to commit crimes.

Confronted with these challenges, we should not only rely on legal systems but also integrate mathematical theories and algorithms in privacy protection. Multiple techniques such as cryptography tools need to be used to prevent privacy leakage in the workload of big data analysis and machine learning and they are at the core of privacy-preserving computation.

1.1.1 Definition of Privacy-preserving Computing

Privacy-preserving computing refers to a series of techniques for computing without breaching raw data, which guarantee the available but invisible property of data during their usage. In this book, we focus on a series of techniques for protecting data privacy and enabling computing tasks at the same time, including secret sharing, homomorphic encryption, oblivious transfer, garbled circuit, differential privacy, and federated learning. Privacy-preserving computing incorporates multiple disciplines including cryptography, statistics, computer architecture, and artificial intelligence. The development of its theory and applications is inseparable from cloud computing, big data, and artificial intelligence. At present, privacy-preserving computing is mainly used in data query and analysis as well as machine learning, which have the following characteristics:

- **Data query and analysis**: This type of application usually consists of simple computing tasks such as searching, summing, averaging, and variance calculation, in which the definition and protection of individuals' data privacy is the most important topic.
- **Machine learning**: Machine learning involves the collection of training data and adopts optimization methods to learn models that can extract features and patterns from training data. The model is then used for tasks such as prediction, classification, or behavior guidance. The training and inference usually involve complex computations such as the sigmoid function. During model training, privacy-preserving computing needs to protect the privacy

of the training dataset. During model inference, i.e., predicting new data, privacy-preserving computing needs to protect the privacy of the incoming data.

1.1.2 Taxonomy of Privacy-preserving Computing

The definition of privacy protection varies with the requirement of computing tasks. For machine learning, privacy protection concentrates on both the training and the inference processes. In the training process, the training data and gradients need privacy protection, because training data usually contains sensitive information and gradients are generated from the private data with the training algorithm. During inference, in addition to the privacy of input data, the model parameters also need protection, because the model parameters are trained by private training data and may be exploited to get sensitive information. For databases, the result of queries may contain sensitive information of the data and need protection from random noise. Also, the column name in the queries may need protection to protect the database users' privacy.

Privacy-preserving computing can be classified into encrypted computation with cryptography-based security protocols at its core and privacy-preserving computation with a broader definition. Table 1.1 presents names and definitions of some concepts frequently used in privacy-preserving computing.

Encrypted computation uses cryptography tools to construct privacy-preserving computing applications so that multiple data owners can collaborate on computing tasks while protecting secret data. Secure Multi-Party Computation (MPC) (Goldreich, 1998) is one of the representatives of such tools. Cryptography tools encrypt data as ciphertext, which is indistinguishable from random numbers during communication. As a result, the plaintext cannot be accessed by participants except for the private key owners. Encrypted computation is formally proven to guarantee the cryptography-level security of data privacy. However, it is inefficient in practice due to the high computational or communication complexity of the cryptography tools. Recent works have focused on optimizing the performance of cryptographic tools in various applications such as machine learning (Hardy et al., 2017; Mohassel and Zhang, 2017) and data mining (Boneh et al., 2013; Chen et al., 2020; Evfimievski et al., 2003). With the development of cryptography tools such as secret sharing (De Santis et al., 1994), oblivious transfer (Rabin, 2005), garbled circuit (Yao, 1986), and homomorphic encryption (Gentry, 2009), encrypted computation still has a wide range of applications.

Table 1.1 *Names and definitions in privacy-preserving computing.*

Name	Definition
Privacy Computing	Encrypted computation based on cryptography tools in a narrow sense. In a broad sense, it refers to all techniques used for protecting data privacy while achieving computational goals.
Privacy-Preserving Computation	Secures data acquisition and management before computing, data privacy protection in computing, and data privacy protection and interest allocation after computing. Some privacy-preserving computing techniques use encryption and can be regarded as part of privacy computing.
Secure Multi-Party Computing	Uses cryptography tools to construct privacy computing protocols at the security protocol layer so that multiple data owners can collaborate on computing a specific function without disclosing any other private information.
Secret Sharing	A tool dividing private data into multiple partitions for distribution and computation.
Homomorphic Encryption	A cryptographic scheme allowing cipher computing. After encrypting raw messages, only private key owners can decrypt the ciphertext to obtain results. It is a common tool in encrypted computation.
Oblivious Transfer	A commonly used data transmission model considering privacy protection. It ensures that, at the time of transferring private data from a sender to a receiver, the sender does not know the choice of the receiver and the receiver does not know other private data transferred by the sender either.
Garbled Circuit	Protects plaintext electronic signals by encrypting the input and output signals of logic gates. It is one of the most widely used privacy encryption techniques.
Differential Privacy	A flexible and effective privacy protection technique. It differs from cryptography-based schemes in that it does not encrypt data but protects privacy by adding random noise.
Trusted Execution Environment	A scheme providing privacy computing at a hardware level. It gives users a running environment that separates programs from data so that they cannot be stolen or tampered with by potential intruders.
Federated Learning	A privacy-preserving scheme proposed in the field of machine learning. The information required for model training is transferred between participants while the raw data is not. Federated learning can utilize privacy protection techniques such as homomorphic encryption to provide strict protection to the transferred information.

In encrypted computation, given input data from each participant $X_1, X_2, \ldots$ and computing task $Y = f(X_1, X_2, \ldots)$, all participants collaborate on private computing with various cryptography tools. Encrypted computation guarantees that no information other than the final output Y is disclosed in computing, ensuring that each participant's private data is kept secret. Note that cryptographic tools do not offer privacy protection in multiple independent tasks. Taking the millionaire problem as an example, suppose two millionaires are comparing their properties using encrypted computation so that they do not know how much the other's property is worth. Nonetheless, the intermediate results produced in multiple rounds of comparison can be combined to deduce each millionaire's property with high precision. Furthermore, in machine learning, when multiple data owners collaborate on the training of machine learning models, although the whole training process is encrypted by cryptography tools, a participant can still gather the gradients of the training data transmitted by other participants by analyzing the parameter updating process of its local model. Subsequently, some private information may be inferred from these gradients.

Privacy-preserving computation. Some works adopt noncryptographic tools or compromise on encryption for better performance. In this book, such new privacy-preserving computing techniques are called privacy-preserving computation to distinguish them from the traditional encrypted computation techniques based purely on cryptography tools.

Each participant's privacy leakage after a computing task is finished is closely related to the task's property. The subject of privacy-preserving computation is to study the possibility and degree of each participant's privacy leakage in the entire computing process and to measure and protect data privacy from the perspective of the whole task, which is also a focus of the research in this field.

Privacy-preserving computing techniques can be divided into multiple categories. These include Secure Multi-Party Computation (MPC) (Goldreich, 1998), Homomorphic Encryption (HE) (Gentry, 2009), Differential Privacy (DP) (Dwork, 2008), Trusted Execution Environment (TEE) (Pinto and Santos, 2019), and Federated Learning (FL) (Yang et al., 2019c), based on the development tracks, algorithm basis, and application characteristics of the techniques.

This book provides a comprehensive and in-depth overview and analysis of the aforementioned technologies for encrypted and privacy-preserving computation, allowing readers to gain a complete understanding of privacy-preserving computing. The book focuses on introducing the principles and implementations of technical approaches for privacy protection. Untechnical methods such as supervising companies or organizations by legislation and institutions are not covered in the book.

1.1.3 History of Privacy-preserving Computing

The development of privacy-preserving computing dates back to the time before the invention of computers. Some statistical agencies often used questionnaires to study social phenomena. To protect respondents' privacy on data such as names, ages, and replies, they usually promised that the collected information would only be used for research purposes and would be strictly supervised. At that time, the protection of the respondents' privacy relied mainly on institutions and public regulations. Additionally, in the early days, cryptography played an important role in certain key fields such as military intelligence (Singh, 1999). These small-scale cases of using simple cryptography tools can be seen as early examples of privacy-preserving computing.

The development of modern privacy-preserving computing can be divided into four stages. In each stage, new computing schemes are proposed from different perspectives to solve the omissions and defections in the previous stage. These schemes provide many different views and ideas to solve privacy-preserving computing problems so as to enrich the selections of techniques in different application scenarios. Figure 1.1 presents several critical moments and the corresponding functional features.

The first stage is the development of theories and applications of Secure Multi-Party Computation (MPC) (Goldreich, 1998). Multi-Party Computation is a type of encrypted computation that uses cryptography tools to construct a secure computational model under which multiple participants can collaborate on a computing task using their own data without the fear of leaking data to others. The proposal of Shamir Secret Sharing (Shamir, 1979) heralded the birth of MPC. Following that, a system with secret sharing (Yao, 1982) and garbled circuit (Yao, 1986) as its fundamental protocols was built to implement privacy protection through generating and exchanging random numbers and ensure the validity of computational results via predefined computing protocols. The idea of MPC is well-suited for precise computing and database queries, the security of which is provable. Some privacy-preserving legislation such as GDPR (Europe, 2019) requires that the data shall be kept locally, and MPC satisfies the requirement of not publishing local data. However, its main disadvantage is the enormous performance disparity with unencrypted computing. In the worst case, MPC runs 10^6 times slower than unencrypted

	Stage 1: Secure Multi-Party Computing (MPC)	Stage 2: Differential Privacy (DP)	Stage 3: Centralized Encrypted Computing	Stage 4: Federated Learning (FL)
Technical Design	Exchange data in ciphertext to protect privacy in precise computing and database queries	Obfuscate individuals to protect privacy in database queries and model publishing	Centralize data computing to improve performance and encrypt data or programs to prevent breaches	Designed for machine learning involving multiple participants and satisfying the requirements of heterogeneous data's training, inducing, security, and incentives
Development History	**1979** Secret Sharing Shamir & Blakley **1982** MPC Andrew Chi-Chih Yao **1986** Garbled Circuit Andrew Chi-Chih Yao	**2006** DP Dwork	**2006** TEE/TrustZone ARM **2009** FHE Gentry **2013** TEE/SGX Intel	**2016** Horizontal FL Google McMahan **2018** Vertical FL Federated Transfer Learning QiangYang
Compliance	Does not publish local data Compliant with privacy legislation	Publishes local data Partially compliant with privacy legislation	Publishes local data Conflict with most privacy laws	Does not publish local data Compliant with privacy legislation
Hardware Dependence	No specific dependence	No specific dependence	SGX depends on Intel's CPU TrustZone depends on ARM's CPU	No specific dependence
Computing Performance	10^6 times slower than plaintext computing	Nearly the same as plaintext computing	TEE is nearly the same as plaintext computing FHE is 10^6 times slower than plaintext computing	Depends on implementation techniques
Communication Overhead	Extra overhead for transmitting encrypted information	No extra overhead	Extra overhead for data centralizing	Extra overhead for transmitting intermediate results
Computing Mode	Distributed	Distributed querying, local computing	Centralized	Distributed

Figure 1.1 History of privacy-preserving computing (along the time dimension).

computing. The exact cost varies with different computing tasks and network environments. The bottleneck is the communication overhead.

The second stage is the theories and applications of differential privacy (DP). Differential privacy has long been applied to customer surveys. It differs from MPC in that it perturbs user data by adding random noise to the process or results of a computing task. Differential privacy is based on the obfuscation of data distribution (Dwork, 2008) and evaluates its privacy protection capability at a more flexible level than the cryptography-based techniques relying on the difficulty of solving NP-hard problems. From a legal compliance standpoint, DP satisfies certain privacy protection laws. Meanwhile, it runs at nearly the same speed as computing in plaintext, which is significantly faster than cryptography-based schemes because it does not encrypt data or require extra intensive communications. As a result, DP is initially applied to various artificial intelligence applications, such as Google Keyboard (Google, 2020) and Apple Siri (Apple, Differential Privacy Team, 2017; Ding et al., 2017), to protect end users' privacy.

The third stage is centralized encrypted computation such as trusted execution environment (TEE) and fully homomorphic encryption (FHE). Unlike the previous stages, this stage aims to find a manner to publish data securely. One technical route is TEE, which builds an isolated running environment where users can upload their data without worrying about it being stolen by other programs or computer devices. The implementation of TEE depends on specific hardware produced by different manufacturers, such as Intel SGX (Costan and Devadas, 2016) and ARM TruestZone (Pinto and Santos, 2019). Therefore, its security is not 100 percent guaranteed. However, it runs nearly as fast as plaintext computing,[1] making it more practical than homomorphic encryption. As for FHE, the earliest development of HE can be traced back to the privacy-preserving computing scheme proposed by Rivest. The first version of FHE was not published until 2009 (Gentry, 2009). Homomorphic encryption enables us to perform effective computations directly on ciphertext without decrypting it. However, the effectiveness needs to be paid for by increasing the communication time for ciphertext transmission. Additionally, homomorphic encryption consumes a significant amount of computational time, typically six orders of magnitude more than plaintext computing. Both TEE and FHE provide mechanisms for secure data publishing. However, they may conflict with privacy protection laws that prohibit publishing local data (Europe, 2019).

---

[1] Performing computation without encryption, in contrast to computing on ciphertext with homomorphic encryption.

The fourth stage is federated learning designed for machine learning model training and inference tasks. In contrast to conventional technical roadmaps, federated learning allows data owners to store their data locally and exchange only the protected parameters to accomplish a training process. Therefore, private local data is not exposed in the framework of federated learning. Moreover, the exchange of model parameters does not expose raw data and model contents. Additionally, federated learning protects the privacy of model inference. It focuses on the design of data heterogeneity and security mechanism for distributed machine learning and its performance optimization to avoid performance issues like those encountered in MPC. Federated learning can be implemented based on many privacy-preserving computing techniques such as MPC, DP, TEE, and FHE. Meanwhile, it needs to consider the characteristics of specific modeling and prediction tasks when developing methods for parameter protection. The security of federated learning is usually analyzed jointly with specific machine learning tasks. Compared to the third stage, federated learning guarantees that the local data is kept locally and will not be shared in any form. When regarded as a training paradigm, federated learning can be divided into horizontal and vertical federated learning (Yang et al., 2019c). Compared with the traditional centralized machine learning paradigm, the cost of federated learning comes primarily from cipher computation and the additional communications for transferring intermediate results.

Today, with the deepening of communication and cooperation between multiple research fields, a growing number of startups and large companies enter the privacy-preserving computing industry and release products such as WeBank's FATE and OpenMinded's Syft. Privacy-preserving computing is applied in a wide variety of fields including database query (Microsoft, 2016), vote counting (Xia et al., 2008), and machine learning (Google, 2020).

1.2 Main Technologies of Privacy-preserving Computing

This book introduces the mainstream privacy-preserving computing technologies in the following chapters. Chapters 2–5 introduce common cryptography tools in privacy-preserving computing, including secret sharing, homomorphic encryption, oblivious transfer, and garbled circuit. Differential privacy, trusted execution environment, and federated learning, which are the core techniques of privacy-preserving computation, are discussed in Chapters 6–8. Figure 1.2 illustrates the relationships between the techniques. Federated learning can realize more flexible privacy protection by integrating more privacy protection techniques, such as DP and TEE, than those based on traditional encrypted computation.

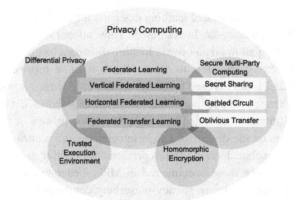

Figure 1.2 Technical framework of privacy-preserving computing.

Chapter 2: Secret Sharing. Secret sharing is an important implementation of encrypted computation, which allows a participant to split private data randomly into multiple parts and send them to other participants. The raw data can be revealed only when a certain number of participants reach an agreement.

Chapter 3: Homomorphic Encryption. Homomorphic Encryption (HE) is an encryption method that supports computing on the ciphertext. Unlike non-homomorphic encryption methods, it allows users to encrypt private data and send ciphertext to an untrusted computer and perform computation on the ciphertext. In the view of an adversary, the input data of programs using HE contains no private information. Privacy will never be disclosed provided that the private keys of HE are not leaked.

Chapter 4: Oblivious Transfer. Oblivious Transfer (OT) defines a privacy-preserving data transmission model that divides participants into a sender and a receiver. The sender possesses private data and the receiver selects messages from the received data. They agree on sending a piece of the sender's private data to the receiver on the assumption that the sender is unaware of the receiver's choice and the receiver does not know the sender's other private data either. Oblivious transfer has been widely applied to solving simple privacy-preserving computing problems and developing complex privacy-preserving computing protocols.

Chapter 5: Garbled Circuit. Garbled Circuit (GC) is one of the most adaptable privacy-preserving computing protocols, since it applies to all computing tasks that circuits can express. GC protects plaintext signals in circuits by encrypting the input and output signals of logic gates. A GC protocol classifies participants into a generator and an operator, who are responsible for garbling circuits and computing on the garbled circuits, respectively. GC is used very widely because circuits can represent most computing tasks.

Chapter 6: Differential Privacy. Differential Privacy (DP) is a flexible and efficient privacy protection scheme. Unlike cryptography-based schemes, DP protects data privacy by adding random noise to data instead of encrypting it. From the perspective of a potential attacker, DP restricts their capability to steal information by reducing the probability of their obtaining true data to a certain degree.

Chapter 7: Trusted Execution Environment. Trusted execution environment (TEE) is a scheme providing privacy-preserving computing at the hardware level. It constructs privacy-preserving computing solutions from the perspective of system architecture. By protecting user programs at the hardware level and employing cryptography tools, TEE provides an environment that separates programs from data, thus preventing them from being stolen or tampered with by potential attackers such as other programs or even system administrators.

Chapter 8: Federated Learning. Federated learning (FL) is a privacy-preserving computing scheme proposed in the field of machine learning. The information required for training models is transferred between participants, not including their local data. Furthermore, FL adopts specific privacy-preserving techniques such as HE to protect the information exchanged between participants to provide high privacy. When model training is accomplished, trained models will be deployed to each participant for subsequent tasks.

1.3 Privacy-preserving Computing Platforms and Cases

In order to promote the commercialization of privacy-preserving computing technology, it is necessary to build privacy-preserving computing platforms based on practical application requirements to facilitate the development and operation of privacy-preserving computing applications.

Chapter 9: Privacy-preserving Computing Platforms. These platforms, including FATE, CryptDB, and Conclave, combine the techniques introduced in Chapters 2–8 to provide privacy protection and interfaces to facilitate application development for different tasks such as machine learning, database query, and web searching.

Chapter 10: Case Studies of Privacy-preserving Computing Cases. These cases deal with applications of privacy-preserving computing in financial marking, risk management, advertisement, data querying, medical treatment, voice recognition, government affairs, and data statistics. From the cases introduced in this chapter, we can see that privacy-preserving computing is not only the traditional style of computing task integrated with privacy protection but also an important precondition for the wide application of new technology.

1.4 Challenges and Opportunities in Privacy-preserving Computing

Chapter 11: Future of Privacy-preserving Computing. In this chapter we discuss the significance of data rights confirmation and the future development of privacy-preserving computing, especially with heterogeneous architecture.

At present, numerous privacy-preserving computing schemes based on techniques such as cryptography exist. But privacy-preserving computing still faces challenges such as security compliance, inferior performance, and the lack of unified standards.

First, no existing privacy-preserving computing schemes guarantee unconditional security. Even schemes that employ cryptography are developed based on the difficulty of NP-hard problems, which may be broken with increase of computational power in the future. Furthermore, while different security protocols provide different levels of protection, their improper use may lead to privacy breaches. For example, if simple hash functions are employed to protect binary-valued data, an attacker can easily infer the data's binary property from the ciphertext.

Second, privacy-preserving computing techniques inevitably cause extra computation costs. For example, the computation cost of ciphertext computing in HE is several orders of magnitude greater than that of plaintext computing, and so is its extra communication overhead. Taking into account that modern computing applications usually involve massive data processing, the computing performance and communication efficiency of privacy-preserving computing still face huge challenges even though computational resources are abundant today.

Finally, there are still barriers to the interconnection between different enterprises' privacy-preserving computing platforms. The APIs and algorithms are not unified. These impediments hinder data interconnection between different privacy-preserving computing platforms and bring in an extra cost for developing additional middleware.

2

Secret Sharing

This chapter introduces the technique of secret sharing. First, starting from the very first problem of secret sharing, we give the definition of secret sharing and describe the development of secret sharing methods and schemes. Then, we introduce the applications of secret sharing in privacy-preserving computing scenarios such as federated learning and analyze the advantages and disadvantages of secret sharing techniques.

Let us start with a story. Once upon a time, there was a rich man. With his good business acumen and continuous efforts, he accumulated countless gold and silver treasures. In his old age, the rich man wanted to find the smartest one of his three sons to inherit his wealth. Because the rich man liked studying math in his spare time, he asked his sons a question, "If one of you inherits my estate, how would you protect the wealth as well as make the other two brothers participate in the management? I hope you can get along with each other. Each of you will provide a plan for me. The one who offers the most reasonable plan will have the right to manage my wealth." The eldest son, a reckless man, blurted out without even thinking, "Father, this is a simple question. We only need to find a vault to lock up all your wealth, and I will keep the key." The rich man listened with his brow wrinkling. The second son snickered and said, "Brother, I am not saying that we do not trust you. But according to our father's requirements, this is not a reasonable plan. I think it is better to divide the key into three parts, one for each of us. Only when we all agree to open the lock and restore the original key can we take the treasure out." The rich man nodded approvingly. The smartest and youngest son added, "This is not good enough. If we urgently need the money but one of us happens to be absent, then the other two will not be able to open the lock. I will design a new lock and make three keys, one for each of us, so that none of us can open the lock with his own key alone, but if two of us are present at the same time, they can take out the treasure." The rich man laughed, looked at his youngest son, and said, "Good idea! My wealth will be managed by the method you propose."

This example reflects the idea of secret sharing. In cryptography-related fields such as secure communications, one core problem is the safekeeping of keys. Key management will directly affect the security of the system. Generally speaking, the most secure way to manage keys is to store them in a high-security place such as a computer, a person's memory, or a safe deposit box. In practice, however, computer failure, the sudden death of the person, or damage to the safe box often renders this method ineffective. A more effective remedy is to repeatedly back up keys while keeping them in different places. However, this still does not essentially solve this type of problem, whereas using secret sharing techniques can solve the problem completely.

The purpose of what is called a secret sharing system is to provide the secrets that need to be kept to all members of a participant set and to maintain each secret separately. The shared secret can be recovered only when all members of an authorized subset of the set have demonstrated their secret sharing, and no information about the secret is available to any unauthorized subset member. Secret sharing schemes are important tools in cryptography and have been used as a framework for the construction of many security protocols, such as generic multiparty computation protocols, Byzantine protocols, threshold cryptography, access control, attribute-based encryption, and oblivious transfer. Secret sharing is also widely used in real-life activities, such as setting up banks or confidential government warehouses and missile launches. It would be extremely dangerous if important information is kept by only one person. The information could be easily damaged, tampered with, or lost. Therefore, multiple people should be independently responsible for keeping it.

2.1 Problem and Definition

Secret sharing is a technique in cryptography for splitting and storing secrets to spread the risk of disclosure and tolerating intrusions to a certain extent. In the following two subsections, we present the problem of secret sharing and its definition separately. Now, we return to the example given at the beginning of this chapter, in which a rich man asked his three sons to give a method for managing access to his treasure. We will explain how to design a perfect key distribution scheme step by step.

2.1.1 Secret Sharing Problem

The three sons explained to the rich man the plan they had designed for managing access to the wealth. In fact, they were discussing the allocation of treasury keys. The rich man wants a fair plan, which should also be capable of emergence. At this point, how should the keys of the treasury be kept?

Option 1: Giving only one person the key to the treasury for safekeeping.
The eldest son took over this custodial task. He leaned on his seniority and forced the other two brothers to accept his offer. In this case, we use the number S to represent the key to the treasury. The eldest son, who keeps the key, has the number S_1,

$$S = S_1. \tag{2.1}$$

The next day, the second son and the youngest son found the treasury empty. The reason was that their eldest brother did not want to share the wealth with them, so he took the treasure and left the country.

It seems that the first plan is the simplest but has a serious disadvantage. If the only person who keeps the key were to defect (for example, the eldest son is rapacious and wants to take the treasure only for himself), the treasure in the treasury would no longer be safe.

Option 2: Giving the key to everyone for safekeeping, and only when all three sons are present can the treasury be opened.
It is very insecure to give the key to only one person for safekeeping. It would be better to distribute keys to three people, which would require all of them to be present to open the treasury. Therefore, the second son's proposal was accepted. The one key was divided into three, and each of the three sons got a key. In this way, none can open the treasury by himself. The number S is needed to open the treasury, and the people who keep the keys have the numbers $S_1, S_2, S_3, \ldots$, respectively, and so

$$S = S_1 + S_2 + S_3 + \cdots . \tag{2.2}$$

The next day, a sudden emergency happened at home, causing an urgent need for money. The rich man's eldest and youngest sons could not find the middle son, who had gone on a trip. They were so upset because, without the key kept by the second son, the treasury could not be opened.

After analysis, the second plan also has certain problems. The people keeping the keys must all be present in order to open the lock. If any person loses the key or is not present, the others will not be able to open the treasury to take out the treasure. Therefore, the second plan is also not a perfect solution.

Option 3: Giving the key to everyone for safekeeping, and only a subset of keepers can open the treasury if they arrive.
In the end, the rich man accepted the scheme proposed by the youngest son. A new lock was designed together with a total of three keys, one for each of the three sons. Any two of them are able to open the treasury. Therefore, even if one of them loses the key or happens to be not at home, the remaining two sons can open the treasury. Besides, none of them can open the treasury on their own.

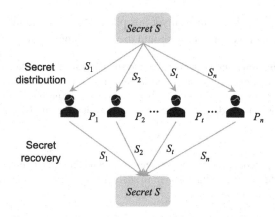

Figure 2.1 Illustration of secret sharing.

As shown in Figure 2.1, the core idea of the plan is to split a secret S into n parts $S_1, S_2, \ldots, S_t, \ldots, S_n$, which are then distributed to different participants $P_1, P_2, \ldots, P_t, \ldots, P_n$. Only when more than t participants cooperate can the secret be recovered. On the one hand, a single participant cannot recover the secret by himself; on the other hand, the secret can be recovered without the cooperation of all participants.

Based on the preceding properties, secret sharing is mostly used for important tasks such as missile launches and check signing. In recent years, with the development of privacy-preserving computing techniques such as federated learning, secret sharing has also been applied in scenarios such as secure aggregation of gradients across participants. ⸱

2.1.2 Definition of Secret Sharing

In this subsection we define secret sharing. Drawing upon different sources (Beimel, 2011; Beimel and Chor, 1994; Bellare and Rogaway, 2007; Blundo et al., 1997; Capocelli et al., 1993; Karnin et al., 1983), we provide two definitions and prove that they are equivalent.

Definition 2.1 Access Structure: Define $\{p_1, \ldots, p_n\}$ as the set of participants and $\mathcal{A} \subseteq 2^{\{p_1, \cdots, p_n\}}$ as a collection of sets of participants. A collection of sets $\mathcal{A}$ is monotone if $B \in \mathcal{A}$ and $B \subseteq C$ imply the set $C \in \mathcal{A}$. An access structure is a monotone collection $\mathcal{A}$ of nonempty subsets of $\{p_1, \ldots, p_n\}$. The sets inside the access structure $\mathcal{A}$ are authorized sets, and the sets outside the access structure $\mathcal{A}$ are unauthorized sets.

A distribution scheme $\Sigma = \langle \Pi, \mu \rangle$ with domain of secret K is determined by Π and μ. Here μ is a probability distribution on some finite set R called the set of random strings, and Π is a mapping from $K \times R$ to a set of n-tuples $K_1 \times K_2 \times \cdots \times K_n$, where K_j is called the domain of the secret shares of p_j. A secret distributor shares the secret $k \in K$ to each participant according to Π. First, the secret distributor samples a random string $r \in R$ according to μ; next, the secret distributor computes the secret share vector $\Pi(k, r) = (s_1, \ldots, s_n)$; finally, the secret distributor securely sends each secret share s_j to the corresponding participant p_j.

In some references (Beimel and Chor, 1994; Bellare and Rogaway, 2007; Blundo et al., 1997), secret sharing is defined in the following way.

Definition 2.2 Secret Sharing: Define K as the finite set of secrets, $|K| \geq 2$. A distribution scheme $\langle \Pi, \mu \rangle$ with domain of secrets K is a secret sharing scheme that implements the access structure $\mathcal{A}$ if the following two requirements hold:

Correctness: The secret k can be recovered by any authorized set of participants. That is, for any set $B = \{p_{i_1}, \ldots, p_{i_{|B|}}\} \in \mathcal{A}$, there exists a reconstruction function $\mathrm{RECON}_B \colon K_{i_1} \times \cdots \times K_{i_{|B|}} \to K$, such that, for each $k \in K$,

$$\Pr[\mathrm{RECON}(\Pi(k, r)_B) = k] = 1. \tag{2.3}$$

Privacy: Each unauthorized set of participants cannot recover any information about the secrets from their secret-shared shares. For any set $T \notin \mathcal{A}$, any two secrets $a, b \in K$, and any vector of possible secret shares $\langle s_j \rangle_{p_j \in T}$:

$$\Pr[\Pi(a, r)_T = \langle s_j \rangle_{p_j \in T}] = \Pr[\Pi(b, r)_T = \langle s_j \rangle_{p_j \in T}]. \tag{2.4}$$

Remark 2.3 The preceding definition requires 100 percent correctness and perfect privacy protection: for any two secrets a, b, the distribution schemes $\Pi(a, r)_T$ and $\Pi(b, r)_T$ are the same. We can relax these two requirements by only requiring that correctness holds with high probability or that the statistical distance between $\Pi(a, r)_T$ and $\Pi(b, r)_T$ is small. A secret sharing scheme that meets these two broad requirements is called a statistical secret sharing scheme.

Next, we give a definition of secret sharing given elsewhere in the literature (Capocelli et al., 1993; Karnin et al., 1983), which uses the entropy function.

Definition 2.4 Secret Sharing (alternative): A distribution scheme is a secret sharing scheme realizing an access structure $\mathcal{A}$ with respect to a given probability distribution on the secrets S, if the following conditions hold:

Correctness: For each authorized set $B \in \mathcal{A}$,

$$H(S|S_B) = 0. \tag{2.5}$$

Privacy: For each unauthorized set $T \notin \mathcal{A}$,

$$H(S|S_T) = H(S). \tag{2.6}$$

Definition 2.2 and Definition 2.4 are equivalent, and the proof will be given in Theorem 2.5. The advantage of Definition 2.2 is that it is not necessary to assume a probability distribution of the secret. This distribution is already known. Besides, Definition 2.2 can be generalized to statistical secret sharing and computational secret sharing. On the other hand, it is more convenient for Definition 2.4 to prove lower bounds. Therefore, the equivalence of the two definitions allows us to choose the more appropriate one for a particular task.

In addition, the equivalence of the preceding two definitions of secret sharing proves a result of Blundo et al. (1998) that the privacy of a scheme based on Definition 2.4 is actually distribution independent: if a scheme realizes an access structure with respect to one distribution of the secrets, then under the same conditions, the scheme can realize the access structure with respect to any distribution.

Theorem 2.5 *For a distribution scheme Σ, the following claims are equivalent:*

(1) According to Definition 2.2, the distribution scheme Σ is secure.
(2) There exists some distribution on the secrets with support K, i.e., $\Pr[S = a] > 0$ for any $a \in K$, such that the distribution scheme is secure according to Definition 2.4.
(3) For any distribution on the secrets whose support is contained in K, the distribution scheme is secure according to Definition 2.4.

Proof We first prove that Theorem 2.5(1) can be derived from Theorem 2.5(3), in which case Theorem 2.5(1) can also be derived from Theorem 2.5(2). In the following proof, $\Sigma = \langle \Pi, \mu \rangle$ denotes a secret sharing scheme whose security is provided by Definition 2.2; S denotes a random variable based on some distribution over K. Therefore, for any set $T \notin \mathcal{A}$, any secret $a \in K$, and any shares $\langle s_j \rangle_{p_j \in T}$ for the participants in T:

$$\begin{aligned}
\Pr[S_T = \langle s_j \rangle_{p_j \in T} | S = a] &= \Pr[\Pi(a, r)_T = \langle s_j \rangle_{p_j \in T}] \\
&= \sum_{b \in K} \Pr[S = b] \cdot \Pr[\Pi(b, r)_T = \langle s_j \rangle_{p_j \in T}] \\
&= \sum_{b \in K} \Pr[S = b] \cdot \Pr[S_T = \langle s_j \rangle_{p_j \in T} | S = b] \\
&= \Pr[S_T = \langle s_j \rangle_{p_j \in T}],
\end{aligned} \tag{2.7}$$

where S_T and S are independent random variables, and by the properties of the entropy function, $H(S|S_T) = H(S)$. Thus, this scheme is secure according to Definition 2.4 with respect to the distribution on S.

For some fixed distribution on the secrets with support K, assume $\Sigma = \langle \Pi, \mu \rangle$ is a secret-sharing scheme that is secure according to Definition 2.4, that is, assume Theorem 2.5(2) holds. Then, for any set $T \notin \mathcal{A}$, the random variables S_T and S are independent, in particular, for any two secrets $a, b \in K$ and any secret shares $\langle s_j \rangle_{p_j \in T}$,

$$
\begin{aligned}
\Pr_r[\Pi(a, r)_T = \langle s_j \rangle_{p_j \in T}] &= \Pr_{r,k}[\Pi(k, r)_T = \langle s_j \rangle_{p_j \in T}] \\
&= \Pr_r[\Pi(b, r)_T = \langle s_j \rangle_{p_j \in T}].
\end{aligned}
\tag{2.8}
$$

The first and third probabilities are for fixed secrets, both of which are taken over the randomness of Π. The second probability is taken over the randomness of both Π and the secret k chosen according to the fixed distribution. Therefore, by Definition 2.2, the secret sharing scheme is secure. $\square$

2.2 Principle and Implementations

The concept of secret sharing was first introduced by the famous cryptographers Adi Shamir and George Blakley. Shamir's scheme was implemented based on polynomial interpolation, while Blakley's scheme was built using the properties of multidimensional spatial points.

2.2.1 Development of Secret Sharing

There are many algorithms to achieve secret sharing, including the classical Shamir's threshold secret sharing scheme and the secret sharing scheme based on the Chinese remainder theorem. Secret sharing schemes can be roughly classified into ten categories (Yu and Li, 2014): threshold scheme, scheme on general access structure, multispan scheme, multisecret scheme, verifiable scheme, dynamic scheme, quantum scheme, visual scheme, scheme based on multiresolution filtering, and scheme based on generalized self-shrinking sequences. These ten kinds of secret sharing schemes are described separately in the following discussion.

Threshold Scheme

In the (t, n)-threshold secret sharing scheme design, the authorized subset is defined as any set containing at least t participants, while the unauthorized subset is the set containing $t - 1$ or fewer participants. In addition to Shamir's and Blakley's secret sharing scheme, the Asmuth–Bloom method based on the Chinese remainder theorem and the Karnin–Greene–Hellman method using matrix multiplication are also methods to achieve (t, n) threshold secret sharing.

Scheme on General Access Structure

The threshold secret sharing scheme implements a threshold access structure, which has restrictions on other more general access structures, such as sharing a secret among four parties A, B, C, and D so that only parties A and D or parties B and C can recover the secret. Threshold secret sharing schemes are not suitable for this situation. To deal with such problems, cryptography researchers proposed a secret sharing scheme for general access structures in 1987 (ITO, 1987). In 1988, a simpler and more effective method, the monotonic circuit construction method, was proposed and it was shown that any access structure could be implemented using this method (Benaloh and Leichter, 1988). Later, more experts started to study the problem of general access structures.

Multispan Scheme

In the multispan secret sharing scheme, each participant's subsecret can be used for sharing multiple secrets, but only one secret can be shared in a single secret sharing process. After the concept was proposed, many multispan secret sharing schemes have been designed. For example, in the l-span generalized secret sharing scheme proposed by Harn and Lin (1992) on access structure, each participant's subsecret can be reused one time to recover one secret separately. In addition, there is also a threshold multispan secret sharing scheme based on the RSA public key system proposed by XU and XIAO (2004), and the threshold multispan secret sharing scheme based on geometric properties proposed by Pang and Wang (2005).

Multisecret Scheme

The multisecret sharing scheme also solves the problem of reusing participants' subsecrets; however, multiple secrets can be shared in a secret sharing process. In 2000, Chien et al. (2000) proposed a new threshold multisecret sharing scheme based on the systematic block codes. In one sharing process, multiple secrets can be shared and subsecrets can be reused, which has important application values. Later, Yang et al. (2004) also proposed a threshold multisecret sharing scheme. The scheme proposed by Pang et al. (2005) retains the advantages of the previous two schemes. In fact, many results of the theory of single-secret sharing schemes have been extended accordingly in multisecret sharing schemes.

Verifiable Scheme

Parties involved in secret sharing can verify the correctness of their own sub-secrets by using public variables, thus effectively preventing the problem of mutual deception between distributors and participants, as well as between participants. Verifiable secret sharing schemes are classified as interactive and noninteractive ones. An interactive verifiable secret sharing scheme means that participants need to exchange information with each other when verifying the correctness of secret sharing; a noninteractive verifiable secret sharing scheme means that participants need not exchange information. Noninteractive verifiable secret sharing schemes can reduce the cost of network communication and the probability of secret leakage, therefore its application area is more extensive.

Dynamic Scheme

The dynamic secret sharing scheme, which has good security and flexibility, was proposed by Laih et al. (1989). It allows adding or removing participants, updating participants' subsecrets periodically or irregularly, and restoring different secrets at different times. The previous five schemes are some classic secret sharing schemes. It should be noted that a specific secret sharing scheme is often a combination of several types.

Quantum Scheme

Hillery et al. first proposed the concept of a quantum secret sharing scheme based on the three-particle entangled state (1999). There are three important quantum secret sharing schemes: the classic secret sharing scheme HBB based on the entangled states (Hillery et al., 1999), the classic secret sharing scheme based on the nonentangled states (Guo and Guo, 2003), and the scheme based on the quantum state (Hillery et al., 1999).

Visual Scheme

At the EUROCRYPT conference in 1994, Naor and Shamir (1994) presented a visual secret sharing scheme. Three years later, Naor and Pinkas (1997) introduced the related applications of visual secret sharing.

Scheme Based on Multiresolution Filtering

In 1994, Santis et al. proposed the concept of the secret sharing scheme based on multiresolution filtering (De Santis et al., 1994). Multiresolution filtering borrows the idea of a bilateral channel filter. A signal sequence can be decomposed into two groups of sequence after being filtered by the bilateral channel filter, and then the decomposed two groups of signals will continue passing through the bilateral channel filter. Thereby, a variety of signal representations of different "resolution" levels can be obtained. With these signals, the original signal (secret) can be accurately recovered.

Scheme Based on Generalized Self-shrinking Sequences

The secret sharing scheme based on generalized self-shrinking sequences (Hu et al., 2001) is an extension of the Lagrangian interpolation polynomial system. The idea is to construct two Lagrangian polynomials, one for recovering the secret and the other for testing the effectiveness of the shares and the secret. The coefficients of the latter one are derived from generalized self-shrinking sequences. Due to its good pseudorandomness, this secret sharing scheme is safe and reliable, and it is convenient for updating the secret shares.

2.2.2 Classic Secret Sharing Schemes

Here we introduce four classic secret sharing schemes: Shamir's scheme, the scheme based on the Chinese remainder theorem, Brickell's scheme, and Blakley's scheme.

Shamir's Scheme

Shamir's secret sharing scheme is called (t, n)-threshold secret sharing scheme (Shamir, 1979), or threshold scheme for short, where t is the threshold value. Shamir's scheme is one of the most classic ones and is widely used because of its simplicity and practicality. The implementation of Shamir's scheme is based on the Lagrangian interpolation method. Given t points $(x_1, y_1), \ldots, (x_t, y_t)$ in the two-dimensional space, where x_i are different. For each x_i, there is a unique $t-1$ degree polynomial $q(x) = a_0 + a_1 x + \cdots + a_{t-1} x^{t-1}$ such that $q(x_i) = y_i$. In the secret splitting stage, we first determine t and n; assign $a_0 = S$, where S is the secret you want to share; and generate $a_1, \ldots, a_{t-1}$ at random to compute the following:

$$S_1 = q(1), \ldots, S_i = q(i), \ldots, S_n = q(n). \tag{2.9}$$

Obtaining any t values of S_i, the coefficients $a_0, \ldots, a_{t-1}$ of the polynomial $q(x)$ can be calculated by the interpolation method, where a_0 is the recovered secret S. But it is impossible to solve the polynomial to recover the original secret with less than t values of S_i. To make the preceding calculation more accurate, Shamir's scheme replaces the real number operation with the modulo operation. First, a large prime p is determined to ensure that p is larger than both S and n, and the coefficients $a_0, \ldots, a_{t-1}$ of the polynomial $q(x)$ are randomly taken from a uniform distribution in the range $[0, p)$, and $S_1, \ldots, S_n$

are also obtained by taking the modulus of p. An example is given in what follows to further illustrate Shamir's secret sharing scheme.

(1) Secret distribution

Step 1: Assume the secret $S = 13$, determine $n = 5$, $t = 3$, and choose the modulus $p = 17$.
Step 2: Generate $t - 1$ random numbers smaller than or equal to p, $a_1 = 10$, $a_2 = 2$, and assign the value of S to $a_0 = 13$.
Step 3: Calculate separately:

$$S_1 = (13 + 10 * 1 + 2 * 1^2) \bmod 17 = 8,$$

$$S_2 = (13 + 10 * 2 + 2 * 2^2) \bmod 17 = 7,$$

$$S_3 = (13 + 10 * 3 + 2 * 3^2) \bmod 17 = 10,$$

$$S_4 = (13 + 10 * 4 + 2 * 4^2) \bmod 17 = 0,$$

$$S_5 = (13 + 10 * 5 + 2 * 5^2) \bmod 17 = 11.$$

Step 4: Distribute (S_i, i) as a key to the ith party.

(2) Secret recovery

Step 1: Gather the keys of any $t = 3$ parties, e.g., (8, 1) of the first party, (7, 2) of the second person, and (11, 5) of the fifth party.
Step 2: List the system of equations:

$$(a_0 + a_1 * 1 + a_2 * 1^2) \bmod 17 = 8,$$

$$(a_0 + a_1 * 2 + a_2 * 2^2) \bmod 17 = 7,$$

$$(a_0 + a_1 * 5 + a_2 * 5^2) \bmod 17 = 11.$$

Step 3: Solving the system of equations to get $a_0 = 13$, $a_1 = 10$, and $a_2 = 2$, the original secret $S = a_0 = 13$.

Scheme Based on the Chinese Remainder Theorem

The Chinese remainder (or Sun Tzu's) theorem is a theorem on the system of linear congruence equations in number theory that states the criterion for a system of linear congruence equations to have a solution and the method of solving it. The problem of a system of linear congruence equations was first presented in "Sun Tzu's Book of Arithmetic," written during the North and South Dynasties of China (around the fifth century AD). The problem goes as follows. There is an integer, the remainder of which divided by three is two, divided by five is three, and divided by seven is two. What is this integer?

In the encryption phase, the algorithm generates a polynomial of order $n - 1$ based on the Chinese remainder theorem and uses the polynomial to encrypt the confidential number so that only the authorized group of parties can access the number. In the decryption phase, the parties combine the private shares, then restore the original number that the authorized parties want to access. In the following, we give a concrete example so that the reader can better understand the secret sharing scheme based on the Chinese remainder theorem.

(1) Secret distribution

Step 1: Assume the secret $S = 117$, determine $n = 5$, and $t = 3$.
Step 2: Generate n mutually prime random numbers and make sure the multiplication of the t smallest random numbers is greater than the secret S, while the multiplication of the $t - 1$ largest random numbers is less than the secret S. For example,

$$d_1 = 4, d_2 = 5, d_3 = 7, d_4 = 9, d_5 = 11,$$

where $d_1 d_2 d_3 > S > d_4 d_5$.
Step 3: Calculate separately:

$$S_1 = 117 \bmod 4 = 1,$$
$$S_2 = 117 \bmod 5 = 2,$$
$$S_3 = 117 \bmod 7 = 5,$$
$$S_4 = 117 \bmod 9 = 0,$$
$$S_5 = 117 \bmod 11 = 7.$$

Step 4: Distribute (S_i, d_i) as a key to the ith party.

(2) Secret recovery

Step 1: Gather the keys of any $t = 3$ parties, e.g., $(1, 4)$ for the first party, $(2, 5)$ for the second party, and $(7, 11)$ for the fifth party.
Step 2: List the system of equations:

$$S \bmod 4 = 1,$$
$$S \bmod 5 = 2,$$
$$S \bmod 11 = 7.$$

Step 3: To solve the system of equations, we can calculate the secret step by step. First, 165 is a common multiple of 5 and 11, whose remainder of division by 4 is also 1. Second, 132 is a common multiple of 4 and 11, whose remainder of division by 5 is 2. Third, 40 is a common multiple of 4 and 5, whose remainder of division by 11 is 7. Then, $165 + 132 + 40 - 4 * 5 * 11 = 117$ is the value of the original secret S.

Brickell's Scheme

Brickell's secret sharing scheme is a generalization of Shamir's secret sharing scheme, moving from one-dimensional equations to thinking about multidimensional vectors. Again, we give a concrete example to help you understand.

(1) Secret distribution

Step 1: Assume the secret $S = 99$, determine $n = 4$, vector dimension $d = 3$, and choose the modulus $p = 127$.

Step 2: Determine the decryption rule $\{(v_1, v_2, v_3), (v_1, v_4)\}$, where v_i denotes the ith d-dimensional vector and this decryption rule indicates that the first, second, and third parties and the first and fourth parties can cooperate to recover the secret, respectively.

Step 3: Determine the $n = 4$ vectors $\{v_1, \ldots, v_n\}$ shared by all, requiring that any set of vectors in the decryption rule can be linearly composed $(1, 0, 0)$, while combinations not in the decryption rule cannot be composed. For example, $v_1 = (0, 1, 0)$, $v_2 = (1, 0, 1)$, $v_3 = (0, 1, -1)$, and $v_4 = (1, 1, 0)$, satisfying the following requirement:

$$\begin{aligned} (1, 0, 0) &= v_2 + v_3 - v_1, \\ (1, 0, 0) &= v_4 - v_1. \end{aligned} \tag{2.10}$$

Step 4: Generate $d - 1$ random numbers less than p, $a_2 = 55$, $a_3 = 38$, and assign the value of S to $a_1 = 99$.

Step 5: Compute $S_i = a \cdot v_i$, respectively, where $a = (a_1, a_2, a_3)$:

$$S_1 = (99, 55, 38) \cdot (0, 1, 0) \bmod p = 55,$$
$$S_2 = (99, 55, 38) \cdot (1, 0, 1) \bmod p = 10,$$
$$S_3 = (99, 55, 38) \cdot (0, 1, -1) \bmod p = 17,$$
$$S_4 = (99, 55, 38) \cdot (1, 1, 0) \bmod p = 27.$$

Step 6: Distribute (S_i, i) as a key to the ith party.

(2) Secret recovery

Step 1: Set any key that satisfies the decryption rule, e.g., $(S_1 = 55, S_2 = 10, S_3 = 17)$ for the first, second, and third parties.

Step 2: Construct $(1, 0, 0)$ using the first, second, and third vectors:

$$c_1 v_1 + c_2 v_2 + c_3 v_3 = (1, 0, 0),$$

where $c_1 = -1, c_2 = 1, c_3 = 1$.

Step 3: Bring the parameters into $c_1 * S_1 + c_2 * S_2 + c_3 * S_3 = S$ to get the original secret S value:

$$(-1 * 55 + 1 * 10 + 1 * 17) \bmod 127 = 99.$$

Blakley's Scheme

Finally, we give a brief introduction to Blakley's secret sharing scheme (Blakley, 1979). The secret sharing scheme independently proposed by Blakley in 1979 is one of the earliest secret sharing schemes. Unlike Shamir's secret sharing scheme, Blakley's secret sharing scheme is based on the Gaussian elimination method.

(1) Secret distribution

Step 1: Determine $n = 5$ and $t = 3$ and assume that the secret $S = (3, 10, 5)$ is a point in the t-space.
Step 2: Construct the $n = 5$ planes passing through this point:

$$x + y + z = 18,$$
$$x + y + 2z = 23,$$
$$x + y + 3z = 28,$$
$$x + 2y + z = 28,$$
$$x + 3y + z = 38.$$

Step 3: Distribute the ith plane as a key to the ith party.

(2) Secret recovery

Step 1: Collect any keys that satisfy the decryption rules, such as the first, second, or fifth party's key.
Step 2: List the system of equations:

$$x + y + z = 18,$$
$$x + y + 2z = 23,$$
$$x + 3y + z = 38.$$

Step 3: Solve the system of equations containing t variables in t equations yielding $S = (3, 10, 5)$ as the original secret.

2.2.3 Homomorphic Properties of Secret Sharing

The most widely used Shamir secret sharing scheme has the additive homomorphism property itself. Suppose A and B have secrets S^A and S^B, respectively, as shown in Figure 2.2, and their values are randomly split into $S_1^A, \ldots, S_n^A$ and $S_1^B, \ldots, S_n^B$, which are assigned to different nodes $P_1, \ldots, P_n$, and the sum of the operation results of each node can be equal to the sum of the original secrets S^A and S^B. In layman's terms, secret sharing homomorphism means that the combination of the secret shares is equivalent to the secret sharing shares of the combination.

The homomorphic secret sharing scheme allows participants to process the addition and multiplication of the received multiple subshares, and thus the addition or multiplication of multiple secrets can be reconstructed while

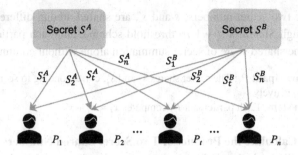

Figure 2.2 Homomorphic properties of secret sharing.

a single secret is kept in privacy. Therefore, the secret sharing scheme has the property of homomorphism (Benaloh, 1986; Rong et al., 2015). For the (t, n) threshold secret sharing scheme, define S as the original secret space and T as the secret share space, and the function $F_I : T^t \to S$ restores any t secret shares $(s_{i_1}, \ldots, s_{i_t})$ to the original secret $s = F_I(s_{i_1}, \ldots, s_{i_t})$, where $I = \{i_1, \ldots, i_t\} \subseteq \{1, 2, \ldots, n\}$, and $|I| = t$.

Definition 2.6 Secret sharing homomorphism: assume that $\oplus$ and $\otimes$ correspond to binary functions in the secret space S and the share space T, respectively. The (t, n) threshold secret sharing has $(\oplus, \otimes)$ homomorphism if, for any subset I,

$$s = F_I(s_{i_1}, \ldots, s_{i_t}),$$
$$s' = F_I(s'_{i_1}, \ldots, s'_{i_t}),$$
(2.11)

then

$$s \oplus s' = F_I(s_{i_1} \otimes s'_{i_1}, \ldots, s_{i_t} \otimes s'_{i_t}).$$
(2.12)

In the following subsection, we will focus on the additive and the multiplicative using Shamir's threshold scheme as an example. (Other homomorphisms include division homomorphism, power product homomorphism, and comparison homomorphism.) The properties of these homomorphisms allow secret sharing to be utilized in a wide range of different scenarios.

Calculate the Sum of Two Secret Shared Numbers

From Definition 2.6, we know that Shamir's threshold scheme has the property of $(+, +)$ homomorphism:

$$s + s' = F_I(s_{i_1}, \ldots, s_{i_t}) + F_I(s'_{i_1}, \ldots, s'_{i_t}) = F_I(s_{i_1} + s'_{i_1}, \ldots, s_{i_t} + s'_{i_t}). \quad (2.13)$$

Suppose two secret numbers, s and s', are shared among different participants through Shamir's $(t + 1, n)$ threshold scheme, and each participant can compute the shared share of secret summation alone without communication.

Input of participant P_j: The secret shares s_j and s'_j, corresponding to secret numbers s and s', respectively.
Calculation steps: Each participant P_j computes $x_j = s_j + s'_j$.

Calculate the Product of Two Secret Shared Numbers

Still using Shamir's threshold scheme as an example, we can make the secret sharing also satisfy the multiplicative homomorphism property (Beaver, 1991) by adding more computing mechanisms.

As we did in calculating the sum, suppose two secrets s and s' are shared among different participants through Shamir's $(t + 1, n)$ threshold scheme. In the absence of communication, the participants can compute the shared share of the secret product using Shamir's $(2t + 1, n)$ threshold scheme. That is, the Shamir threshold scheme has the $(\times, \times)$ homomorphism property, i.e., there are:

$$s \times s' = F_I(s_{i_1}, \ldots, s_{i_t}) \times F_I(s'_{i_1}, \ldots, s'_{i_t}) = F_I(s_{i_1} \times s'_{i_1}, \ldots, s_{i_t} \times s'_{i_t}). \quad (2.14)$$

However, in the following example, we will introduce an alternative construction mechanism by which we can also compute the shared share of the secret product through Shamir's $(t + 1, n)$ threshold scheme through communication among the participants. In this example, we assume that there are t dishonest participants in total, but most of them, $n = t + 1$, are honest.

Input of participant P_j: The secret shares s_j and s'_j, corresponding to secret s and s', respectively.
Calculation Step I: Each participant P_j computes $x_j = s_j * s'_j$ and shares the secret to other participants through Shamir's $(t + 1, n)$ threshold scheme, whose shares are denoted as $x_{j,1}, \cdots, x_{j,n}$. The participant P_j will send share $x_{j,l}$ to the participant P_l.
Calculation Step II: Each participant P_j computes $u_l = \sum_{j=1}^{n} \beta_j x_{j,l}$. where $\beta_1, \ldots, \beta_n$ are constants defined to recover the secret in Shamir's $(2t + 1, n)$ threshold scheme, and $\alpha_1, \ldots, \alpha_n \in F^q$ are nonzero unique elements known to all participants.

$$\beta_j = \prod_{1 \leq l \leq t, l \neq j} \frac{\alpha_{i_l}}{\alpha_{i_l} - \alpha_{i_j}}. \quad (2.15)$$

Other homomorphism properties, such as the division homomorphism (Catrina and Saxena, 2010), the power multiplication homomorphism (Hart, 1978), and the comparison homomorphism (Catrina and Saxena, 2010; Catrina and De Hoogh, 2010), can also be implemented by new designs of the secret sharing scheme. We do not discuss them in this book.

2.3 Advantages and Disadvantages

In general, secret sharing is a cleverly conceived and widely used cryptographic technique. Besides, different secret sharing schemes have their own advantages and disadvantages.

Advantages of Secret Sharing The t secret shares can be determined for the entire polynomial, and additional secret shares can be computed. New sharers can be added while the secret shares of the original sharers remain unchanged, as long as the total number of sharers after the addition does not exceed t. It is also possible to recalculate the secret shares of the sharers in a new round by constructing tth-order polynomials with new coefficients where the constant term is still the shared key before the original shared key is exposed to nullifying the original secret shares of the sharers. Secret sharing owns the advantanges such as no loss of precision, much higher computational efficiency compared to homomorphic encryption methods, relatively simple implementation, many protocol options, and low computational cost.

Disadvantages of Secret Sharing During the secret distribution phase, dishonest secret distributors may distribute invalid secret shares to participants. During the secret reconstruction phase, some participants may submit invalid secret shares, making it impossible to recover the correct secret. A peer-to-peer secure channel needs to be constructed between the secret distributors and the participants. Besides, secret sharing must generate and store a large number of random numbers offline before performing online computation, resulting in high communication costs.

2.4 Application Scenarios

There are many application scenarios of secret sharing in privacy-preserving computation, which include key negotiation, digital signatures, e-commerce, federated learning, and secure multiparty computing. In this subsection, we will introduce the applications of secret sharing in horizontal federated learning, vertical federated learning, and secure multiparty computation.

2.4.1 Secret Sharing in Horizontal Federated Learning

In horizontal federated learning, secret sharing is often used instead of homomorphic cryptography to design secure aggregation protocols for gradients. For example, an efficient secure aggregation method was proposed by Google's Federated Learning team at CCS'2017 (Bonawitz et al., 2017). Secret sharing techniques are used to enable servers to securely aggregate gradients from different users, while individual parties' gradients are not disclosed.

Horizontal Federated Learning Scenarios

Horizontal federated learning considers training a deep neural network to predict the next word that the user wants to type when writing a text message. Such networks are typically used to improve the typing efficiency of cell phone keyboards. Researchers may want to train such a model for all text messages across a large number of users. However, SMS messages often contain sensitive information. Users do not want to upload their data to the central server. Instead, we consider training such a model with federated learning, where each user securely maintains a private database of his/her text messages on his/her mobile device and trains a shared global model coordinated by a central server. Horizontal federated learning systems face several practical challenges. Mobile devices only have occasional access to power and network connections, so the set of users involved in each update step is unpredictable. Therefore, the system must be robust to user dropout. Since neural networks can be parameterized by millions of numbers, the amount of updates can be large, representing a direct cost to the user in terms of measuring network costs. Mobile devices are often unable to establish direct communication channels with other mobile devices (relying on servers or service providers to coordinate such communication) or to authenticate to other mobile devices locally. Thus, horizontal federated learning has stimulated the need for secure aggregation protocols that have the following advantages: they can operate on high-dimensional vectors; they are very efficient in communication, even if a new set of users is available at each instantiation; and they provide the strongest security within the constraints of an unauthenticated network of servers.

Secure Aggregation Protocol

In this chapter, we divide entities into two categories: a single server S that does aggregation operations, and a set $\mathcal{U}$ that includes n clients. Each user u in the set $\mathcal{U}$ has a private m-dimensional vector x_u and $\sum_{u \in \mathcal{U}} x_u$ is in the domain $\mathbb{Z}_R$. The goal of the protocol is to compute $\sum_{u \in \mathcal{U}} x_u$ safely: the server is guaranteed to learn only the final aggregation result, and the user learns nothing. Assuming that there is now an order of users and that there is a random vector $s_{u,v}$ between each pair of users $(u, v), u < v$, then the following blinding operation can be done on the data x_u:

$$y_u = x_u + \sum_{v \in \mathcal{U}: u < v} s_{u,v} - \sum_{v \in \mathcal{U}: u > v} s_{v,u} (\mathrm{mod}\ R). \qquad (2.16)$$

Then y_u is sent to the server, which calculates

$$z = \sum_{u \in \mathcal{U}} y_u$$

$$= \sum_{u \in \mathcal{U}} (x_u + \sum_{v \in \mathcal{U}:u<v} s_{u,v} - \sum_{v \in \mathcal{U}:u>v} s_{v,u}) \qquad (2.17)$$

$$= \sum_{u \in \mathcal{U}} x_u (\mathrm{mod}\ R).$$

It can be seen that the common vectors between users eventually offset and the task of secure aggregation is completed. However, this approach has two drawbacks: firstly, users must exchange random vectors $s_{u,v}$. If done directly, it will require a large communication overhead ($|\mathcal{U}| \times |x|$); second, the party that cannot complete the protocol is not tolerated. If user u quits after exchanging vectors with other users and before submitting y_u to the server, the vector masks associated with u will not be offset in the sum z. The communication overhead can be reduced by replacing the shared entire vector $s_{u,v}$ with the seeds of a shared pseudorandom number generator. These shared seeds will be computed by having each party broadcast a different Diffie–Hellman public key and participate in key negotiation. One way to handle dropout users is notifying them to all existing users, and then the existing users reply to the server with the random seeds they shared with the dropout users. However, it is also possible that the users quit before transmitting the random seeds. The chapter solves this problem by using a threshold secret sharing scheme and asking each user to send their different Diffie–Hellman secret shares to all other users. As long as the minimum number of participants (determined by the threshold) remains online and responds with a share of the discarded user keys, the pair of seeds can be recovered, even if the other participants drop out during the recovery period. The general steps for a secure aggregation protocol for secret sharing are shown in Figure 2.3.

Another double-blinding operation is to prevent security problems caused by the server regarding the user as an offline user because the user is too slow in sending messages. The specific operation is to add the vector generated by users when blinding with the vector $s_{u,v}$. First, the user generates a random seed b along with the random number s. In the secret sharing phase, the user shares b with other users. In the recovery phase, the server must make an explicit choice for the user, requesting the random number s or b; the user does not share s and b of the same user. After collecting at least t s and t b from online users, the server can subtract all b to display the sum. The calculation formula is as follows:

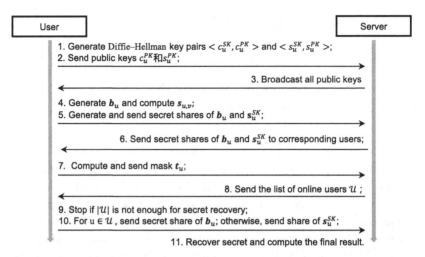

Figure 2.3 General steps for a secure aggregation protocol for secret sharing.

$$y_u = x_u + \text{PRG}(b_u) + \sum_{v \in \mathcal{U}:u<v} \text{PRG}(s_{u,v}) - \sum_{v \in \mathcal{U}:u>v} \text{PRG}(s_{v,u})(\bmod R). \quad (2.18)$$

2.4.2 Secret Sharing in Vertical Federated Learning

In 2020, Wu et al. applied the technique of secret sharing in a vertical federated tree model, named Pivot (Wu et al., 2020). Compared to the Secure-Boost (Cheng et al., 2021a) algorithm, Pivot does not leak intermediate results, improving security, and has higher efficiency than the related secure multiparty computation approaches.

Vertical Federated Learning Scenarios

The work in Wu et al. (2020) is based on the classification and regression tree (CART) algorithm (Loh, 2011). With the CART algorithm, integrated models with higher accuracy such as random forest (Breiman, 2001) and gradient boosting decision tree (Friedman, 2001) can also be implemented. Suppose there are n data points $\{x_1, \ldots, x_n\}$ in the training data D, and each data point contains features in d dimensions, and there is also a corresponding set of labels $Y = \{y_1, \ldots, y_n\}$. The CART algorithm constructs a decision tree by recursion, and for each node of the tree, the algorithm determines whether the branch-and-prune condition is satisfied. If the condition is satisfied, the algorithm returns the label with the highest number in the current sample of leaf nodes; if the condition is not satisfied, the CART algorithm will select the

u_1		
ID	income	label
1	2500	Class 1
2	1500	Class 2
3	3500	Class 1
4	5000	Class 1
5	2000	Class 2

u_2	
ID	age
1	30
2	20
3	45
4	35
5	55

u_3	
ID	deposit
1	10000
2	5000
3	30000
4	12000
5	25000

Figure 2.4 Vertical tree model scenarios.

best splitting point. Then, the two newly generated subtrees will be recursively constructed according to the same way.

In the federated learning scenario, suppose there exist m participants $\{u_1, \ldots, u_m\}$ who want to jointly train the decision tree model without leaking their own data $\{D_1, \ldots, D_m\}$. Define n as the number of samples, and let d_i represent the feature dimension in the ith participant's dataset $D_i = \{x_{it}\}_{t=1}^{n}$, where x_{it} is the tth sample in D_i and $Y = \{y_t\}_{t=1}^{n}$ denotes the set of labels of the samples. For example, when $m = 3$, as shown in Figure 2.4, the Pivot algorithm solves the tree model training problem in a vertical federation scenario. In this scenario, each participant shares the same sample id, but has different features. Moreover, we assume that the sample labels exist only in one of the participant's datasets, and these local data cannot be shared directly to other participants.

Pivot for Privacy-preserving Vertical Federated Decision Trees

The Pivot algorithm combines the privacy-preserving techniques of homomorphic encryption and secret sharing. Since secret sharing incurs additional communication overhead, each participant tries to use homomorphic encryption for all local computations and switches to secret sharing only when homomorphic encryption cannot complete a certain computation (e.g., a comparison operation is needed to decide the best partition). Therefore, the most important part in this scheme is how to convert the numbers in the homomorphic encryption state obtained from the local computation to the numbers in the secret sharing state, and the conversion method is shown in algorithm 1.

The homomorphic encryption and secret sharing techniques used in the Pivot are the multikey semihomomorphic encryption in the Paillier ecosystem

(Paillier, 1999) and the additive secret sharing scheme in the SPDZ (Damgård et al., 2012), respectively. The input of this transformation algorithm is a number in the homomorphically encrypted state. First, each participant u_i locally generates a random number r_i and does a homomorphic encryption operation on it, and they all send the encrypted random number to the participant u_1; then, the participant u_1 computes the sum $[e]$ of the input number and each participant's random number in the ciphertext state; then, all participants decrypt the sum e together; finally, each participant computes its own secret shared share in the way that u_1 computes its shared share as $e - r_1 \bmod q$, and the remaining participants u_i compute their shared share as $-r_i \bmod q$.

Input : $[x]$ is the number in the homomorphic encryption state, $\mathbb{Z}_q$ is the secret shared space, pk is the homomorphic encryption public key, and $\{sk_i\}_{i=1}^m$ is the partial key;
Output: $\langle x \rangle = (\langle x \rangle_1, \ldots, \langle x \rangle_m)$ for x in the secret shared state;
for $i \in [1, m]$ **do**
　　$[r_i] \leftarrow u_i$ randomly chooses $r_i \in \mathbb{Z}_q$ and encypts it;
　　u_i sends $[r_i]$ to u_1;
end
u_1 computes $[e] = [x] \oplus [r_1] \oplus \cdots \oplus [r_m]$;
$e \leftarrow$ parties collaboratively decrypt $[e]$;
u_1 computes $\langle x \rangle_1 = e - r_1 \bmod q$;
for $i \in [2, m]$ **do**
　　u_i computes $\langle x \rangle_i = -r_i \bmod q$;
end
Algorithm 1: Homomorphic encryption to secret sharing conversion algorithm

2.4.3 Secret Sharing in Secure Multiparty Computation

Secret sharing also has many applications in secure multiparty computing. For example, ABY[3] (Mohassel and Rindal, 2018) uses a three-server architecture where the secret is divided into three parts and stored on each of the three servers, e.g., we divide the secret numbers x and y into three parts and put them on servers A, B, and C, respectively.

$$[[x]] := (x_1, x_2, x_3),$$
$$[[y]] := (y_1, y_2, y_3). \tag{2.19}$$

With a secret sharing architecture based on three servers, we can easily implement additive operations on ciphertexts. For example, suppose we want to compute the sum z of x and y:

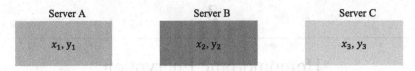

Figure 2.5 Illustration of ABY^3's addition operation.

Figure 2.6 Illustration of ABY^3's multiplication operation.

$$[[z]] = [[x]] + [[y]] = (x_1 + x_2 + x_3) + (y_1 + y_2 + y_3). \qquad (2.20)$$

The multiplication operation is slightly more complicated. Suppose we want to compute the product z of x and y. We cannot simply multiply the secret shares on each server because there are some intermediate computation results involving the multiplication of shares between servers:

$$\begin{aligned}
[[z]] = [[x]] * [[y]] &= (x_1 + x_2 + x_3)(y_1 + y_2 + y_3) \\
&= x_1y_1 + x_1y_2 + x_1y_3 \\
&\quad + x_2y_1 + x_2y_2 + x_2y_3 \\
&\quad + x_3y_1 + x_3y_2 + x_3y_3. \qquad (2.21)
\end{aligned}$$

The design of ABY^3 makes use of "duplicate secret sharing" to solve the ciphertext multiplication problem. As shown in Figure 2.6, each server has two different shares of the same secret. The multiplication operation in the ABY^3 scheme is more convenient compared to the previous secret sharing scheme.

Under this duplicate secret sharing mechanism, servers A, B, and C can compute z_1, z_2, and z_3 locally, respectively:

$$\begin{aligned}
z_1 &= x_1y_1 + x_1y_3 + x_3y_1, \\
z_2 &= x_2y_2 + x_1y_2 + x_2y_1, \qquad (2.22) \\
z_3 &= x_3y_3 + x_3y_2 + x_2y_3.
\end{aligned}$$

Then, in order to perform other computations afterward, the three servers communicate the previous computation results. In the mechanism of duplicate secret sharing, any two servers can reconstruct the secret, so in the face of semi-honest security models, or even malicious models, ABY^3 allows only up to one server corruption. In addition, ABY^3 also considers other challenges, such as the computational bottlenecks of switching back and forth between binary computation (binary secret sharing) and arithmetic computation (arithmetic secret sharing).

3

Homomorphic Encryption

Homomorphic Encryption (HE) is an encryption scheme with special properties: the ciphertexts encrypted by the HE schemes support various algebraic operations, without the participation of the key owner. Homomorphic Encryption has been hailed as the holy grail of cryptography since it was proposed in 1978. On one hand, through HE technology, the data owner can send the data to cloud service providers or other private computing parties for arbitrary processing without worrying about the original information of the data being leaked. The fact that it does not require the participation of the key owner makes it naturally have a high affinity with cloud computing. Thus, it is becoming a strong candidate technology for privacy-preserving computing solutions today when cloud computing is in full swing. On the other hand, the construction of HE schemes is extremely challenging. After decades of development, current HE schemes still have challenging problems such as security and efficiency. It is certain that once an efficient and secure fully HE scheme that supports arbitrary operations is proposed, it will greatly promote the implementation of privacy-preserving computing in various practical scenarios. This chapter introduces the problem HE tries to solve, the principles and theoretical foundation of popular implementations as well as their advantages and disadvantages. Finally, the current development trend and application scenarios are discussed in detail.

3.1 Definition

Homomorphic Encryption is a general term for a class of encryption methods. Encryption methods are generally used to protect data content during data storage and transmission. Homomorphic Encryption aims to answer a question: can we perform operations on encrypted data to complete various computing tasks on remote servers while ensuring the security of user data? In practical scenarios, servers need to collect user data for storage, query, processing, and performing various machine learning tasks. During the process, there are often concerns from users that their privacy will be leaked to the server. Gentry uses the jewelry store problem to describe this problem model vividly: the jewelry store owner wants his workers to be able to process expensive gold into jewelry, but he does not want the gold to be exposed to the workers and stolen by them (Gentry, 2010). If computing tasks can be completed on encrypted data, users can safely upload the encrypted data to the server for arbitrary operations. As long as users keep their private keys, they do not have to worry about their original data being leaked. It is like putting gold in a black box: workers can only put on gloves and stick their hands into the box through small windows to handle the gold, but not take it away. Homomorphic Encryption is proposed to solve this kind of problem.

The HE schemes discussed in this chapter are all asymmetric encryption ones, that is, public key encryption schemes. Encryption and decryption in this arrangement use different keys: the encryption operation uses the public key, and the decryption operation uses the private key. The public key can be distributed to others for encryption operations, while the private key remains with the data owner for decryption to obtain the plain data. Homomorphic Encryption schemes using symmetric encryption are rare in practical applications and will not be discussed.

We give the definition of HE as follows:

Definition 3.1 (Homomorphic Encryption) An HE solution consists of four components: KeyGen, Encrypt, Decrypt, and Evaluate.

- KeyGen(λ) $\rightarrow$ (pk, sk): Key generation function. Given encryption parameters λ, it generates the private/public key pair (pk, sk).
- Encrypt(pt, pk) $\rightarrow$ ct: Encryption function. Given public key pk, it encrypts the plaintext pt into ciphertext ct.
- Decrypt(sk, ct) $\rightarrow$ pt: Decryption function. Given private key sk, it decrypts the ciphertext ct into plaintext pt.
- Evaluate(pk, Π, ct_1, ct_2, $\cdots$) $\rightarrow$ (ct_1', ct_2', $\cdots$): Evaluation function. Given the public key pk, the input ciphertexts (ct_1, ct_2, $\cdots$) and the computing function Π, it will perform Π on the input ciphertexts and output the results (ct_1', ct_2', $\cdots$), also in ciphertext.

The evaluation function as part of the scheme is what makes HE different from traditional encryption schemes. The type of operation function Π supported determines the homomorphic operations supported by a specific HE scheme. In HE, this operation function can also be represented by a computing circuit.

Given the preceding four components, an HE scheme should also satisfy correctness and semantic security.

Definition 3.2 (Correctness) Generally, an HE scheme is correct for operation Π if it correctly decrypts ciphertexts on the two following conditions:

- It correctly decrypts a ciphertext that has not been evaluated before (which is also called "fresh"):

$$\Pr[\text{Decrypt}(\text{sk}, \text{Encrypt}(\text{pk}, \text{pt})) = \text{pt}] = 1. \qquad (3.1)$$

- It correctly decrypts ciphertexts evaluated on Π. Namely, the decryption results are equal to those obtained by directly performing the operation function Π on the original plaintexts of the input ciphertexts:

$$\Pr[\text{Decrypt}(\text{sk}, \text{Evaluate}(\text{pk}, \Pi, \text{ct}_1, \text{ct}_2, \cdots)) = \Pi(\text{pt}_1, \text{pt}_2, \cdots)] = 1,$$
$$(3.2)$$

where $\text{ct}_i = \text{Encrypt}(\text{pt}_i)$ for all i.

The first condition of correctness guarantees that when an HE scheme is used as the encryption method, the encrypted data can be decrypted correctly. The second, as a unique property of HE schemes, ensures that the evaluation function can be used to perform data processing operations on the ciphertext. $\text{Evaluate}(\text{pk}, \Pi, \text{ct}_1, \text{ct}_2, \cdots)$ is called the homomorphic operation of Π on ciphertext.

It should be noted that the parameter of the operation function Π is plaintext, and the parameter of the evaluation function is ciphertext. The evaluation function of HE does not directly execute the operation function Π on the ciphertext, but uses some specific operations corresponding to the homomorphic method Evaluate in the ciphertext domain. The two operations can be the same or not. Taking the Cheon–Kim–Kim–Song (CKSS) scheme as an example, its ciphertext is in the form of a vector, and the homomorphic operation corresponding to the vector addition operation on the ciphertext domain is vector modulo addition. Also, some HE schemes that support floating-point operations (e.g., CKKS) can only guarantee that the decrypted result is approximately correct due to the influence of noise, truncation operation, and precision error in the decryption process.

Like the general encryption scheme, the HE scheme also needs to satisfy security to ensure that the attacker cannot retrieve information about the original plaintext from the ciphertext. Whether an encryption scheme is secure is determined by proving its *semantic security*. The core idea of semantic security is that different plaintexts are encrypted so that the probability distributions of their generated ciphertexts are indistinguishable in polynomial time. Thus, it is hard to distinguish which plaintext is the original data of a specific ciphertext. With practical security proofs, we ensure the security level of an encryption scheme by demonstrating the types of attacks the scheme can resist. Specifically, we define two parties: a challenger and an attacker. With specific given information, the attacker attempts to distinguish and crack the ciphertext generated by the challenger. There are two kinds of attack scenarios commonly used depending on the information the attacker holds: Chosen Plaintext Attack (CPA) and Chosen Ciphertext Attack (CCA).

- Chosen Plaintext Attack (CPA): the attacker sends any two plaintext messages m_0, m_1 to the challenger, the challenger encrypts one of the plaintexts at random, generates ct_i, and sends it to the attacker. The attacker tries to distinguish whether the ciphertext ct_i corresponds to m_0 or m_1.
- Chosen Ciphertext Attack (CCA): In addition to the chosen-plaintext attack, the attacker can also send any number of ciphertexts to the challenger for decryption to assist in cracking. It can also be subdivided into two types of attacks: CCA1 and CCA2. The CCA1 scenario only allows the attacker to send ciphertexts to the challenger for decryption before the chosen plaintext attack challenge. But CCA2 also allows the attacker to send ciphertexts after the challenge, as long as the chosen ciphertext is not the received ciphertext ct_i obtained in CPA. Thus, the attacker can deliberately design the ciphertext for decryption based on ct_i to retrieve more useful information in CCA2.

In a chosen plaintext attack, after the attacker obtains the ciphertext ct_i returned by the challenger and the given public key pk, the attacker can use an arbitrary algorithm $A(pk, ct) \rightarrow 0, 1$ to identify whether the plaintext corresponds to ciphertext m_0 or m_1. If for any polynomial-time function A, we have

$$|\Pr(A(pk, ct_0) = 1) - \Pr(A(pk, ct_1) = 1)| < \epsilon, \qquad (3.3)$$

the attacker does not have a probabilistic polynomial time (PPT) algorithm to distinguish between two different ciphertexts, and the encryption scheme is said to satisfy the semantic security under CPA (IND-CPA). Also, if the encryption scheme satisfies the preceding semantic security under the CCA1 or CCA2 attack scenario, it is said to satisfy the semantic security under CCA1 or CCA2 (IND-CCA1 or IND-CCA2). The more complex the attack scenario with greater attacker authority a challenger can defend, the higher the security level of the encryption scheme. In the preceding scenarios, IND-CCA2 has the highest security level. At present, researchers have only successfully constructed an HE scheme that satisfies IND-CPA.

In addition to the basic properties of correctness and security, a practical HE scheme must satisfy more properties. For instance, we can design the following HE scheme: when evaluating with the Evaluate function, operations are not performed but recorded in ciphertexts. Then, in the process of decryption, the series of recorded operations are extracted and executed on the decrypted plaintext to generate the evaluated result. Though this scheme satisfies correctness and semantic security, it is completely different from what we expect from a HE scheme. The essential difference is that the ciphertext processed after Evaluate in the preceding scheme is different from a fresh ciphertext with a larger memory requirement due to the accumulation of recorded operations. Thus, if we can ensure that the evaluated ciphertext is indistinguishable from a fresh ciphertext, the storage and computation complexity of subsequent decryption and evaluation operations will be independent of the number of times Evaluate has been called before.

Definition 3.3 (Strong Homomorphism) If ciphertexts generated by Encrypt encryption have the same distribution as the ciphertexts generated by Evaluate, the HE scheme is called strong homomorphism.

Strong homomorphism is often hard to satisfy. Generally, we fall back on a weaker notion, *compactness*, which ensures that the size of ciphertexts after evaluation does not grow indefinitely.

Definition 3.4 (Compactness) A homomorphic encryption scheme is compact if the size of evaluated ciphertext size(ct) is always less than some polynomial functions of its encryption parameters λ and independent of the complexity of the evaluation operation Π.

In addition to the privacy preservation of the original data, in certain private computing scenarios, we may also want to protect the operations performed on the ciphertext against users. Specifically, if an evaluated ciphertext looks the same as a fresh ciphertext with the same value, the attacker cannot expect to extract any useful information about the evaluation function from it. This property is called *circuit privacy*.

Definition 3.5 (Circuit Privacy) A homomorphic encryption scheme satisfies circuit privacy, if, for any given plaintexts $(m_1, m_2, \cdots)$ and their corresponding ciphertexts $(ct_1, ct_2, \cdots)$, Evaluate$(pk, \Pi, ct_1, ct_2, \cdots)$ and Encrypt$(\Pi(m_1, m_2, \cdots), pk)$ are indistinguishable.

With a HE scheme that satisfies circuit privacy, the attacker cannot obtain the specific information of the homomorphic operation through the result ciphertext of the homomorphic operation. Thus it not only protects user privacy for the server, but also protects the server's evaluation algorithm against the user.

Depending on the homomorphic operations supported, the existing HE schemes can be divided into the following types:

• Partially Homomorphic Encryption (PHE): homomorphic encryption schemes that only support single homomorphic operations (such as addition or multiplication). We also call the homomorphic encryption schemes that only support homomorphic addition additively homomorphic encryption.
• Somewhat Homomorphic Encryption (SWHE): homomorphic encryption schemes support multiple kinds of homomorphic operations (e.g., addition and multiplication), but the number of allowed operations on ciphertexts is limited.
• Leveled Homomorphic Encryption (LHE): homomorphic encryption schemes support multiple kinds of homomorphic operations. We can define the upper bound of the number of homomorphic operations allowed arbitrarily in the security parameters. Generally, the larger the number of homomorphic operations allowed, the greater the ciphertext storage overhead and the time complexity of these operations.
• Fully Homomorphic Encryption (FHE): homomorphic encryption schemes support an unlimited number of any kind of homomorphic operation, as long as the operation can be represented as Boolean circuits.

The difference between LHE and SWHE is that the former can take the supported computational upper bound as an input parameter to construct an encryption scheme. In this way, in practical applications, the LHE scheme can be utilized to replace the FHE scheme according to the maximum number of operations (i.e., the depth of the operation circuit) required by the specific application.

Practically, the current mainstream HE schemes mainly consider the support for addition and multiplication.[1] The primary goal of HE researchers is to construct an efficient and reliable FHE scheme that supports any arithmetic operations.

---

[1] A HE scheme that satisfies infinite additions and multiplications can support arbitrary operations by constructing an OR gate operation circuit.

3.2 Principle and Implementation

Like general encryption schemes, HE schemes are also constructed based on various difficult problems. They are characterized by the asymmetry in the difficulty of constructing and solving problems. Taking the difficult problem of large number decomposition used by RSA as an example, given two large prime numbers p and q, it is straightforward to calculate $n = p * q$. However, inversely identifying the prime factors p, q from the given n is very difficult. Encryption schemes generally complete the construction part of the difficult problem in the encryption process and then use the additional information provided by the private key to solve the problem in the decryption process. In this process, the homomorphism presented from some special construction methods becomes the basis of HE schemes.

In this section, we will introduce the four types of HE schemes and some of their representatives. We refer readers to Martins et al. (2017) and Acar et al. (2018) for a comprehensive survey of various HE methods in history. Before introducing various types of HE schemes in further detail, we need to understand some basic concepts in number theory, such as groups, rings, and lattices.

3.2.1 Groups

A group is a basic algebraic structure consisting of a set of elements G and a binary operation $\cdot$. It satisfies the following conditions: closure, associativity, identity element, and inverse element.

- Closure: for any two elements $a, b \in G$, the element $a \cdot b$ is also in G.
- Associativity: for any $a, b, c \in G$, $(a \cdot b) \cdot c = a \cdot (b \cdot c)$.
- Identity: there exists an element $e \in G$ that for any element $a \in G$, we have $e \cdot a = a \cdot e = a$.
- Inverse: for any element $a \in G$, there is an element in G that satisfies $a \cdot b = b \cdot a = e$.

If a group also satisfies the commutative law, i.e., $a \cdot b = b \cdot a$ for any $a, b \in G$, it can be further called a *commutative group* or an *abelian group*. Common groups include the additive group of integers, the additive group of integers modulo n, the multiplicative group of integers modulo n, and elliptic curves that are usually used in cryptography. Here, we use $\cdot$ to refer to the group operation, and define the power of the element a^2 as $a \cdot a$, which can be used to generate polynomials of elements.

A finite group is a group with a finite number of elements. We define the *order* of a finite group as the number of elements in the group $|G|$.

If every element of a group G can be expressed as a power g^m of a certain element g in the group G, then G is called a cyclic group, denoted by $G = (g) = \{g^m | m \in \mathbb{Z}\}$, where g is called a generator of G, as it can be used to generate all the elements in the group. The smallest positive integer n that satisfies $a^n = e$ is called the order of the elements of a, which is equal to the order of the group if and only if a is a generator of the group.

Take the additive group of integer modulo 6 $\mathbb{Z}_6 = \{0, 1, 2, 3, 4, 5\}$ as an example. The order of the group is 6, the identity is 0, and 1 and 5 are generators. The order of all the elements in the group is 1, 6, 3, 2, 3, 6. Take element 5 as an example; after addition modulo 6, we have

$$
\begin{aligned}
5^1 &= 5, \\
5^2 &= (5 + 5) \pmod 6 = 4, \\
5^3 &= (5 + 5 + 5) \pmod 6 = 3, \\
5^4 &= (5 + 5 + 5 + 5) \pmod 6 = 2, \\
5^5 &= (5 + 5 + 5 + 5 + 5) \pmod 6 = 1, \\
5^6 &= (5 + 5 + 5 + 5 + 5 + 5) \pmod 6 = 0 = e.
\end{aligned}
\tag{3.4}
$$

Thus, the order of element 5 is 6, which makes it a generator of this additive group $\mathbb{Z}_6$.

If there is a subset G' of the group G and the conditions for the group also hold for the subset on the same operation $\cdot$, G' is called a subgroup of G, denoted as $G' \subseteq G$. It can be observed that the generation of powers of any elements in a finite group G results in a subgroup of G (generator generates G itself), and the order of the subgroup is equal to the order of the element used for generation. Here, we call the element the generator of the subgroup. In the preceding example, generating from element 2, the subset $\{2, 4, 0\}$ is a subgroup of $\mathbb{Z}_6$, and its order is equal to the order of the element, which is 3.

3.2.2 Rings

Based on commutative groups, we can construct rings with the element set by adding a new binary operation. Generally, we denote the element set in a ring by R, and the two operations $+$ and $\cdot$. In addition to the properties and commutative law of the original operator symbol $+$, the new operator symbol $\cdot$ also needs to satisfy:

- Closure: for all elements a, b in R, the result of $a \cdot b$ is also in R.
- Associativity: $(a \cdot b) \cdot c = a \cdot (b \cdot c)$ holds for any $a, b, c \in R$.
- Identity: there exists an element $e \in R$ that satisfies $e \cdot a = a \cdot e = e, \forall a \in R$.

- Distributive Law: Multiplication operations can be distributed among additions. That is, given any $a, b, c \in R$, there are $a \cdot (b + c) = a \cdot b + a \cdot c$ and $(b + c) \cdot a = b \cdot a + c \cdot a$.

In a ring $(R, +, \cdot)$, if its subset I and its addition operation form a subgroup $(I, +)$ and satisfy $\forall i \in I, r \in R, i \cdot r \in I$, then I is called a *right ideal* of the ring R. If $\forall i \in I, r \in R, r \cdot i \in I$, then I is called a *left ideal* of the ring R. If the left and right ideals are satisfied at the same time, then I is called an *ideal* on the ring R. The ideal is closed under multiplication.

3.2.3 Lattice

Given a n-dimensional vector space $\mathbb{R}^n$, any discrete additive subgroup on it is a *lattice*. According to the basic knowledge of linear algebra, we can construct a set of n linearly independent vectors $v_1, v_2, v_3, \ldots, v_n \in \mathbb{R}^n$ in $\mathbb{R}^n$. Based on the linear combinations of these vectors with integer coefficients, we can generate a series of discrete points:

$$L(v_1, v_2, v_3 \cdots v_n) = \left\{ \sum_{i=1}^{n} \alpha_i v_i | \alpha_i \in \mathbb{Z} \right\}. \tag{3.5}$$

These sets of elements together with the addition operations $(L, +)$ are called lattices. This set of linearly independent vectors $\boldsymbol{B}$ is called the basis of the lattice, and the number of vectors is called the dimension of the lattice. Although the lattice is also obtained by basis expansion, it differs from a continuous vector space in that its coefficients are restricted to integers, resulting in a series of discrete vectors.

The discrete nature of vectors in lattices has given rise to a new set of hard problems. The main problems on lattices are the shortest vector problem (SVP) and the closest vector problem (CVP).

Definition 3.6 (Shortest vector problem) Given a lattice L, the shortest vector problem aims to find a shortest nonzero vector $v \in L$.

Definition 3.7 (Closest vector problem) Given a lattice L and a vector w in the vector space but not necessarily in the lattice L, the closest vector problem aims to find a vector $v \in L$ that is closest to w, i.e., minimizing $\|w - v\|$.

The difficulty of solving these problems, to a large extent, depends on the properties of the basis of the lattice. There are efficient ways to solve SVP and CVP approximately if the basis of the lattice is *good*, which means it consists of reasonably short and orthogonal base vectors. Otherwise, the current fastest algorithms for solving SVP and CVP still require exponential computation time. Therefore, by using a basis with poor orthogonality as the public key and another with good orthogonality as the private key, we can design lattice-based encryption algorithms where the decryption problems are based on these hard problems.

3.2.4 Partially Homomorphic Encryption

The history of HE begins with partially homomorphic encryption schemes. As one of the most popular encryption methods in cryptography, RSA is not only the first practically designed public key encryption scheme, but also the first encryption technology discovered to have homomorphic properties. Two years after the asymmetric encryption scheme proposed by Diffie and Hellman (1976), Rivest et al. proposed the RSA encryption algorithm based on the factorization of large numbers (1978a). Then, Rivest et al. pointed out the multiplicative homomorphism of RSA (1978b), and proposed the concept of privacy homomorphism for the first time. Subsequently, a series of PHE works has sprung up. Goldwasser et al. (1982) proposed the first probabilistic public key encryption scheme GM based on the quadratic residuosity problem (explained in detail in the introduction to Paillier later), where randomness is introduced into the encryption process. The GM encryption system encrypts the bits one by one and satisfies the homomorphic addition on bit level: for two-bit messages m_1, m_2, there are $Enc(m_1)*Enc(m_2) = Enc(m_1 + m_2)$. Benaloh proposed an improved version of the GM scheme in Benaloh (1994), which is based on the higher residuosity problem, which supports encrypting the entire message and is additively homomorphic: $Enc(m_1) * Enc(m_2) = Enc(m_1 + m_2 \pmod{n})$.

In addition, based on Diffie and Hellman (1976), Taher ElGamal proposed an extended asymmetric encryption scheme, El-Gamal, in 1985 (ElGamal, 1985). This scheme is based on the hard problem in the discrete logarithm algorithm and is often used for symmetric encryption to transmit the private key. El-Gamal supports multiplicative homomorphism, $Enc(m_1) * Enc(m_2) = Enc(m_1 * m_2)$. Later, Paillier (1999) proposed a probabilistic homomorphic encryption scheme called Paillier, which is based on the assumption of the composite residuosity problem. While satisfying additive homomorphism, it also supports a series of other operations on the ciphertext to modify the encrypted message. Paillier implements its encryption mechanism based on the Decision Composite Residuosity Assumption (DCRA). This section will further introduce the PHE algorithm Paillier in detail.

Given a positive integer m, we can classify all integers by their residues (mod m). For example, if $m = 3$, then the residues of $-2, 1, 4, 7, 10 \ldots$ modulo

3 are all 1, so they all belong to the same residue class modulo m. These classes are called residue classes modulo m. The higher residuosity problem can also be defined as follows. For the integers a and n, if there exists a solution to the equation

$$x^n \equiv a \pmod{m}, \tag{3.6}$$

then a is called an nth residue modulo m. As mentioned before, the GM scheme is based on the quadratic residuosity problem, which attempts to determine whether an integer a is a quadratic residue modulo m. Here, the DCRA that Paillier relies on refers to the assumption that, given a composite n and an integer $a \in \mathbb{Z}_{n^2}$, it is hard to determine whether a is an nth residue modulo n^2, namely, whether there exists an integer x to satisfy $x^n \equiv a \pmod{n^2}$.

The implementation of its encryption scheme is as follows:

- Key generation function: Selects two large prime numbers (p, q) such that $gcd(pq, (p-1)(q-1)) = 1$ (the preceding requirements can be satisfied by selecting two prime numbers with identical bit length). Calculate $n = pq$ and the least common multiple of $p-1$ and $q-1$, $\lambda = \text{lcm}(p-1, q-1)$. Then, select a random integer $g \in \mathbb{Z}^*_{n^2}$ so that n is divisible by the order of g. This condition can be achieved by guaranteeing the existence of the multiplicative inverse of $L(g^\lambda \bmod n^2) \bmod n$, where $L(x) = \frac{x-1}{n}$. Then, the scheme uses (n, g) as the public key and (p, q) as the private key.
- Encryption function: for the given plaintext message m, randomly select a number r and generate the following ciphertext:

$$c = \text{Enc}(m) = g^m r^n \pmod{n^2}. \tag{3.7}$$

- Decryption function: for a given ciphertext c, decrypt the plaintext m according to the following formula:

$$m = \text{Dec}(c) = \frac{L(c^\lambda(\bmod n^2))}{L(g^\lambda(\bmod n^2))} \bmod n. \tag{3.8}$$

The ciphertexts of Paillier have the following properties:

$$\text{Enc}(m_1) * \text{Enc}(m_2) = g^{m_1+m_2}(r_1 * r_2)^n \pmod{n^2} = \text{Enc}(m_1 + m_2). \tag{3.9}$$

Thus, Paillier is an additive homomorphic encryption scheme. The homomorphic operation of the plaintext addition is multiplication over the ciphertext space. The evaluation function can be designed as $\text{Evaluate}(pk, +, ct_1, ct_2) = ct_1 * ct_2$. In addition, Paillier also supports the following mixed operations of ciphertext and plaintext messages:

$$\mathrm{Enc}(m_1) * g^{m_2} \quad (\mathrm{mod}\ n^2) = \mathrm{Enc}(m_1 + m_2 \quad (\mathrm{mod}\ n)), \tag{3.10}$$

$$\mathrm{Enc}(m_1)^{m_2} \quad (\mathrm{mod}\ n^2) = \mathrm{Enc}(m_1 * m_2 \quad (\mathrm{mod}\ n)). \tag{3.11}$$

3.2.5 Somewhat Homomorphic Encryption

Somewhat homomorphic encryption schemes (SWHE) can support both addition and multiplication homomorphic operations. However, since the size of the ciphertext keeps increasing when performing operations, the number of homomorphic operations that can be performed on the ciphertext is limited. Most of the SWHE schemes focus directly on the homomorphic operation, trying to transform and restrict the homomorphic operation to a certain standard computational structure (such as computational circuits, expressions, branching programs, finite automata, truth tables, etc.), and then propose specific solutions for HE.

The first SWHE scheme that supports both homomorphic addition and homomorphic multiplication was proposed by Fellows and Koblitz (1994), whose ciphertext size increases exponentially with the number of homomorphic operations. Its homomorphic multiplication is computationally expensive and can hardly be put into practical use. Sander, Young, and Yung (1999) proposed SYY approximate homomorphic encryption. The encryption scheme supports a certain type of homomorphic operation in the form of simple circuits and can support multiple AND gate operations and one NOR gate operation. After each NOR gate operation, the length of the ciphertext will increase exponentially, thereby limiting the circuit depth.

Later, Boneh et al. (2005) proposed the Boneh–Goh–Nissim (BGN) encryption scheme. BGN supports any number of additions and one multiplication while keeping the ciphertext size unchanged. Yuval Ishai and Anat Paskin proposed IP to extend homomorphic operations to branching programs (Ishai and Paskin, 2007). A branch program is another approach to express computation functions besides circuits. Its conditional branch supports performing the next operation according to the previous calculation result, which is more suitable for expressing functions with conditional branch logic. The ciphertext length of IP encryption is only related to the program depth and plaintext size, and is independent of the size of the program (specifically, it is not affected by the number of branches in the conditional statement). Therefore, IP can support homomorphic operations in the form of branching programs of any size under the condition of limited depth. Due to space limitations, this section only introduces the representative SWHE algorithm BGN in detail. The implementation of BGN is based on the hard *subgroup decision problem*. The subgroup decision problem attempts to determine whether an element belongs to a subgroup of order p in a group of order $n = pq$ (p, q are prime numbers).

The key reason why BGN can support both addition and multiplication is that it proposes a set of methods that can construct a bilinear map $e: G \times G \rightarrow G_1$ between two groups G and G_1. The bilinear map satisfies that when fixing one input element, there is a linear relationship between the other input element and the output. That is, $\forall u, v \in G$, and $a, b \in \mathbb{Z}$, there are $e(u^a, v^b) = e(u, v)^{ab}$. The method proposed by BGN can generate two multiplicative cyclic groups G, G_1 of equal order and establish their bilinear mapping relationship e. It also satisfies that, when g is the generator of G, $e(g, g)$ is the generator of G_1. Before the multiplication is performed, the ciphertext belongs to the elements in the group G, and the homomorphic addition operation of the ciphertext can be performed using the binary operation of the group G. The multiplicative homomorphic operation of the ciphertext maps the ciphertext from the group G to the elements of G_1 through the bilinear mapping function. After performing the multiplication homomorphic operation, the ciphertexts in G_1 still support homomorphic addition. The specific implementation of the BGN encryption scheme is as follows:

- Key generation function: Given security parameters, BGN selects two large prime numbers q_1, q_2 and obtains the composite $n = q_1 q_2$. It will then construct two cyclic groups G, G_1 of the order n and the bilinear mapping relationship (q_1, q_2, G, G_1, e). Then, select two generators g, u randomly from G, and obtain $h = u^{q_2}$. It can be known that h is the generator of a subgroup of G with the order q_1. The public key is set to (n, G, G_1, e, g, h), and the private key is set to q_1.

- Encryption function: for the plaintext message m (a natural number less than q_2), randomly extract an integer r between 0 and n to generate the following ciphertext:

$$c = \text{Enc}(m) = g^m h^r \in G. \tag{3.12}$$

- Decryption function: use the private key q_1 to firstly calculate $c^{q_1} = (g^m h^r)^{q_1} = (g^{q_1})^m$, and then the discrete logarithm $m = \text{Dec}(c) = \log_{g^{q_1}} c^{q_1}$.

The preceding ciphertext satisfies homomorphic addition: for two ciphertexts c_1, c_2, the homomorphic addition is the ciphertext multiplication $c_1 c_2 h^r$. Its homomorphic multiplication is realized by a bilinear mapping function. Let $g_1 = e(g, g)$ and $h_1 = e(g, h)$, and write h as $h = g^{\alpha q_2}$ (because g can generate $u: u = g^\alpha$), the homomorphic multiplication of c_1, c_2 is as follows:

$$e(c_1, c_2)h^r = e(g^{m_1} h^{r_1}, g^{m_2} h^{r_2})h_1^r = g_1^{m_1 m_2} h_1^{\hat{r}} \in G_1, \tag{3.13}$$

where $\hat{r} = m_1 r_2 + r_2 m_1 + \alpha q_2 r_1 r_2 + r$ is also uniformly distributed between 0 and n, like those r randomly selected before.

It can be seen that the ciphertext after homomorphic multiplication is transferred from G to G_1, and its decryption process is completed on G_1 (replace g with the generator $g_1 = e(g, g)$ of G_1). The homomorphic addition operation can still be performed on the group G_1, so BGN supports homomorphic addition after the homomorphic multiplication. However, because there is no more group to continue the transferring, the ciphertext encrypted by BGN can only support only one multiplication homomorphic operation.

3.2.6 Fully Homomorphic Encryption

Although many PHE and SWHE solutions had arisen after the concept of HE was proposed, there had not really been a fully homomorphic encryption scheme that can support unlimited types of homomorphic operations until 2009, when Craig Gentry, a doctoral student at Stanford University, proposed the first practical FHE scheme (Gentry, 2009). He gave a detailed elaboration of the scheme in his doctoral dissertation. Based on SWHE schemes, Gentry creatively proposed a technique he called "bootstrapping," which can be used to transform an SWHE scheme that meets specific conditions into an FHE scheme.

As mentioned earlier, SWHE schemes can support various types of homomorphic operations for a limited number of times. However, because these schemes do not satisfy strong homomorphism, the size of their ciphertext increases with the progress of homomorphic operations, until they no longer meet the requirements of homomorphic operations. If we want to keep performing homomorphic operations, a straightforward way is to decrypt the ciphertext and encrypt it again, so that you can get a *fresh* ciphertext. This process is simply called *refreshing*. The refreshed ciphertext can be regarded as being reset to a fresh ciphertext just encrypted, thus continuing to support homomorphic operations. However, in this method, the ciphertext needs to be decrypted using the private key, which violates the principle of HE that performs operations on ciphertexts. Gentry was acutely aware that if we can design an encryption scheme where its decryption operation itself could be made a homomorphic operation, we can perform the "refresh" operation without decryption. The process can be briefly described as follows:

- For a given HE scheme $\mathcal{E}$, after generating the public–private key pair, encrypt the private key sk with the public key pk again to obtain $\overline{sk}$.
- When performing the homomorphic operation on a ciphertext ct, use the public key to perform another encryption to obtain ciphertext $\overline{ct}$ that is

encrypted twice. Given the decryption operation as $D_{\mathcal{E}}$, since $\mathcal{E}$ supports homomorphic decryption operation, we use the double encrypted ciphertext $\overline{ct}$ and the encrypted private key $\overline{sk}$ for homomorphic decryption Evaluate(pk, $D_{\mathcal{E}}, \overline{ct}, \overline{sk}$). After the operation, the inside ciphertext before the second encryption has been decrypted, thus the result now can be regarded as a fresh ciphertext on the original plaintext message.[2]

- Continue to perform a series of homomorphic operations on the new ciphertext.

If the HE scheme employed supports KDM-Security (Key-Dependent Message Security, the security in the case where the attacker knows the encrypted ciphertext of the private key), the preceding scheme is safe. It can be observed that, even if the input ciphertext is an *old* ciphertext that has been going through multiple homomorphic operations to reach the upper limit, by performing homomorphic decryption with the above algorithm, we decrypt the *old* ciphertext inside the newly encrypted black box and then continue to perform homomorphic operations on the new ciphertext. In this way, an SWHE scheme that can only support a limited number of homomorphic operations can be transformed into a fully homomorphic scheme that can support an infinite number of homomorphic operations. This technique is called *bootstrapping*. An SWHE scheme that can be bootstrapped is bootstrappable. All in all, as long as a bootstrappable SWHE scheme that satisfies KDM-security is given, the corresponding fully homomorphic scheme can be constructed by combining the bootstrapping technique. Under this core idea, Gentry proposed his ideal lattice-based FHE scheme.

Lattice-based encryption systems have been widely used in recent years, mainly due to the high efficiency of encryption and decryption and the high difficulty of the problems they are based on. Its encryption and decryption mainly use linear algebra operations, which are relatively efficient and easy to implement. In order to achieve a security level of k bits, encryption and decryption of traditional encryption systems (Elgamal, RSA, and ECC) based on large integer factorization or discrete logarithm problems generally require $O(k^3)$ time complexity, while lattice-based encryption systems only require $O(k^2)$. In addition, the advent of quantum computing has greatly increased the capability of solving difficult problems. Classical hard problems, such as factoring large numbers, have been shown to be solvable by quantum computers in polynomial time. However, no quantum algorithm can solve the lattice-based hard problems in polynomial time for now.

---

[2] The influence of homomorphic decryption operation on ciphertexts is ignored here.

Firstly, Gentry proposed a somewhat encryption scheme based on ideal lattices. Ideal lattices are a special type of lattice that are also ideals in rings. On the polynomial ring $\mathbb{Z}[x]/(f(x))$, the ideal can be constructed through cyclic lattices. Cyclic lattices are a special class of lattice. Given a vector $v_0 = (v_1, v_2, v_3, \ldots, v_n)^\mathrm{T}$, you can perform rotational shift operation on it to obtain a series of vectors: $v_1 = (v_n, v_1, v_2, \ldots, v_{n-1})^\mathrm{T}$, $v_2 = (v_{n-1}, v_n, v_1, \ldots, v_{n-2})^\mathrm{T}$, $\ldots$. A lattice generated based on the preceding n generated vectors is called a cyclic lattice. On a polynomial ring, the basis of a cyclic lattice is obtained by giving a polynomial $v \in L$ and then successively modular multiplying x, that is, $\{v_i = v_0 * x^i \pmod{f(x)} | i \in [0, n-1]\}$. It is proved that the cyclic lattices constructed on the polynomial ring are also the ideals of the ring, and thus are called ideal lattices.

Gentry's ideal lattice–based SWHE scheme is implemented as follows:

- Key generation function: Given a polynomial ring $R: \mathbb{Z}[x]/(f(x))$ and a fixed basis B_I of a ideal $I \subset R$, generate its ideal lattice J by cyclic lattice to satisfy $I + J = R$, and generate two bases of J: $(B_J^{\mathrm{sk}}, B_J^{\mathrm{pk}})$ as a public–private key pair. One basis B_J^{sk} has a high degree of orthogonality and is used as a private key; another basis B_J^{pk} has a very low degree of orthogonality and is used as a public key. Additionally, a random function $\mathrm{Samp}(B_I, x)$ is provided for sampling from the coset of $x + B_I$. The final public key is $(R, B_I, B_J^{\mathrm{pk}}, \mathrm{Samp}())$, and the private key is B_J^{sk}.
- Encryption function: use B_J^{pk} to encrypt the input plaintext $m \in \{0, 1\}^n$ with randomly selected vector r, g:

$$c = \mathrm{Enc}(m) = m + r \cdot B_I + g \cdot B_J^{\mathrm{pk}}. \tag{3.14}$$

- Decryption function: decrypt the ciphertext c with B_J^{sk}:

$$m = c - B_J^{\mathrm{sk}} \cdot \left\lfloor (B_J^{\mathrm{sk}})^{-1} \cdot c \right\rceil \pmod{B_I}. \tag{3.15}$$

In the formula, $\lfloor \rceil$ indicates that the coordinates of each dimension of the vector are rounded.

In the preceding encryption scheme, c can be regarded as the sum of an element $g \cdot B_J^{\mathrm{pk}}$ in lattice J, the plaintext message m, and a noise $r \cdot B_I$. In the decryption process, the problem to be solved is based on the closest vector problem, that is, to find the closest vector of the ciphertext vector in the lattice J, so that the plaintext message m can be extracted. The decryption function uses $B_J^{\mathrm{sk}} \cdot \left\lfloor (B_J^{\mathrm{sk}})^{-1} \cdot c \right\rceil$ to obtain the closest vector in the lattice through rounding, and subtracts it from the ciphertext modulo B_I to get the plaintext m. This method can only be used when the basis of the lattice is highly orthogonal, so using the public basis B_J^{pk} cannot decrypt the ciphertext. In addition, this method requires the noise term $m + r \cdot B_I$ to be small enough to guarantee that the closest lattice element found during decryption is the same as the lattice element $g \cdot B_J^{pk}$ in encryption.

Since the ciphertext and plaintext in this scheme have a linear relationship, its homomorphic operation is easy to implement. Homomorphic addition can be realized directly with ciphertext addition as follows:

$$c_1 + c_2 = m_1 + m_2 + (r_1 + r_2) \cdot B_I + (g_1 + g_2) \cdot B_J^{pk}. \qquad (3.16)$$

The result is still in ciphertext space, and as long as $m_1 + m_2 + (r_1 + r_2) \cdot B_I$ is relatively small, we can obtain $m_1 + m_2$ by the preceding decryption function. The homomorphic multiplication is also based on ciphertext multiplication:

$$c_1 \cdot c_2 = e_1 e_2 + (e_1 g_2 + e_2 g_1 + g_1 g_2) \cdot B_J^{pk},$$
$$e_1 = m_1 + r_1 \cdot B_I,$$
$$e_2 = m_2 + r_2 \cdot B_I. \qquad (3.17)$$

The result is still in the ciphertext space, and when $|e_1 \cdot e_2|$ is small enough, we can obtain $m_1 \cdot m_2$ with the preceding decryption function. With the accumulation of homomorphic addition and multiplication, the noise term in the ciphertext gradually accumulates until the plaintext can no longer be deciphered. Therefore, the encryption scheme is an SWHE scheme. By further using other designs with the scheme, Gentry combines the preceding scheme with the bootstrapping technique to realize the first FHE scheme that can support an infinite number of homomorphic addition and multiplication operations.

Gentry's pioneering work has rekindled researchers' enthusiasm for FHE. Subsequently, Smart and Vercauteren (2010) further optimized the FHE scheme proposed by Gentry. Van Dijk et al. (2010) propose an FHE scheme in the integer field based on the approximate greatest common divisor problem. Brakerski and Vaikuntanathan (2011) proposed an FHE scheme based on the Ring Learning with Error (RLWE) problem. López-Alt et al. (2012) proposed an improved FHE scheme based on the NTRUEncrypt public key encryption scheme.

3.2.7 Leveled Homomorphic Encryption

Leveled homomorphic encryption is a weaker version of FHE. The LHE scheme can support any circuit depth, input size, and circuit size defined in the security parameters. After Gentry proposed the bootstrapping method, the fully homomorphic problem of supporting an infinite number of homomorphic operations has been solved. As long as an efficient and available LHE algorithm is given, combined with the bootstrapping method, researchers can construct a corresponding FHE scheme. Therefore, most researchers have aimed to design faster and more efficient LHE algorithms since then. Among them, the schemes based on the RLWE problem have become the mainstream scheme for FHE in the current industry because of their simple implementation, high performance, and ability to support batch operations.

According to the supported circuits and underlying mathematical foundations, the current LHE schemes based on the RLWE problem are mainly divided into two classes: one is derived from the GSW encryption scheme originated from Gentry et al. (2013), which mainly focuses on the calculation of Boolean circuits. Among the important subsequent works are FHEW (Ducas and Micciancio, 2015) and TFHE (Chillotti et al., 2020). The other class originated from BGV (Brakerski et al., 2014) mainly focusing on numerical calculation. The main subsequent works are FV (Fan and Vercauteren, 2012) and HEAAN (or CKKS) (Cheon et al., 2017). In addition, a series of recently proposed schemes, such as CHIMERA (Boura et al., 2018) and PEGASUS (Jie Lu et al., 2020), have designed operations to transform ciphertext between different encryption schemes to utilize their benefits on different operations to accelerate the computation speed. This section will introduce CKKS in detail. It supports approximate homomorphic operations based on floating-point numbers, which fits popular machine learning applications and thus has received a lot of attention and has been widely used. Before introducing CKKS, we need to give a basic introduction to LWE and RLWE problems. The Learning with Error (LWE) problem was proposed by Oded Regev in 2009 in his paper "On Lattices, Learning with Errors, Random Linear Codes, and Cryptography" (Regev, 2009), for which he won the 2018 Gödel Prize. LWE is also a problem constructed on the lattice problems. The LWE problem can be viewed as solving a noisy system of linear equations: given a random vector $s \in \mathbb{Z}_q^n$, a random coefficient matrix $A \in \mathbb{Z}_q^{n \times n}$, and random noise $e \in \mathbb{Z}_q^n$, we can generate linear operation output$(A, bmA \cdot s + e)$. The LWE problem attempts to infer the value of s from this output. Regev (2009) has proven that LWE is at least as difficult as the problems in lattices, and thus also resistant to attacks from quantum computers.

The simplicity of the LWE problem makes the implementation of cryptosystems built on top of it also very simple. For example, we can use $(-A \cdot s + e, A)$ as the public key and s as the private key. For messages that need to be encrypted $m \in \mathbb{Z}_q^n$, we can use the public key encryption function $(c_0, c_1) = (m - A \cdot s + e, A)$. Cracking this ciphertext is at least as difficult as cracking the LWE problem, so its security is guaranteed. When decrypting with the private key, we only need to calculate $c_0 + c_1 \cdot s = m + e$. When the noise e is small enough, the plaintext m can be recovered with limited information loss.

Based on LWE, Lyubashevsky et al. (2010) further proposed the ring learning with errors (RLWE) problem, extending the LWE problem to the ring structure. Ring learning with errors replaces the n-dimensional vector space on the ring $\mathbb{Z}_q$ in LWE with an n-order polynomial ring $\mathbb{Z}_q[X]/(X^N + 1)$. Therefore, the vectors s, e, m in the preceding LWE problem are replaced by polynomials in the polynomial ring. The $n \times n$ coefficient matrix A is replaced by the 1×1 polynomial $a \in \mathbb{Z}_q[X]/(X^N + 1)$. Through the replacement, the public key size of RLWE is reduced from $O(n^2)$ to $O(n)$ without reducing the amount of data carried by the message m (as the n-dimensional vector is replaced by an n-order polynomial). In addition, polynomial-based multiplication operations can be accelerated by a discrete Fourier transform algorithm to achieve $O(n \log(n))$ computational complexity, which is faster than matrix–vector multiplication.

Based on the RLWE problem, the HEANN/CKKS leveled homomorphic encryption scheme is implemented as follows:

- Key generation function: given security parameters, CKKS generates private key $s \in \mathbb{Z}_q[X]/(X^N + 1)$ and public key $p = (-a \cdot s + e, a)$. a, e both are randomly selected from the polynomial ring $a, e \in \mathbb{Z}_q[X]/(X^N + 1)$, and e is small.
- Encryption function: For a given message $m \in \mathbb{C}^{N/2}$ (represented as a complex vector), CKKS first needs to encode it and map it to a polynomial ring to generate $r \in \mathbb{Z}[X]/(X^N + 1)$ (see the original paper for the specific method). Then, CKKS encrypts r with the public key as follows:

$$(c_0, c_1) = (r, 0) + p = (r - a \cdot s + e, a). \tag{3.18}$$

- Decryption function: For the ciphertext (c_0, c_1), CKKS uses the private key for decryption as follows:

$$\tilde{r} = c_0 + c_1 * s = r + e. \tag{3.19}$$

$\tilde{r}$ needs to be decoded and mapped back from the polynomial ring to the vector space $\mathbb{C}^{N/2}$. When the noise e is small enough, an approximate result of the original message can be obtained.

The CKKS scheme supports floating-point arithmetic operations. In order to save the floating-point numbers in the message, CKKS sets a scaling factor $\Delta > 0$ during the encoding process and multiplies the floating-point numbers by the scaling factor to generate an integer polynomial term whose exponent is stored in the scaling factor Δ.

The CKKS scheme also supports homomorphic addition and multiplication. Given two ciphertexts ct_1 and ct_2, the corresponding homomorphic addition is as follows:

$$ct_1 + ct_2 = (c_0, c_1) + (c_0', c_1') = (c_0 + c_0', c_1 + c_1'). \quad (3.20)$$

The corresponding homomorphic multiplication is as follows:

$$ct_1 \cdot ct_2 = (c_0, c_1) \cdot (c_0', c_1') = (c_0 \cdot c_0', c_0 \cdot c_1' + c_1 \cdot c_0', c_1 \cdot c_1'). \quad (3.21)$$

After each homomorphic multiplication, CKKS needs to perform *relinearization* and *rescaling* operations to enable further multiplication. It can be observed that after a homomorphic multiplication operation is performed, the size of the ciphertext is increased by half. The CKKS scheme provides a relinearization technique (Chen et al., 2019), which can convert the amplified ciphertext $(c_0 \cdot c_0', c_0 \cdot c_1' + c_1 \cdot c_0', c_1 \cdot c_1')$ back to the binary pair (d_0, d_1) allowing for more homomorphic multiplication operations. In addition, because the scaling factor Δ is used in the encoding process, when the homomorphic multiplication operation is performed, the ciphertexts whose two scaling factors are both Δ are multiplied, and the resulting scaling factor becomes Δ^2. If homomorphic multiplication is used successively, the scaling factor will increase exponentially. Therefore, after each multiplication operation, CKKS will perform a rescaling operation, dividing the ciphertext value by Δ to restore the scaling factor from Δ^2 to Δ, which is implemented by truncating the polynomial coefficients. In the process of successively rescaling and dividing by Δ, the available bits in polynomial coefficients will drop by $\log(\Delta)$ bits each time until eventually exhausted, and no more homomorphic multiplication is allowed. Therefore, the modulo q used in the polynomial ring determines the depth of the computational circuit.

During the process of encryption, decryption, relinearization, and rescaling of CKKS, the accumulated noise will affect the precision and accuracy of the final decrypted message. Therefore, while CKKS supports floating-point operations, trade-offs are made to the accuracy of the results. The CKKS scheme is suitable for floating-point-based computation applications that are tolerant of small errors, such as machine learning tasks.

3.3 Advantages and Disadvantages

Compared with other tools used in privacy-preserving computing such as secret sharing and garbled circuits, one benefit of HE is its noninteractive property. The ciphertext encrypted by HE schemes can theoretically support an unlimited number of various homomorphic operations in the cloud and can continue to be transmitted to other endhosts for further operations without compromising the user's privacy. The parties holding private keys are not required to participate in the computation process, thereby freeing users from the private computing task over their data.

Taking the machine learning inference service provided by the cloud as an example, users can encrypt their own data with HE and upload the ciphertexts to the cloud server for machine learning inference tasks. The entire inference process does not require the participation of the user. Finally, the cloud server returns the generated encrypted inference result to the user, which the user decrypts to get the result. If using secure multiparty computing protocols, users usually need to continuously interact with the server during the computing process to provide auxiliary computing, greatly increasing communication and computing overhead at the client side. When the client computation power and network bandwidth are limited, the interaction will become the bottleneck of the entire privacy-preserving computing process. On the other hand, the encryption, decryption, and homomorphic operations of HE can be completed without the participation of multiple parties. Thus, compared with other solutions, HE-based solutions generally require fewer participants to achieve the same function and generally do not require a trusted third party to provide computing certification. This makes HE also one of the basic tools for ciphertext exchange and calculation in various multiparty secure protocols.

For now, HE is still in development with some disadvantages: (i) even though Gentry proposed the first FHE scheme in 2009, the existing schemes still suffer from excessive computational and communication overhead. Particularly, the overhead of bootstrapping technique is very large. Therefore, in practical applications, researchers and engineers tend to step back to choose the LHE algorithm with a limited number of homomorphic operations. Table 3.1 gives the running time of homomorphic operations of CKKS under the HE framework SEAL 3.6.

On the other hand, due to the limitation of computing power, most current HE schemes can only support homomorphic addition and multiplication. To support more complex operations, HE schemes need to use security parameters supporting deep circuits whose overheads are heavy. The size and computational cost of the ciphertext are proportional to the number of homomorphic multiplications that can be performed by the ciphertext. Thus, users often need to compromise between efficiency and homomorphic calculation capability. In addition, the security of HE is also often questioned compared to traditional encryption algorithms. Currently, an FHE scheme that can satisfy IND-CCA1

Table 3.1 *The running time of homomorphic operations of LHE scheme CKKS in SEAL 3.6. N and L represent the order of the cyclic polynomial and the ciphertext level, respectively. The former determines the dimension of the ciphertext vector, and the latter determines the upper bound of supported homomorphic multiplication operation number.*

Operation	Running Time μs		
	$N = 2^{12}$ $L = 1$	$N = 2^{13}$ $L = 3$	$N = 2^{14}$ $L = 7$
Add	21	83	330
Multiply	228	906	3682
Rescale	441	1894	8254
Relinearization	1257	6824	44273
Encode	414	1144	3926
Encrypt	2034	29947	20947
Decode	520	1922	8898
Decrypt	72	288	1293
Rotate	1297	6958	44616

has not yet been implemented. And in theory, HE cannot achieve the security level of IND-CCA2 because the attacker can send the ciphertext after the homomorphic operation back to the challenger for decryption. Although this ciphertext is different from the original one, the attacker can perform a simple inverse function to obtain the value of the original ciphertext. In addition, Li and Micciancio (2020) discovered the vulnerability in the floating-point arithmetic-based HE scheme CKKS, and an attacker can conversely derive the private key by analyzing the added noise.

3.4 Applications

According to the techniques used and the supported computations (such as Boolean circuits, integer operations, and floating-point operations), existing HE solutions are divided into multiple branches. For each branch there are lots of available open HE libraries. Table 3.2 gives the mainstream HE libraries and their supported schemes. Readers can find the open-source codes and usage documentations for most of these frameworks on GitHub.

Homomorphic Encryption technology is not only often used as a basic tool in various secure multi-party computing frameworks, but also has a wide range of applications in scenarios such as distributed private computing and cloud private computing. The following section mainly introduces the application examples of HE in two scenarios: private database query and cloud machine learning service.

Table 3.2 *Mainstream homomorphic encryption libraries and supported schemes.*

HE Library	FHEW	TFHE	BGV	BFV	CKKS
HEAAN					✓
cuFHE		✓			
FHEW	✓				
SEAL			✓	✓	✓
TenSEAL				✓	✓
HElib			✓		✓
PALISADE			✓	✓	✓
TFHE	✓	✓		✓	✓

3.4.1 Private Database Query

With HE techniques, servers could provide private database query service, where the clients issue private queries to the database on the server side, and the server cannot learn any information about the query. For example, a user can generate a query "height > 168cm AND height < 180cm AND weight < 65kg" to the server, and the server returns to the user all entries whose height is between 168 cm and 180 cm and whose weight is less than 65 kg. Private queries based on other privacy-preserving computing techniques can only process simple queries, and it is hard to process complex request operations with AND and OR. Dan Boneh proposed a method for private database query based on the SWHE scheme in Boneh et al. (2013), which can effectively support various complex queries.

The three-party protocol between the client, the server, and the proxy is given as follows:

- The server encodes and encrypts the database with the SWHE scheme. Specifically, the server encodes every set of indices (attr = value) into a polynomial $\prod_{s \in S} (x - s)$. In this way, the server has encoded all the possible sets of indices as query output into polynomials, where the roots are the queried indices. The coefficients of the polynomials are encrypted with the SWHE scheme. Then, the server encrypts the (attr, value) as key, uses the encrypted polynomials as value, and sends the key-value pairs to the proxy for further computation.
- When the client issues a private database query, it engages a protocol based on oblivious transfer to obtain all the needed keys representing the index sets (attr, value).
- The client sends all the keys (attr, value) obtained to the proxy to request the actual sets of indices, and the proxy obtains the corresponding encrypted

polynomial A_i. Then, the proxy uses all collected polynomials to generate a linear combination $B(x) = A_1(x)R_1(1) + A_2(x) R_2(x) + \cdots$ with random coefficients. It can be proved that when the range of indices is limited, the root of the linear combination $B(x)$ is the intersection of the roots of each polynomial $A_i(x)$, that is, the intersection of the corresponding index sets. Through the preceding operations, the proxy executes the AND operations in the query. The operations are all performed in the ciphertext under HE. The proxy then returns the ciphertext $B(x)$ to the client.

- After getting $B(x)$, the client performs secure multiparty computation protocol with the server that holds the private key to obtain the decrypted result of $B(x)$. Then, the client performs factorization on it to calculate the roots and obtain the queried indices.

The private database query system implemented on the Brakerski SWHE scheme can process queries on databases with millions of entries in minutes. Overall, the system proposed by Boneh has the following characteristics:

- In traditional private database query systems, when the database server processes queries, it will traverse all the entries in the database indiscriminately. Otherwise, the server can infer the entry requested by the user from the processing record. Also, when returning the query result, the server must also return the information at the level of the entire database, so that no information can be deduced from the result. In this way, when the database volume is large, there will be serious performance and communication overheads. Boneh introduces a proxy as a third party to assist in the query processing, which stores the indices information. The proxy performs homomorphic operations on the encrypted indices and directly sends the result back to the user, thus avoiding the risk of leaking query information on the server side from the processing and transmission procedures.

- The mainstream HE methods are probabilistic encryption schemes, where the output ciphertext of the encryption on the same plaintext at each time is different. Therefore, the ciphertext encrypted by the HE cannot directly perform homomorphic operations based on equivalence, such as element pairing and calculating the intersection of sets. Based on Kissner and Song's method of using polynomials for private intersection calculation (Kissner and Song, 2005), Boneh uses polynomials to represent the index sets in the simplest queries and then uses the linear combination of polynomials to calculate the intersection of sets, so as to process conjunction queries. Both polynomial encryption and private linear operations can be implemented using SWHE schemes.

3.4.2 Machine Learning Service over the Cloud

In recent years, with the development of deep learning technology and the increase of hardware computation power, machine learning applications are playing an increasingly important role in all aspects of people's lives, especially in natural language processing and computer vision. Deep learning has become an infrastructure and core function of many applications. However, with the increase in deep learning model size and the amount of training data, the computation costs for model training and inference are also increasing. Therefore, many cloud service providers have launched cloud-based machine learning services. Companies, organizations, and individuals can upload their data to cloud servers for model training. Also, cloud servers can maintain deep learning models and provide online inference service, and users can upload their data to the cloud for real-time inference. In this process, how to protect data privacy in the training and inference processes has become a significant problem that needs to be solved in privacy-preserving computing. Homomorphic Encryption is one of the techniques providing privacy-preserving machine learning services over the cloud, due to its noninteractive property.

Privacy-preserving machine learning methods based on HE are mainly divided into two categories: private training methods providing centralized training and private inference methods providing privacy-preserving inference services. The majority of these works focus on private inference. For private inference service, the server maintains the model trained in advance to provide online real-time inference service for users. It assumes that the model is public to the server and thus is stored on the server as plaintext. In HE-based private inference methods, the users will upload the encrypted data to the server with HE, which are then calculated with the plaintext model to generate the encrypted inference result. The more popular of these works are CryptoNets (Gilad-Bachrach et al., 2016), Gazelle (Juvekar et al., 2018), and nGraph (Acar et al., 2018; Boemer et al., 2019). Here we will introduce CryptoNets in detail. In CryptoNets, users use LHE to encrypt the input of deep neural networks. The encrypted input is sent to the server, which performs inference on the ciphertext to generate the model output. The encrypted model output is then sent back to users and decrypted to get the inference result. During the inference on deep neural networks, several types of operations/layers are involved according to their characteristics:

- Convolutional layer: This layer performs convolution operation on the input image to extract important features of the image. Each layer consists of a series of convolution kernels, and each convolution kernel performs window sliding and linear operation on local features in the window to check whether the features considered by the kernel exist in each window of the input image.

- Pooling layers: Pooling layers are a type of downsampling technique. This layer divides the input image into several subregions, and then compresses these regions by downsampling to reduce the dimension of the input as well as the model complexity. Common pooling operations include max pooling layer that selects the maximum value in subregions and average pooling layer that selects the average value.
- Activation function: In addition to the linear transformation provided by the convolutional layer, the activation function provides nonlinear transformation between linear layers, thereby improving the model capabilities for extracting nonlinear features. The activation function often uses the Sigmoid or ReLU function.

At present, HE schemes can only support homomorphic addition and multiplication. Thus, they can only support polynomial activation functions. CryptoNets transforms general neural networks as follows: for pooling layers, CryptoNets replaces all nonlinear max-pooling layers with linear average pooling layers; for nonlinear activation functions, CryptoNets uses a square function x^2 instead of other nonlinear activation functions, which can be calculated with homomorphic operations. Then, CryptoNets performs homomorphic inference with encrypted image inputs on the modified neural network model.

CryptoNets can achieve 99 percent prediction accuracy on the digital image dataset MNIST. The work also discusses more problems that may be encountered when applying HE schemes to machine learning models and corresponding optimization methods. For now, there is still limited work providing cloud training services using HE schemes. In the training phase, in order to protect the model parameters and input features from the cloud, the model parameters need to be encrypted, and its model training requires homomorphic arithmetic operations between the encryption layer and the encrypted input, whose computation overhead is much heavier than the operations between model plaintexts and input ciphertexts in private inference services. In addition, current HE methods accumulate noise when performing arithmetic operations and require computationally expensive bootstrapping operations to support successive model update operations on encryption model parameters. Thus, most current privacy-preserving training models based on HE are limited to simple models, such as logistic regression and linear regression models (Crawford et al., 2018; Kim et al., 2018; Nikolaenko et al., 2013;

Wang et al., 2016). Nandakumar et al. (2019) attempted to train deep neural networks in a non-interactive manner on encrypted data using FHE and took more than 10 hours to train just one step on a simple MLP. How to effectively use HE for machine learning model training is still an important question waiting to be solved.

4

Oblivious Transfer

Oblivious Transfer (OT) is one of the basic primitives for building secure multiparty computation (MPC) protocols. In theory, OT is equivalent to MPC, which means MPC can implement OT, and OT can also implement MPC protocols (Kilian, 1988). In this chapter, we first introduce Oblivious Transfer's basic definition and implementation. Then we briefly introduce its application in Garbled Circuit (GC) as an essential building block.

4.1 Definition

The participants of Oblivious Transfer are classified as Sender (S) and Receiver (R). Sender S holds two messages, noted as m_0 and m_1; Receiver R holds one selection bit $b \in \{0, 1\}$. At the end of this protocol, R gets m_b. S learns nothing about b, and R learns nothing about m_{1-b}. Oblivious Transfer gets its name because at the end of the protocol, S is oblivious about the selection bit b, and R is oblivious to the other message. The formal definition of OT is as follows:

Definition 4.1 "1-out-of-2" Oblivious Transfer
  Parties: Sender S and Receiver R.
  Parameters: Sender S owns two messages $x_0, x_1 \in \{0, 1\}^n$, Receiver R owns selection bit $b \in \{0, 1\}$.
  Output: Receiver R gets x_b.

Besides the preceding definition, OT can also be defined as two parties jointly computing the function $f(X, b) = X[b]$, in which X is the data owned by the sender and b is the private input provided by the receiver. Since X is owned by the sender, it makes no difference whether the output is revealed to the sender.

63

There have been various types of OT and different implementations. For example, 1-out-of-2 OT can be extended to 1-out-of-k OT, meaning the sender owns k private messages, and the receiver selection is extended to $0, 1, 2, \ldots, k - 1$. Later in this chapter, we will discuss the implementation of this extension of OT.

4.2 Implementation

It has been proven that OT must be achieved by public key cryptography (Beaver, 1995; Naor and Pinkas, 2001). Even though we could optimize the performance of OT with private key cryptography, we assume that the parties are honest but curious in the following content.

Oblivious Transfer Based on Public Key Cryptography

The instinct of public-key-based OT is to encrypt the message on the sender S with different keys, and the receiver holds only one of the private keys. At the same time, the corresponding public key is used to encrypt the wanted message of the receiver, and the sender S does not know the corresponding private key. With the preceding assumption, we give the implementation of 1-out-of-2 Oblivious Transfer as follows:

Parameters:

- Two participants: Sender S and receiver R
- Sender with two private messages x_1, x_2
- Receiver with private selection bit $b \in \{0, 1\}$

Protocol:

- The receiver generates a public–private key pair using cryptography tools such as RSA. Noted as (pk, sk), it generates a random public key rk, but the receiver does not own the corresponding private key.
- The receiver reorders the keys according to the bit $b \in \{0, 1\}$. For example, if $b = 0$, it generates (pk, rk). If $b = 0$, it generates (rk, pk). The receiver sends the keys to sender S.
- The sender encrypts the messages with the key in the same position. For example, if the received keys are (k_0, k_1), the sender encrypts x_0 with key k_0 and encrypts x_1 with key k_1. Note that the keys are denoted as (k_0, k_1) because the sender S cannot distinguish two keys. After encryption, sender S sends encrypted messages to the receiver R.

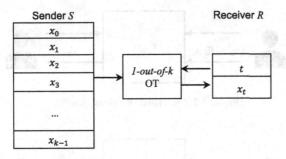

Figure 4.1 1-out-of-k Oblivious Transfer.

- The receiver R decrypts the messages with private key sk. The receiver can decrypt only one ciphertext successfully since it only holds one of the private keys. The other ciphertext, after decryption, will be random garbage. The decrypted message is x_b, which is the desired message of the receiver.

The preceding Oblivious Transfer protocol relies on the security of public key cryptography, in which the private key cannot be calculated from the public key in polynomial time. If we assume that the participants are honest, the protocol is secure because the sender S only knows two public keys from the sender but does not know which private key the receiver holds. The probability that the sender S successfully guesses b of the receiver is no greater than 1/2. The receiver only has one private key, meaning it can decrypt only one of the messages successfully. Decrypting the other message is as difficult as calculating the private key with the public key.

Extension and Optimization of OT

"1-out-of-k" Oblivious Transfer

"1-out-of-2" OT can be extended into "1-out-of-k" OT, as shown in Figure 4.1. The sender S now has k private messages, and the receiver R holds $t \in \{0, 1, \ldots, k - 1\}$. At the end of the protocol, the receiver gets x_t without knowing other messages, and the sender S is oblivious of t.

Based on the protocol in the previous section, it is straightforward to extend "1-out-of-2" OT into "1-out-of-k" OT. The random public key is generated for $k - 1$ times, and the two parties perform "1-out-of-2" OT for $\lceil \log k \rceil$ times.

Correlated OT and Random OT

Sometimes, the sender's message satisfies some conditions, such as correlation or randomness, which can be exploited to improve efficiency (Ishai et al.,

Figure 4.2 Correlated Oblivious Transfer.

Figure 4.3 Random Oblivious Transfer.

2003). In Correlated Oblivious Transfer (C-OT), message x_0 and x_1 on sender satisfy $x_0 = x_1 \oplus T$, in which T is value agreed upon by two parties, as shown in Figure 4.2. C-OT is widely used in secure protocols such as Garbled Circuit (GC) and secret sharing.

In Random Oblivious Transfer (R-OT), the sender's message is generated randomly, as shown in Figure 4.3. Some optimizations have been applied to R-OT and C-OT to improve efficiency. For example, since we know the relationship between the two messages, the data sent to the receiver can be halved in C-OT.

Another optimization of OT lies in symmetric cryptography tools. Public key cryptography (or asymmetric cryptography) is the bottleneck for a large set of OT operations. In this case, symmetric cryptography can be adapted to improve performance without compromise.

Assume that there are m 1-out-of-2 OT operations, and each message contains l bits. The optimized OT uses l basic OT operations and some symmetric encryptions. The OT-Extension gives the following implementation.

Assume that there are m independent OTs between the sender S and the receiver R. The receiver R has m selection bits $r \in \{0, 1\}^m$. The sender S has m pairs of messages, which can be represented by an $m \times 2$ matrix X. At the end of the OT protocol, the receiver R gets the results of n OTs, which are $X_{0,b_0}, X_{1,b_1}, \ldots, X_{n-1,b_{n-1}}$.

First, the receiver R generates random matrices U and T, which satisfies:

- the sizes of U and T are $m \times l$;
- the columns of U and T satisfy $t_j \oplus u_j = r_j \cdot 1^k$.

Then, the sender S generates random bits $s \in \{0, 1\}^k$. The sender S and the receiver R perform k 1-out-of-2 OTs, in which the sender and receiver switch roles. The sender S receives k bits from the sender S with selection bit $s_i \in s, (i = 0, 1, \ldots, k - 1)$ and s_i is used to select from two columns $(u_i, t_i), u_i \in U, t_i \in T$. After k OTs, the sender builds a new matrix Q with received messages. It can be concluded that for column $q_j \in Q$, if $s_j = 0$, $q_j = t_j$; if $s_j = 1, q_j = t_j \oplus s$.

Denote H as some random oracle function (such as a hash function). With the hash function, the sender S generates a set of new matrixes: for the row I, $y_{i,0} = X_{i,0} \oplus H(i, q_i), y_{i,1} = X_{i,1} \oplus H(i, q_i \oplus s)$. And the sender sends all $y_{i,0}, y_{i,1}$ to the receiver R. Finally, the receiver calculates $z_i = y_{i,r_i} \oplus H_j, t_j$. In this protocol, we only conduct k OTs. Later operations only involve the random oracle function and bit-wise operations. When $m \gg k$, which means the number of OTs is far greater than the length of the ciphertexts, the extended version of OT performs better.

4.3 Applications

OT in Other MPC Protocols

At the beginning of this chapter, we mentioned that MPC could be implemented by OT, and OT could be implemented by some protocols of MPC.

In the secret sharing protocols, OT is mainly applied to generate multiplication triples. Compared to other cryptography tools, such as Paillier encryption, generating multiplication triples using OT is much more efficient.

The generation of multiplication triples using OT is as follows:

- Party A generates random data a_0, b_0. Party B generates random data a_1, b_1.
- Party A calculates $a_0 \times b_0$. Party B calculates $a_1 \times b_1$.
- Party A and Party B collaboratively conduct C-OT protocol for l times, in which party A plays as the sender, party B plays as the receiver, and l stands for the bit-length of random data. In the ith OT, b_i in party B is the choice bit, and the correlation function is $f_{\delta_i}(x) = (a_0 \cdot 2^i - x) \mod 2^l$. On the output, Party A gets $(s_{i,0}, s_{i,1})$, in which $s_{i,0}$ is random data and $s_{i,1} = (b_1[i]a_0 \cdot 2^i - s_{i,0}) \mod 2^l$.
- Party A calculates $u_0 = \sum_{i=1}^{l} s_{i,0} \mod 2^l$ and Party B, $u_1 = \sum_{i=1}^{l} s_{i,b_1[i]} \mod 2^l$.

In the preceding protocol, we generate multiplication triples using OT. After the protocol, party A gets $u_0 = (a_1 * b_0)_0$ and party B gets $u_1 = (a_1 * b_0)_1$. Similarly, we may conduct the same protocol again, and party A gets $u_0 = (a_0 * b_1)_0$ and party B gets $u_1 = (a_0 * b_1)_1$.

Notice that in secret sharing, $a * b = (a_0 + a_1) \cdot (b_0 + b_1) = a_0 \cdot b_0 + a_1 \cdot b_0 + a_0 \cdot b_1 + a_1 \cdot b_1$. In these terms, $a_0 \cdot b_0$ and $a_1 \cdot b_1$ can be computed locally, and $a_1 \cdot b_0, a_0 \cdot b_1$ can be calculated with the above protocols. Finally, these factors are added together. Party A gets c_0 and Party B gets c_1, and c_0, c_1 satisfy $c_0 + c_1 = (a_0 + a_1) \cdot (b_0 + b_1)$.

Compared to the MT generation protocol using partially homomorphic encryption, OT-based MT generation is more efficient because OT has shorter communication and computation overhead.

Application in Garbled Circuit

In Garbled Circuit, OT is applied to send the circuit so the other party can evaluate the result. The input of GC is transformed into ciphertexts by garbling, and sending the input will expose the plaintext. Therefore, in GC, the Garbler and Evaluator conduct OT to protect their private input. We will introduce GC in Chapter 5.

5

Garbled Circuit

Garbled Circuit (GC) is an MPC protocol conducted on the circuit level. The computation overhead of the GC is relatively low. Garbled Circuit has a wide range of applications because circuits can express complicated functions. Every function described as a circuit can be collaboratively evaluated in GC. In this chapter, we first introduce the definition and basic primitives of GC. Then, we introduce the implementation and optimization of GC. Finally, we give an analysis of the pros and cons of GC and its applications.

5.1 Definition

Garbled Circuit defines two participants: garbler and evaluator. First, the garbler expresses the task as a circuit and performs garbling. The input and output of the GC are ciphertexts. Then, the garbler sends the circuit to the evaluator, who evaluates the circuit with ciphertexts and sends the result to the garbler. Finally, the garbler decrypts the result as plaintext.

In the following paragraphs, the garbler is noted as Alice and the evaluator as Bob. We explain GC with an analogy to homomorphic encryption.

There are multiple implementations for generating GC, but all these implementations are based on circuit representation. First, consider the table of a single gate. For example, an AND gate has two input signals and one output signal, as shown in Table 5.1.

It can be observed that the table of a gate represents the mapping from input signals to output signals. All kinds of gates can be expressed with these mappings. The mapping can also be converted into ciphertexts, as shown in Table 5.2.

After garbling the input signals, both parties hold their mapping from input signals to ciphertexts. Moreover, Alice has the mapping from output signals to

69

Table 5.1 *Two-input AND gate.*

α	β	Output
0	0	0
0	1	0
1	0	0
1	1	1

Table 5.2 *Garbled AND gate.*

α	β	Output
c_{α_0}	c_{β_0}	c_{o_0}
c_{α_0}	c_{β_1}	c_{o_0}
c_{α_1}	c_{β_0}	c_{o_0}
c_{α_1}	c_{β_1}	c_{o_1}

ciphertexts. In this way, we have built a circuit in which the input signals and output signals are all ciphertexts. The evaluation of this circuit is as follows:

- Both parties provide their input signals. The input signals are generated by encrypting the private input by the parties. To ensure that the plaintext of the input signal is safe, the mapping from ciphertexts to input signals shall not be leaked to the other party.
- The parties get output ciphertexts after evaluation. In practice, this is done by the evaluator.
- Alice gets the plaintext output based on the mapping from ciphertext to output signals, similar to decryption. At last, Alice tells the other party about the plaintext output.

From the preceding process, we know that the idea of GC is still encryption-evaluation-decryption. The difference with other protocols is that the GC does not rely on the cryptography tool's homomorphism. Instead, it regards the gates as a table. Since most privacy-preserving applications can be represented as circuits with truth tables, GC can be adapted to many applications.

Extending from single gates to circuits works as follows. Every circuit can be represented as input, gate, and output signals. If we know how to connect two gates in GC, we can extend the GC to any number of gates because the output signal of the prior gate is the input signal of the next gate.

In practice, the privacy-preserving computing application is regarded as a function f, whose inputs consist of private data from all parties. Since the data in the computer has a finite number of bits, f can be expressed as a circuit that consists of wires and gates. Then it can be evaluated with the GC.

When two gates are connected, in which the last gate's output wire is the input wire of the next gate, the output of the prior gate is a ciphertext of 0 or 1 and can be passed to the next gate. In this way, we have built a GC with multiple connecting gates.

This section has introduced the basic ideas of garbled circuits. In practice, many details, such as choosing encryption schemes and GC generation algorithms, may also be considered. Next, we give the implementation and optimization of GC.

5.2 Implementation

In the previous section, we give a basic construction scheme for GC. To implement GC, some details need to be addressed, such as the party that performs garbling and the algorithms for garbling. We first illustrate the difficulty in garbling and give a simple algorithm. Finally, we introduce some optimizations and analyze the costs.

The mapping from private input to ciphertext is kept private by the party. Otherwise, the privacy data will be leaked to other parties. However, private mapping leads to a dilemma: on the one hand, the data and mapping need to be kept private during garbling; on the other hand, the evaluator needs the mapping to decrypt the result after evaluation.

We introduce an OT-based approach to solve this problem efficiently. In Chapter 4, we give the definition of OT: the sender keeps private messages m_0 and m_1 and sends m_b to the receiver, in which the receiver knows nothing about m_{1-b} and the sender knows nothing about b. In general, the function of OT can be expressed as $f(m, b) = m[b]$, in which m is the array of messages and b is the choice of receiver.

OT-based Implementation

First, we express GC with the key and ciphertexts instead of lookup tables. A two-input AND gate can be expressed as in Table 5.3. Compared to the table, the inputs of the gate are keys, and the outputs become ciphertexts which are generated by encrypting the output signal with corresponding keys iteratively. The ciphertext can only be decrypted by the corresponding combination of key pairs because the combination is unique in the table.

With the preceding character, we can garble the circuit without revealing any private input. The protocol is as follows:

• The parties (noted as Alice and Bob) express the task as a circuit.

Table 5.3 *Garbled AND Gate with Key.*

α	β	Output
k_{α_0}	k_{β_0}	$E(E(0, k_{\alpha_0}), k_{\beta_0})$
k_{α_0}	k_{β_1}	$E(E(0, k_{\alpha_0}), k_{\beta_1})$
k_{α_1}	k_{β_0}	$E(E(0, k_{\alpha_1}), k_{\beta_0})$
k_{α_1}	k_{β_1}	$E(E(1, k_{\alpha_1}), k_{\beta_1})$

- Alice generates key pairs for every input signal, and every key pair is mapped to the 0/1 signals. Note that the key pair is two independent keys instead of a public-private key pair.
- Alice encrypts all possible output signals with the corresponding combination of keys. This step is called garbling.
- Alice sends the corresponding key to Bob.
- Alice and Bob perform OT, where Bob plays the receiver, and Alice plays the sender. Alice holds the key pairs, which are mapped to the input of Bob. Bob holds his private input.
- Alice sends the GC to Bob, who decrypts all the output with his key pair. If the decryption is successful, the decrypted signal is the output signal of the circuit. Bob will send the output signal to Alice if needed.

Here, we also start from a simple AND gate to illustrate the garbling and evaluation. Then we generalize the garbling to all circuits.

Garbling AND Gate

Assume that Alice's input is α and Bob's input is β. The algorithm for garbling is as follows:

- Alice generates key pairs for all inputs and possible signals, namely $k_{\alpha_0}, k_{\alpha_1}$ and k_{β_0}, k_{β_1}.
- Garbling the circuit: Alice iteratively encrypts possible output signals with corresponding key pairs, namely $E(E(0, k_{\alpha_0}), k_{\beta_0})$, $E(E(0, k_{\alpha_0}), k_{\beta_1})$, $E(E(0, k_{\alpha_1}), k_{\beta_0})$, $E(E(1, k_{\alpha_1}), k_{\beta_1})$.
- Alice sends the ciphertexts to Bob.
- Evaluation: Alice sends the corresponding key pairs to Bob. For example, if $\alpha = 1$, Alice will send k_{α_1} to Bob. Then the parties perform OT, in which Alice plays as the sender who owns private data k_{β_0}, k_{β_1} and Bob plays as the receiver who owns β. It can be observed that after OT, Bob has the corresponding key for decryption, and Alice knows nothing about the value of β.

Table 5.4 *General Garbled Circuits.*

α_1	α_2	$\cdots$	α_m	β_1	β_2	$\cdots$	β_n	Output
$k_{\alpha_{10}}$	$k_{\alpha_{20}}$	$\cdots$	$k_{\alpha_{m0}}$	$k_{\beta_{10}}$	$k_{\beta_{20}}$	$\cdots$	$k_{\beta_{n0}}$	$E(E(\cdots E(0,k_{\alpha_{10}})\cdots k_{\beta_{10}})\cdots k_{\beta_{n0}})$
$k_{\alpha_{11}}$	$k_{\alpha_{20}}$	$\cdots$	$k_{\alpha_{m0}}$	$k_{\beta_{10}}$	$k_{\beta_{20}}$	$\cdots$	$k_{\beta_{n0}}$	$E(E(\cdots E(0,k_{\alpha_{10}})\cdots k_{\beta_{10}})\cdots k_{\beta_{n0}})$
						$\cdots$		
$k_{\alpha_{11}}$	$k_{\alpha_{21}}$	$\cdots$	$k_{\alpha_{m1}}$	$k_{\beta_{11}}$	$k_{\beta_{21}}$	$\cdots$	$k_{\beta_{n1}}$	$E(E(\cdots E(0,k_{\alpha_{10}})\cdots k_{\beta_{11}})\cdots k_{\beta_{n1}})$

Next, Bob tries to decrypt the ciphertexts with his keys, and the successful decryption gives the output of the AND gate.

For a concrete example, assume that $\alpha = 0$ and $\beta = 1$. Alice sends k_{α_0} to Bob. Then Alice and Bob perform OT, after which Bob has k_{β_1} without knowing k_{β_0}, and Alice knows nothing about β. Now Bob has the key pair and is able to decrypt $E(E(0,k_{\alpha_0}),k_{\beta_1})$. Other ciphertexts cannot be decrypted because they are encrypted with different key pairs. Note that to ensure security, Alice will randomly sort the ciphertexts so that Bob cannot tell the input signal in the order. Besides, the security of OT ensures that Alice knows nothing about the input signal of Bob.

General Circuits

For any gate, we denote the input of the gate as $\alpha_1, \alpha_2, \ldots, \alpha_m$, and $\beta_1, \beta_2, \ldots, \beta_n$, in which α_i is the private input of Alice and β_i the private input of Bob.

In the general circuit, Alice generates a key pair for every input signal and iteratively encrypts the output signal with the corresponding combination of keys, as shown in Table 5.4. Then Alice sends the keys, which correspond to the private input of Alice. Then, with OT, Bob receives the key pairs, which correspond to Bob's private input. Finally, Bob decrypts all ciphertexts with his key pairs. The successful decryption gives the output of the gate.

If we represent the secure computation task as a circuit, then every bit of input can be regarded as the input signal of the circuit, and the output signal is the output data. So we can build GC with a general description of the gate. However, in practice, this construction brings too much overhead. For example, if we express a 32-bit adder circuit with a single gate, we need 64 key pairs to represent 64 input signals. Moreover, we get 2^{64} possible combinations of inputs that cannot be stored in a computer. So we need a practical protocol for GC. Here we introduce the protocol for the general circuit.

Since the cost for garbling is related to the number of input signals in every gate, we represent the circuit with multiple gates and fewer input signals. For

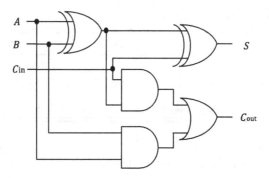

Figure 5.1 Structure of 32-bit adder.

example, we denote the adder circuit with a full-adder circuit as shown in Figure 5.1.

Now every gate in the circuit has two input signals, so the overhead for garbling remains small. However, the output signal of every gate also acts as input for the next gate. So we cannot simply encrypt 0 and 1. The output signals of the gates are expressed as keys so that they can also act as input for the next gates. The protocol for garbling general circuit is as follows:

- The two parties express the task as a circuit.
- Generating keys: Alice generates a key pair for every signal in the circuit.
- Garbling: Based on the true table of the gate, Alice iteratively encrypts the output signal with the corresponding combination of keys. Note that some signals are expressed as keys in order to act as input for the next gates.
- Alice sends the corresponding keys to Bob and then performs OT with Bob to securely send the other key pairs.
- Bob decrypts the ciphertexts for each gate with the corresponding combination of keys. Successful decryption produces a key for the input of the next gate. Finally, the output of the circuit is sent to Alice, who will decrypt the output.

In the protocol, it can be learned that the parties need to tell the difference between a successful decryption and a failed decryption. So, we usually use a key with a smaller length than the ciphertext so that we can tell if the decryption is successful by the length of the output. This protocol has the same security as the protocol in Section 5.1.

Optimizations and Costs

GC has made a great contribution to the application of MPC in the real world. There have been many optimizations on GC which improve the efficiency of

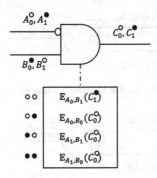

Figure 5.2 Permute-and-point illustration.

garbling and evaluation. In this section, we introduce some optimizations and analyze the costs.

Permute-and-point

In the original implementation of GC, we try to decrypt every ciphertext and find the successfully decrypted one is the output of the circuit. The failed decryption brings extra computation overhead. We hope to save unnecessary decryption and save computation. Beaver–Micali–Rogaway (BMR) protocol (Beaver et al., 1990) provides a solution to save this computation.

First of all, we mark the key pairs with different colors randomly. For example, if we have a pair of keys k_0, k_1, we can mark k_0 as white and k_1 as black, or the reverse. Both schemes are feasible, and we choose one randomly. For two ciphertexts, we use the same color strategy, and different signals have independent coloring schemes.

Then, we sort the ciphertexts based on the coloring scheme. For example, we can sort by WW-WB-BW-BB, as shown in Figure 5.2. Alice sends the sorted ciphertexts to Bob and performs OT to transfer the keys. During decryption, Bob does not decrypt every ciphertext. Instead, Bob decrypts the ciphertext with the same coloring scheme. For example, the coloring scheme of the key is RB, and Bob will only decrypt the second ciphertext. In this way, Bob has only one ciphertext to decrypt during evaluation.

The optimization does not reveal any private information. First, the coloring scheme is totally random, which means Bob cannot get the input of the circuit by the coloring scheme. Second, the ciphertexts are sorted by order of the coloring scheme, which means the order of ciphertexts is random, so Bob cannot tell the input from the position of the ciphertext.

Free XOR

At the beginning of this chapter, we showed that the essence of GC is to replace plain signals with ciphertexts. If we assign some relations to these ciphertexts

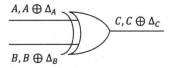

Figure 5.3 Garbled Circuit without fixed offset.

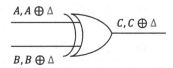

Figure 5.4 Garbled Circuit with fixed offset.

instead of generating them randomly, there could be more opportunities for optimization. Free XOR (Kolesnikov and Schneider, 2008) is one of the techniques that exploit optimization from the relations of ciphertexts. Free XOR proposes zero-cost garbling for XOR gates, which means XOR gates do not need garbling.

To elaborate on the Free XOR scheme, we first introduce a new representation for signals in a circuit. For every signal in the circuit, we use c_0/c_1 to represent $0/1$, respectively. And $c_1 = c_0 \oplus \Delta$, in which Δ is regarded as an offset with respect to the other signal. In the origin implementation, the offset may be different in different wires. For example, in Figure 5.3, the offset of signal A Δ_A and the offset of signal B Δ_B are different. In Free XOR, we set all offsets as the same value so that all wires have the same offset, as shown in Figure 5.4.

For output signal C and input signals A, B in an XOR gate, since we assume that the wires have the same offset, it is observed that

$$A \oplus B = C,$$
$$A \oplus \Delta \oplus B = C \oplus \Delta.$$

Since A and B are input signals for the XOR gate and C is the output signal, the evaluation of the garbled signal is the same as the plain signal. In this case, we do not need to garble the XOR circuit. During garbling, Alice can just XOR the garbled signals of the input, and the result can be used as output signals of the XOR gate.

The optimization will not leak any private data. First, Alice will not tell Bob the value of Δ, which is only used during garbling. Second, Bob cannot tell the plain signal from a garbled signal because even if Δ is the same among all signals, the ciphertexts are random, and it is still random after XORing with Δ.

Although the Free XOR technique optimizes the garbling of XOR gates, other gates, such as AND and NOT gates, still bring computation overhead.

In practice, some optimizations try to convert the circuit into the equivalent circuit with as many XOR gates as possible to improve the performance of garbling.

5.3 Advantages and Disadvantages

Advantages of GC

(i) Computation Efficiency. Garbled Circuit has no restrictions on the encryption scheme, so the programmer can choose an efficient cryptographic system such as AES encryption. Besides, OT is also efficient in terms of computation. As a result, GC is computationally efficient even though it involves a lot of encryption.

(ii) Constant Rounds of Communication. The number of rounds of communication is always constant and has no relevance to the circuit. In other protocols, such as secret sharing, the number of communication rounds is proportional to the depth of the circuit, which brings high communication costs, especially when the RTT (Round Trip Time) is large.

(iii) Generality. As shown in the previous section, GC can be applied to all tasks, which can be expressed as circuits.

Disadvantages of GC

(i) GC cannot be reused. Since every key pair is mapped into a wire and every signal in the wire has only two possible values (0/1), GC can be used only once. A new garbling is needed if the parties want to perform the task again. Otherwise, the parties are able to derive private information from the ciphertexts.

(ii) Huge cost in protocol conversion. In practice, we adopt multiple protocols for the MPC task in order to get the best performance. However, since GC has a bit-level representation, the conversion may bring huge costs, which limit the application of GC in the mixed protocol.

5.4 Applications

Application in Mixed Protocol

Garbled Circuit has great generality and can be applied to all tasks expressed as a circuit. But in many cases, GC is not the most efficient protocol. In practice, we often adopt a mixed-protocol implementation, such as mixing with secret sharing and homomorphic encryption.

Popular frameworks such as ABY(Demmler et al., 2015a) have implemented mixed protocols with both GC and secret sharing. The basic implementation of GC in ABY is as follows:

Assume there are two parties, P_0 and P_1, in which P_0 is the garbler, and P_1 is the evaluator. The protocol adopts permute-and-point and free XOR techniques. Denote the offset as R, and the primitives are as follows:

- Sharing. If P_0 has the secret x, P_0 generates x_0 randomly, sets $k_x = k_0 \oplus xR$, and sends k_x to P_1, in which k_0, k_1 are two keys for the wire. If P_1 has the secret x, P_0 and P_1 perform C-OT, in which P_0 acts as the sender and P_1 acts as the receiver. $f(x) = x \oplus R$. Finally, P_0 gets k_0 and P_1 gets $k_x = k_0 \oplus xR$.
- Reconstruction. P_{1-i} sends the permutation bit $\pi = x_{1-i}[0]$ to P_i, which calculates $x = \pi \oplus x_i[0]$.

Notice that the sharing protocols are different when the secret value is owned by different parties. This is to ensure that the garbler and evaluator stay the same throughout the protocol. The sharing and reconstruction protocol can be regarded as a combination of secret sharing and GC. Since the plaintext of the signal is only relevant to the last bit of the sharing, it can be regarded as the combination of boolean secret sharing and GC. The operations on secret sharings are as follows:

- XOR: With the free XOR technique, XOR can be conducted locally by $z_i = x_i \oplus y_i$.
- AND: P_0 generates the garbled AND circuit and sends it to P_1, who evaluates the gate with corresponding keys.

Since XOR and AND gates are able to build any circuit, we only need these two gates to construct any task as a circuit. XOR gates can be evaluated locally without communication or re-encryption. AND gates involve extra encryption and communication. With this GC protocol based on XOR and AND gates, we can build a circuit with both generality and good performance.

Empirically, GC is also suitable for the following scenarios:

- Problems that cannot be solved in other cryptographic systems. For example, the comparison is not supported in homomorphic encryption, so it can be solved by a comparison circuit in GC.
- Platforms with weak CPU. Compared to other computation-intensive protocols, such as homomorphic encryption, GC has relatively less cost in computation, so it is suitable for platforms with low-performance CPUs, such as mobile devices.

Table 5.5 *Comparison of some GC frameworks.*

Framework	#Parties	Mixed Protocol	Garbling Cost	Communication Rounds	Malicious Security
FairplayMP	≥ 2	No	4	1	Yes
ABY	2	Yes	3	1	No
EMP-Toolkit	2	Yes	2	Multiple	Yes
ObliVM	2	No	3	1	No

- Platforms that prefer fewer communication rounds. Some devices may have large network latency and prefer a protocol with a constant round of communication.
- Hiding the task. After garbling, Bob is unable to tell the semantics of the circuit during evaluation because all wires are encrypted if GC is feasible when one party wants to hide the task from the other party.

Application in General MPC

Some MPC applications can be implemented by pure GC protocol efficiently. Previous works such as FairplayMP (Ben-David et al., 2008) can achieve practical performance on a certain task. Later works such as AgMPC (Wang et al., 2017) focused on optimizations of GC protocol and specific optimizations on different network conditions such as LAN and Internet. Some popular problems are as follows.

- Malicious parties. In this chapter, we assume that the parties are honest but curious. But in practice, the parties may violate the protocol, so authentication is needed to detect the malicious behavior.
- Garbled Circuit protocol for more than two parties.
- Parties with weak CPU or limited bandwidth. Weak CPU or limited bandwidth may cause bottlenecks among parties in GC protocol.

We list some frameworks and their features, as well as their performance. As shown in the table, in practice, we also need to consider the number of parties and malicious security and then select the protocol that has the best performance. Besides, some works have built domain-specific language (Ben-David et al., 2008; Liu et al., 2015) to describe the MPC task and compile it into a circuit.

6

Differential Privacy

In the previous chapters, we have discussed how to achieve the goal of privacy-preserving computing via cryptographic techniques, including secret sharing (SS), homomorphic encryption (HE), and oblivious transfer (OT). In this chapter, we discuss a different approach – differential privacy (DP) – that does not involve cryptography, but instead resorts to randomness. We will introduce problem definitions of differential privacy, compare it with cryptography-based approaches, and discuss its strengths and weaknesses. Finally, we will introduce some real-world applications of differential privacy.[1]

6.1 Introduction

In the previous chapters, we have extensively discussed privacy-preserving techniques based on cryptography. For example, homomorphic encryption (HE) supports additions or multiplications between ciphertexts. Therefore, a data owner D can upload their data in the form of ciphertexts to another party C for computation without leaking any information about the original data to C in the *computation process*. When the computation process finishes, D retrieves the results in ciphertexts, decrypts them, and obtains the results in plaintexts, while C learns nothing about the data owned by D.

However, in real-world applications, the completion of the *computation process* does not necessarily indicate the end of a task. Rather, after the computation process, data owners may need to publish the *computation results*. For example, in financial statements, a corporation should publish all required statistics regarding its financial activities, such as the average salary of employees.

[1] We acknowledge the course *CS 860 – Algorithm for Private Data Analysis* by Dr. Gautam Kamath from the University of Waterloo.

On these occasions, cryptographic techniques are no longer helpful, as results open to the public cannot be published in ciphertexts. Thus, we face another possibility of privacy leakage caused by *computation results*.

We use an example to illustrate the difference between privacy leakage caused by the *computation process* and *computation results*. Let us suppose that a corporation C would like to develop a system that supports querying the average salary of any set of employees. To develop the system, corporation C would like to outsource the task to a cloud computing platform P without leaking information about the salaries. Thus, C can submit encrypted salary data to P with homomorphic encryption to prevent privacy leakage to P. However, privacy risks still linger when the system accepts queries from employees. For example, to compute the salary of Alice, an employee Bob can first query the average salary of the set {*Alice, Bob*} and then subtract his own salary from the result. In this example, the task outsourcing from C to P constitutes the *computation process*, where C can leverage homomorphic encryption to ensure its privacy. The queries processed by the system exemplify the *computation results*, where privacy is easily compromised in the view of any employee.

At this point, readers might be curious about whether it is possible to protect the privacy of computation results with cryptographic techniques. The answer is no, and here is why. In a standard cryptosystem, there are generally three parties, a *sender*, a *receiver*, and an *attacker*, while the goal is to protect privacy against the attacker. For example, by agreeing on a set of keys, a sender Alice can communicate with a receiver Bob, while no attacker without knowledge of the keys can know the contents of their communication. The three-party model also holds for the *computation process*, where the corporation C plays the role of both the sender and the receiver, while the cloud platform P is a potential attacker, and the message is protected from the attacker using homomorphic encryption. However, for the *computation results*, there are only two parties, a data *curator* who publishes the results (analogous to the sender), and an *analyst* who obtains the results (analogous to the receiver) and derives private information about the curator (analogous to the attacker). Correspondingly, protecting privacy information in the *computation results* would, in the three-party cryptosystem, be analogous to (informally) the sender sending a message to the receiver without allowing the receiver to learn what is sent.

At first glance, this may seem impossible. How can a curator publish meaningful results about its data to analysts without leaking privacy on exactly the same data? The concept of Differential Privacy (DP) proposed by Dwork and McSherry (Dwork et al., 2006) addresses the dilemma. For example, in the preceding example, corporation C can leverage homomorphic encryption to prevent privacy leakage to *P*, and can simultaneously leverage DP to prevent privacy leakage to those who query the system. Due to its flexibility and high efficiency, DP has attracted significant attention from both the research community and the industry. In practice, DP has been extensively deployed by major corporations such as Apple, Google, and Microsoft in their most popular applications, such as Safari, Siri, Android, and Windows (Apple, 2017; Ding et al., 2017).

However, as there is no free lunch, we have to pay certain costs for the privacy achieved by DP. More specifically, although DP has appealing properties such as efficiency and flexibility, it suffers from drawbacks such as inaccurate computation results. In this chapter, we will introduce DP, including basic concepts, definitions, and implementations. We will also cover practical applications of DP as well as its strengths and weaknesses.

6.2 Problem Definition

Before going into detailed definitions and concepts, here we would like to emphasize two major differences between DP and cryptographic techniques.

- **Privacy Definition.** As stated in Section 6.1, DP focuses on protecting the privacy of *computation results*, while cryptographic techniques focus on that of the *computation process*.
- **Technical Foundation.** Cryptographic techniques generally build their approaches upon problems that are computationally hard to solve, such as factorization problems and discrete logarithm problems. On the other hand, DP is primarily established upon *probability theory* and *randomness*, as we will show in the following sections.

We begin our discussion with a classical example, called the *Randomized Response*, to intuitively show how randomness leads to privacy.

6.2.1 Randomized Response

Let us suppose that an exam is going on in a large class. The instructor of the class suspects that some students cheated in the exam, and would like to know how many students cheated via a survey. However, achieving this goal is hard, as intuitively, students would not admit cheating even though they might have done so. Thus, directly handing out a survey would not lead to satisfactory results. One solution to address this issue is to design some randomized techniques based upon the answers from the students. In this way, even though a student answers "Yes" in the survey, he could argue that it is randomness, rather than cheating, that leads to the answer. Thus, no students would be held accountable due to their answers, which motivates them to tell the truth (under proper randomness). In this example, whether a student cheated is considered private by the student, who would not like to tell exactly, and proper randomness alleviates the student's concern about privacy leakage.

The preceding story provides an intuitive understanding of how randomness leads to privacy. Formally speaking, suppose there are n people numbered as $i = 1, \ldots, n$, each of which owns a private bit $x_i \in \{0, 1\}$, where $x_i = 1$ indicates cheating. When asked by the instructor, each person sends a properly randomized answer $y_i = \mathcal{A}_{RR}(x_i)$ to the instructor, such that the instructor can get an estimate about how many students cheated, $p = \sum_i x_i$.

In the case where a conventional survey is carried out, $y_i = x_i$, and $p = \sum_i y_i$ accurately. However, the instructor directly observes x_i and can easily hold students who cheated accountable. In other words, there is no privacy. Alternatively, consider the case with complete randomness, where $y_i = 1$ with probability 0.5, and vice versa. In this case, y_i tells nothing about x_i, which indicates complete privacy. However, $\sum_i y_i$ would also be completely independent of p, leaving the result useless.

The preceding discussions provide an intuition that we should strike a balance between full accuracy and full privacy. To implement the intuition, we consider a strategy, called the *Randomized Response*, defined as follows,

Definition 6.1 (Randomized Response) The randomized response $\mathcal{A}_{RR}$ involves the following procedures to compute y_i:

(i) Throw a fair coin with $1/2$ probability of landing on either side.
(ii) If we obtain heads, we reply $y_i = x_i$; if we obtain tails, we throw another fair coin and answer $y_i = 1$ if the second coin is a head, and vice versa.

We provide an analysis on Definition 6.1. Given $p = \sum_i x_i$, $p' = \sum_i y_i$, we have

$$\mathbb{E}[p'] = \frac{1}{4}n + \frac{1}{2}p, \tag{6.1}$$

and thus, we can estimate p via $\hat{p} = 2p' - \frac{n}{2}$. We make the following two remarks.

Remark 6.2 (Unbiasedness of Randomized Response) By showing that $\mathbb{E}[\hat{p}] = p$ (which is straightforward), the randomized response leads to an unbiased estimate about the true value p.

Remark 6.3 ((Informal) Privacy of Randomized Response) Each student replies with a random variable y_i, and thus, the instructor can never retrieve the exact x_i. More specifically, each student can plausibly deny cheating, as they can always claim that $y_i = 1$ is caused by randomness. In this way, the students' privacy is protected.

From Remarks 6.2 and 6.3, we observe that Randomized Response ensures the privacy of *individual* data points, while maintaining usefulness of the *global statistics* by adding proper randomness. These practices provide answers to the question raised in Section 6.1,

"How can a curator publish meaningful results about its data to analysts, without leaking privacy on exactly same data?"

namely that we aim to protect the privacy of *individuals*, rather than the *global statistics*. For example, stating that "Those who smoke are more susceptible to lung cancer" does not violate privacy, as it focuses on the global statistics.

In fact, differential privacy does exactly the same things as the example of the randomized response: randomizing individuals and publishing the global. In the following sections, we move on from the example of Randomized Response to general notions of differential privacy.

6.2.2 Definitions of Differential Privacy

In security and privacy, it is crucial that we precisely specify the setting in which we discuss the results. Thus, we first provide examples and definitions of the setting where we discuss differential privacy.

A common scenario for real-world big data analysis is that a database owner possesses a large amount of data and provides open APIs for relevant users to query related statistics. In the example in Section 6.1, the corporation owns the database and develops a system that allows users to query the average salaries of a certain set of employees, e.g., a certain department. On this occasion, we are confronted with a similar dilemma as students cheating: we would like to provide global statistics as accurately as possible, while protecting the privacy of individuals. Considering the dilemma, we formulate the setting of differential privacy (sometimes called *central differential privacy*) as follows:

Definition 6.4 (Setting of DP) Suppose there are n individuals, each of which i owns a private data point x_i. A data curator C trusted by all individuals owns the data $X = \{x_1, \ldots, x_n\}$ and aims to run an algorithm $\mathcal{A}(D), D \subset X$, such that

$\mathcal{A}(D)$ depicts certain properties of D, while, even though $\mathcal{A}(D)$ is published, protecting the privacy of $X \in \mathcal{X}$.

We explain the definition using the two previous examples used in this chapter.

- In the example of students cheating, each student is an independent data curator C with only one piece of data x_i. The algorithm $\mathcal{A}(D)$, which is essentially $\mathcal{A}(x_i)$, outputs a random variable related to x_i.
- In the example of querying salaries of employees, each employee is an individual with x_i denoting his salary. The corporation is a trusted curator, and $\mathcal{A}(D)$ returns a result related to the average salary of set D.

Given the setting we are interested in, we now move on to precisely formulate the notion of *privacy* in differential privacy. Again, we start with concrete examples to motivate the formulation step by step.

First, before defining *privacy*, we should intuitively understand how privacy is compromised. Consider the example of querying average salaries. Suppose an attacker would like to know the exact salary of Alice; then a simple attacking method would be as follows:

(i) First, the attacker picks an arbitrary set of employees D.
(ii) Second, the attacker queries the average salary of D and $D \cup \{Alice\}$, and subtracts them to obtain the salary of Alice.

The attack is called a *differential attack*, in that the key process in the attack is to construct sets that differ by a single element and to differentiate their results. Contrarily, to ensure privacy against the attack, one feasible way is to ensure $\mathcal{A}(D)$ does not differ a lot from $\mathcal{A}(D \cup \{Alice\})$, such that differentiating them would not lead to extra information regarding Alice. This example provides the first intuition about how to define privacy in DP: *results of neighboring sets should be similar*, or equivalently, *results should not be significantly changed by the presence or absence of a single sample*.

Second, we take a closer look at how the strength of *privacy* will change. Consider the example of randomized response. In Definition 6.1, $\mathbb{E}[y_i] = \frac{1}{2}x_i + \frac{1}{4}$. Suppose we define a variant of Definition 6.1, called the θ-randomized response, which replaces the fair coin in Step 1 with a biased coin with heads probability $\theta < 1/2$. Now, with θ-randomized response, $\mathbb{E}[y_i'] = \theta x_i + \frac{1-\theta}{2}$. We observe that, although both y_i and y_i' are random variables, the correlations between y_i', y_i, and x_i differ, and that, given $\theta < 1/2$, y_i is more related to x_i than y_i'. Thus, by intuition, y_i leaks more privacy than y_i'. The example provides the second intuition about how to define privacy in DP: *the privacy should be quantified, rather than being a yes-no answer.*

Given the two intuitions, we now formally present the definition of differential privacy.

Definition 6.5 (ε-DP) Let $\mathcal{A}$: $2^{\mathcal{X}} \rightarrow \mathcal{Y}$ be a randomized algorithm, where $2^{\mathcal{X}}$ denotes the set of all subsets of $\mathcal{X}$, and $\mathcal{Y}$ is the range of $\mathcal{A}$. We say that $D_1, D_2 \subset \mathcal{X}$ are neighboring if and only if they differ by exactly one element. Then, we say that $\mathcal{A}$ is ε-differentially private (ε-DP) if, for all neighboring D_1, D_2 and all $Y \subset \mathcal{Y}$, the following inequality holds:

$$\frac{\Pr[\mathcal{A}(D_1) \in Y]}{\Pr[\mathcal{A}(D_2) \in Y]} \le \exp(\varepsilon). \tag{6.2}$$

We refer to the parameter $\varepsilon > 0$ as the privacy budget. The randomness in Equation 6.2 is over the randomized algorithm $\mathcal{A}$.

Definition 6.5 is not straightforward to understand, and thus some remarks are necessary.

Remark 6.6 (Similarity between Neighboring Sets) Because we can exchange D_1, D_2, Equation 6.2 implies that

$$\exp(-\varepsilon) \le \frac{\Pr[\mathcal{A}(D_1) \in Y]}{\Pr[\mathcal{A}(D_2) \in Y]} \le \exp(\varepsilon). \tag{6.3}$$

Moreover, when ε is small, $\varepsilon + 1 \approx \exp(\varepsilon)$. We thus have

$$1 - \varepsilon \le \frac{\Pr[\mathcal{A}(D_1) \in Y]}{\Pr[\mathcal{A}(D_2) \in Y]} \le 1 + \varepsilon, \tag{6.4}$$

which exemplifies the first intuition that results of neighboring sets should be similar (in the sense of probability distributions).

Remark 6.7 (Quantification of Privacy) Consider the extreme case where $\varepsilon = 0$. Definition 6.5 states that $\Pr[\mathcal{A}(D_1) \in Y] = \Pr[\mathcal{A}(D_2) \in Y], \forall Y \subset \mathcal{Y}$. In this case, we obtain perfect privacy, i.e., the outputs of $\mathcal{A}$ follow exactly the same distributions for all $D \subset \mathcal{X}$, making it impossible to identify any information from $\mathcal{A}(D)$. However, in the meantime, the algorithm degrades to a uniform random algorithm and fails to reflect the properties of D. Deriving from the extreme case, we observe:

- A smaller ε leads to a smaller divergence between $\mathcal{A}(D_1), \mathcal{A}(D_2)$, leading to a more uniform but less accurate algorithm $\mathcal{A}$ and stronger privacy.

- There exists a trade-off between privacy and performance of algorithm $\mathcal{A}$. In general, we have to sacrifice algorithm accuracy for the privilege of privacy protection.

Finally, regarding proper values of ε, anything between 0.1 and 5 can be reasonable, and we should be skeptical when it comes to claims with significantly larger or smaller ε.

Remark 6.8 (Irrelevance to Computational Power) Differential privacy is established on probability and randomness, as opposed to computational complexity adopted by cryptographic techniques (e.g., factorization, discrete logarithm). Thus, Definition 6.5 represents a worse-case guarantee that holds for arbitrary computational models and power. On the other hand, certain cryptographic techniques may fail upon infinite computational power.

There are many variants of Definition 6.5, of which we introduce two. First, we introduce (ε, δ)-DP, which is a relaxation of ε-DP.

Definition 6.9 $((\varepsilon, \delta)$-DP) Following the notations defined in Definition 6.5, let $\mathcal{A} \colon 2^X \to \mathcal{Y}$ be a randomized algorithm. Let $D_1, D_2 \subset X$ be neighboring datasets. Then, we say that $\mathcal{A}$ is (ε, δ)-differentially private $((\varepsilon, \delta)$-DP) if, for all neighboring D_1, D_2 and all $Y \subset \mathcal{Y}$, the following inequality holds:

$$\Pr[\mathcal{A}(D_1) \in Y] \leq \exp(\varepsilon)\Pr[\mathcal{A}(D_2) \in Y] + \delta. \tag{6.5}$$

Again, the randomness in Equation 6.5 is over the randomized algorithm $\mathcal{A}$.

If $\delta = 0$, (ε, δ)-DP degenerates to ε-DP. Similar arguments to Remarks 6.6, 6.7, and 6.8 hold for (ε, δ)-DP. Additionally, we make the following remark to illustrate the implication of (ε, δ)-DP.

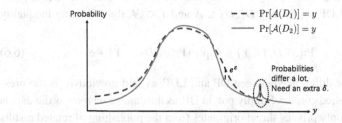

Figure 6.1 Implications of (ε, δ)-DP. The δ indicates the probability where ε-DP cannot hold. At areas where $\Pr[\mathcal{A}(D_1) = y]$ and $\Pr[\mathcal{A}(D_2) = y]$ differ a lot, an extra δ is required to bound the difference.

Remark 6.10 (Implication of (ε, δ)-DP) In (ε, δ)-DP, δ stands for the probability where ε-DP may fail. (See Lemma 3.17 in Dwork et al. (2014).) We illustrate the meaning of δ in Figure 6.1. In most areas, $\Pr[\mathcal{A}(D_1) = y]$ is similar to $\Pr[\mathcal{A}(D_2) = y]$ and can be bounded by $\exp(\varepsilon)$. However, there may exist certain areas where the divergence between $\Pr[\mathcal{A}(D_1) = y]$ and $\Pr[\mathcal{A}(D_2) = y]$ cannot be bounded by $\exp(\varepsilon)$. When that happens, ε-DP is compromised, and if the extra divergence is bounded by δ, (ε, δ)-DP still holds.

From the remark, we also know that values for δ should be small, as we do not want a system that fails with a large probability. In practice, any $\delta \geq \frac{1}{|X|}$ is dangerous, as doing so allows the curator to compromise the privacy of a small fraction of samples $(\delta|X|)$, while still satisfying (ε, δ)-DP.

The second variant we introduce is (ε, δ)-*local differential privacy (LDP)*.

Readers may recall that Definition 6.5 is also referred to as *central differential privacy*. This is because Definitions 6.5 and 6.9 both assume that a trusted curator exists, who manages and directly observes all data X and publishes computation results. In this case, the curator does not pose a privacy threat, and we only need to consider potential leakages caused by the published results. However, in many real-world scenarios, this is not an appropriate setting, as we cannot find a trusted curator to manage all data. For example, consider the case of students cheating where each student owns his private data x_i. In this case, the instructor is not a trusted curator. Similarly, we can also consider the case where corporations like Apple would like to collect user data, in which corporations themselves are considered privacy threats to users and thus cannot be viewed as trusted curators. Thus, it is necessary to consider a different setting from Definitions 6.5 and 6.9, where each individual data sample needs to protect the privacy of itself *without a curator*. The concept of *local differential privacy* is accordingly defined as follows.

Definition 6.11 $((\varepsilon, \delta)$-LDP) Following the notations defined in Definition 6.5, let $\mathcal{A} \colon 2^X \to \mathcal{Y}$ and $\varepsilon, \delta > 0$. We say that $\mathcal{A}$ is (ε, δ)-local differentially private $((\varepsilon, \delta)$-LDP) if, for any $D_1, D_2 \subset X$ and $Y \subset \mathcal{Y}$, the following inequality holds:

$$\Pr[\mathcal{A}(D_1) \in Y] \leq \exp(\varepsilon) \Pr[\mathcal{A}(D_2) \in Y] + \delta. \tag{6.6}$$

The major difference between DP and LDP, as said previously, is the presence of a trusted curator. Simply put, in DP, as the curator who owns the data is trusted, the only privacy threat originates from the publishing of related results from the curator. Thus, DP is commonly used for privately *publishing* data.

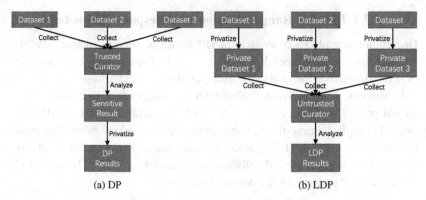

Figure 6.2 The difference between DP and LDP. The major difference is the existence of a trusted curator.

On the contrary, in LDP, no trusted curators exist, and thus each data owner needs to protect its own privacy before moving on to future data processing. Therefore, LDP is commonly used for privately *gathering* data, as we will see in the examples of Google and Apple. We illustrate the difference in Figure 6.2.

There are other variants of DP aside from (ε, δ)-DP and (ε, δ)-LDP. For example, Rényi differential privacy (Mironov, 2017) is another relaxation to ε-DP which uses Rényi divergence to measure the difference between $\Pr[\mathcal{A}(D_1) \in Y]$ and $\Pr[\mathcal{A}(D_2) \in Y]$. Compared with (ε, δ)-DP, Rényi DP offers a strictly stronger privacy guarantee than (ε, δ)-DP and also allows tighter analysis under composition. Interested readers are referred to Mironov (2017).

6.3 Mechanisms for DP

In this section, we present several fundamental mechanisms for DP. As shown in Definition 6.5, DP relies heavily on randomness, and thus, all these mechanisms involve injecting random noises to obfuscate accurate computation results. We discuss these mechanisms according to their application scenarios. For discrete ranges, we revisit the Randomized Response in Definition 6.1 and analyze its DP property; for continuous ranges, we introduce two simple but fundamental mechanisms, the Laplace Mechanism and the Gaussian Mechanism.

6.3.1 Discrete Range: Randomized Response Revisited

One common application scenario of DP would be surveys, where possible replies form discrete ranges $\mathcal{Y} = \{0, 1, \ldots, C - 1\}$. For simplicity, we consider $\mathcal{Y} = \{0, 1\}$, which is the case in the example of students cheating.

In surveys, each individual constitutes an independent data owner and should protect its privacy on its own. Thus, the definition of LDP (Definition 6.11) applies. Interestingly, although the advent of Randomized Response (Definition 6.1, Warner (1965)) is much earlier than LDP (Dwork et al., 2006), Randomized Response itself satisfies the definition of LDP. Theorem 6.12 stated the LDP property of Randomized Response.

Theorem 6.12 (Randomized response is LDP) *The randomized response mechanism in Definition 6.1 is* $(\ln 3, 0)$*-LDP.*

Proof As $\mathcal{Y} = \{0, 1\}$, consider $\Pr[\mathcal{A}_{RR}(x_i) = 0]$ and $\Pr[\mathcal{A}_{RR}(y_i) = 1]$. We have

$$
\begin{aligned}
\frac{\Pr[\mathcal{A}_{RR}(x_i) = 1|x_i = 1]}{\Pr[\mathcal{A}_{RR}(x_i) = 1|x_i = 0]} &= \frac{3/4}{1/4} = 3, \\
\frac{\Pr[\mathcal{A}_{RR}(x_i) = 0|x_i = 0]}{\Pr[\mathcal{A}_{RR}(x_i) = 0|x_i = 1]} &= \frac{3/4}{1/4} = 3.
\end{aligned}
\tag{6.7}
$$

By Definition 6.11, $\mathcal{A}_{RR}$ is $\ln 3$-LDP. $\qquad\qquad\square$

Although Randomized Response is a very simple mechanism, it (as well as its variants) serves as a vital building block for many more complex differentially private systems, such as RAPPOR by Google (Erlingsson et al., 2014).

6.3.2 Continuous Range: Laplace and Gaussian Mechanisms

There are also many computing tasks whose outputs are continuous real values, i.e., $\mathcal{Y} = \mathbb{R}^k$, such as computing mean values, max values, and variances. We introduce two fundamental mechanisms, the Laplace Mechanism and the Gaussian Mechanism. As shown by their names, both mechanisms achieve DP by injecting noise with particular distributions.

First, we present some necessary definitions.

Definition 6.13 (L_1-sensitivity) We define the global L_1-sensitivity of function $f : 2^X \to \mathcal{Y}$ as

$$
\Delta_1 f = \max_{\text{Neighboring } D_1, D_2 \subset X} \|f(D_1) - f(D_2)\|_1.
\tag{6.8}
$$

We define the local L_1-sensitivity of function $f: 2^X \to \mathcal{Y}$ as

$$\Delta_1^L f = \max_{D_1, D_2 \subset X} \|f(D_1) - f(D_2)\|_1. \tag{6.9}$$

We can extend Definition 6.13 to other metrics, such as L_2-sensitivity. It follows by their names that the global sensitivity corresponds to DP, while the local sensitivity corresponds to LDP. In the following discussions, we focus on global sensitivity and DP, while results on LDP can be accordingly obtained.

Definition 6.14 (Laplace Distribution) We denote a Laplace distribution with location parameter 0 and scale parameter b as $\mathrm{Lap}(b)$. The probability density function of $\mathrm{Lap}(b)$ is

$$f(x) = \frac{1}{2b} \exp\left(-\frac{|x|}{b}\right). \tag{6.10}$$

If $x \sim \mathrm{Lap}(b)$, then $\mu(x) = 0$, $\mathrm{Var}(x) = 2b^2$.

Definition 6.15 (Gaussian Distribution) We denote a Gaussian distribution with mean μ and variance σ^2 as $N(\mu, \sigma^2)$. The probability density function of $N(\mu, \sigma^2)$ is

$$f(x) = \frac{1}{\sqrt{2\pi}\sigma} \exp\left(-\frac{(x-\mu)^2}{2\sigma^2}\right). \tag{6.11}$$

We are now ready to introduce the Laplace mechanism.

Definition 6.16 (Laplace Mechanism) Given a function $f: 2^X \to \mathbb{R}^k$, the Laplace mechanism with privacy budget ε is defined as

$$\mathcal{A}_L(D, f, \varepsilon) = f(D) + (Y_1, \ldots, Y_k), \tag{6.12}$$

where $Y_1, \ldots, Y_k$ are independent and identically distributed (i.i.d.) samples from $\mathrm{Lap}(\Delta_1 f / \varepsilon)$.

We make the following remark on the Laplace mechanism.

Remark 6.17 As shown in Definition 6.16, the only extra cost of the Laplace mechanism is to sample independent random variables from a Laplace distribution. Thus, the Laplace mechanism is efficient in both computation and communication.

However, the price paid to achieve privacy is accuracy. As shown, we have to inject a greater level of noise $\Delta_1 f / \varepsilon$ for a higher level of privacy (small ε), and the results get more inaccurate.

We show that the Laplace mechanism is ε-DP as follows.

Theorem 6.18 (Laplace mechanism is DP) *The Laplace mechanism in Definition 6.16 is ε-DP.*

Proof We let $D_1, D_2 \subset X$ be neighboring datasets, and p_1, p_2 be the probability density functions of $\mathcal{A}_L(D_1, f, \varepsilon)$ and $\mathcal{A}_L(D_2, f, \varepsilon)$. Consider $z \in \mathcal{Y}$,

$$
\begin{aligned}
\frac{p_1(z)}{p_2(z)} &= \prod_{i=1}^{k} \left(\frac{\exp\left(\frac{-\varepsilon|f(D_1)_i - z_i|}{\Delta_1 f}\right)}{\exp\left(\frac{-\varepsilon|f(D_2)_i - z_i|}{\Delta_1 f}\right)} \right) \\
&= \prod_{i=1}^{k} \exp\left(\frac{\varepsilon(|f(D_2)_i - z_i| - |f(D_1)_i - z_i|)}{\Delta_1 f} \right) \qquad (6.13) \\
&\leq \prod_{i=1}^{k} \exp\left(\frac{\varepsilon|f(D_1)_i - f(D_2)_i|}{\Delta_1 f} \right) \\
&\leq \exp(\varepsilon),
\end{aligned}
$$

where the first inequality follows from the triangle inequality, and the second follows from the definition of L_1-sensitivity. We note that $\Pr[\mathcal{A}_L(D, f, \varepsilon) \in Y] = \int_y p_1(y) dy$, and thus

$$
\begin{aligned}
\frac{\Pr[\mathcal{A}_L(D_1, f, \varepsilon) \in Y]}{\Pr[\mathcal{A}_L(D_1, f, \varepsilon) \in Y]} &= \frac{\int_y p_1(y) dy}{\int_y p_2(y) dy} \\
&\leq \frac{\int_y \exp(\varepsilon) p_2(y) dy}{\int_y p_2(y) dy} \qquad (6.14) \\
&= \exp(\varepsilon). \qquad \square
\end{aligned}
$$

While DP can be achieved via the Laplace mechanism, in practice, Gaussian distributions are more frequently used due to better smoothness and composability (the sum of Gaussian variables also follows a Gaussian distribution, while the sum of Laplacian variables does not). Thus, a natural question arises: can DP be achieved via Gaussian mechanisms? The answer would be yes, which is stated in the following definitions and theorems.

Definition 6.19 (Gaussian Mechanism) Given a function $f : 2^X \to \mathbb{R}^k, D \subset X$, the Gaussian mechanism with variance σ^2 is defined as

$$
\mathcal{A}_N(D, f, \sigma) = f(D) + (Y_1, \ldots, Y_k), \qquad (6.15)
$$

where $Y_1, \ldots, Y_k$ are i.i.d. random variables sampled from $N(0, \sigma^2)$.

Theorem 6.20 (Gaussian mechanism is (ε, δ)-DP) *Given* $\varepsilon \in (0, 1)$. *If* $c^2 >$ $2\ln(1.25/\delta)$, *then, if* $\sigma > c\Delta_2 f/\varepsilon$, *the Gaussian mechanism is* (ε, δ)-*DP.*

The proof to Theorem 6.20 relies on tail inequalities such as Chernoff bounds, and thus we omit the proof here. We refer interested readers to Appendix A in Dwork et al. (2006) for a detailed proof.

6.3.3 Beyond the Basics

This section only covers basic and the most popular mechanisms of DP. Other implementations of DP include the exponential mechanism (McSherry and Talwar, 2007) and the sparse vector techniques (Hardt and Rothblum, 2010). Interested readers are referred to the references.

6.4 Properties of DP

In the previous section, we introduce basic building blocks of differentially private algorithms, including the randomized response for discrete ranges, and Laplace and Gaussian mechanisms for continuous ranges. However, in real-world applications of DP, we generally need to combine multiple such building blocks to build more complex DP algorithms. Thus, it is necessary to study how privacy is preserved under such combinations. In this section, we introduce how DP algorithms maintain privacy under composition.

6.4.1 Postprocessing

Postprocessing is often necessary for real-world data analysis. For example, after an organization obtains the differentially private average salaries of some corporations, it may need to further compute other statistics of the average salaries, such as max, min, and quantiles. In these scenarios, one convenient fact about DP is that the private results cannot be "un-privatized." Strictly speaking, DP cannot be compromised without accessing raw private data, as stated in the following theorem.

Theorem 6.21 (Postprocessing maintains DP) *Let* $\mathcal{A}: 2^X \to \mathcal{Y}$ *be* (ε, δ)-*DP, and let* $f: \mathcal{Y} \to \mathcal{Z}$ *be an arbitrary random mapping, then* $f \circ \mathcal{A}: 2^X \to \mathcal{Z}$ *is* (ε, δ)-*DP.*

Proof We prove Theorem 6.21 under $\delta = 0$. For $z \in \mathcal{Z}$ and $D_1, D_2 \subset X$ be neighboring datasets, the following inequalities hold:

$$
\begin{aligned}
\Pr[f(\mathcal{A}(D_1)) = z] &= \sum_{y \in \mathcal{Y}} \Pr[f(\mathcal{A}(D_1)) = z | \mathcal{A}(D_1) = y] \Pr[\mathcal{A}(D_1) = y] \\
&= \sum_{y \in \mathcal{Y}} \Pr[f(y) = z] \Pr[\mathcal{A}(D_1) = y] \\
&\leq \exp(\varepsilon) \sum_{y \in \mathcal{Y}} \Pr[\mathcal{A}(D_2) = y] \Pr[f(y) = z] \\
&= \exp(\varepsilon) \sum_{y \in \mathcal{Y}} \Pr[\mathcal{A}(D_2) = y] \Pr[f(\mathcal{A}(D_2)) = z | \mathcal{A}(D_2) = y] \\
&= \exp(\varepsilon) \Pr[f(\mathcal{A}(D_2)) = z].
\end{aligned}
$$

(6.16)

□

We omit the proof for $\delta > 0$. Theorem 6.21 allows us to arbitrarily postprocess differentially private results as long as we do not revisit the private data. For example, suppose we want to find the department in a company with the highest average Salary. We can decompose the query into two steps. First, we compute the average salaries of departments under DP. Second, we take the max among departments. As the second step does not revisit the original data, so the whole process is as DP as the first step.

6.4.2 Group Privacy

So far, we have introduced what happens to neighboring D_1, D_2 for DP algorithms. However, one might wonder what happens for D_1, D_2 differing in multiple data samples. The property is called the "group privacy," which states that the privacy budget grows linearly with increasing distance.

Theorem 6.22 (Group Privacy) *Let $\mathcal{A}: 2^X \to \mathcal{Y}$ be ε-DP, and D_1, D_2 differ in exactly k data samples; then, for any $Y \subset \mathcal{Y}$, the following inequality holds:*

$$
\Pr[\mathcal{A}(D_1) \in Y] \leq \exp(k\varepsilon) \Pr[\mathcal{A}(D_2) \in Y].
$$
(6.17)

Proof Consider a sequence of datasets $D^{(0)}, D^{(1)} \ldots D^{(k)}$ with $D^{(0)} = D_1, D^{(k)} = D_2$, and $D^{(i)}, D^{(i+1)}$ differing by only one data sample. We have

$$
\begin{aligned}
\Pr[\mathcal{A}(D^{(k)}) \in Y] &\leq \exp(\varepsilon) \Pr[\mathcal{A}(D^{(k-1)}) \in Y] \\
&\leq \exp(2\varepsilon) \Pr[\mathcal{A}(D^{(k-2)}) \in Y] \\
&\cdots \\
&\leq \exp(k\varepsilon) \Pr[\mathcal{A}(D^{(0)}) \in Y].
\end{aligned}
$$
(6.18)

□

Similar results hold for (ε, δ)-DP, whose composition is not quite as clean as ε-DP. Specifically, group privacy with group size k under (ε, δ)-DP is $(k\varepsilon, k \exp((k-1)\varepsilon)\delta)$-DP (Dwork et al., 2014).

6.4.3 Parallel Composition

In real-world data analysis, we often care about more than one result. For example, for a set of data, we may care about mean values, variances, and medians. We are thus interested in how private it will be if we release all these results simultaneously.

Intuitively, the more results we publish, the greater amount of information will be revealed about the data. For example, even if the same DP algorithm is performed on the same set of data repetitively, the privacy is still compromised, as we can easily cancel out the noise by taking an average. Formally, the following theorem states the composition rules for publishing multiple results in parallel.

Theorem 6.23 (Parallel Composition) *Let* $\mathcal{A}_1, \mathcal{A}_2 : 2^X \to \mathcal{Y}$ *be* $(\varepsilon_1, \delta_1), (\varepsilon_2, \delta_2)$ *-DP respectively, then* $\mathcal{A} = (\mathcal{A}_1, \mathcal{A}_2) : 2^X \to \mathcal{Y} \times \mathcal{Y}$ *is* $(\varepsilon_1 + \varepsilon_2, \delta_1 + \delta_2)$*-DP.*

The proof for Theorem 6.23 also requires using Chernoff bounds. We refer interested readers to appendix B in Dwork et al. (2014) for the detailed proof. By induction, Theorem 6.23 holds for arbitrary k compositions. Theorem 6.23 indicates that, if we want to privately publish multiple results on a dataset, we need to bound the privacy budget of each individual result.

6.4.4 Sequential Composition

There are also scenarios in data analysis where we need to iteratively query the private dataset. For example, suppose we want to know the number of data samples whose values exceed the average value of the dataset. To do so, we need to first iterate through the dataset to obtain the (differentially private) mean value μ, and then iterate through the dataset again to count the (differentially private) number of samples whose values exceed μ. Theorem 6.24 ensures that such sequential composition of DP algorithms also preserves DP. More importantly, Theorem 6.24 allows arbitrary dependency on previous results.

Theorem 6.24 (Sequential Composition) *Let* $\mathcal{A}_1 : 2^X \to \mathcal{Y}$ *be* ε_1-DP, $\mathcal{A}_2 : 2^X \times \mathcal{Y} \to \mathcal{Y}'$ *be* ε_2-DP. *Then* $\mathcal{A} = \mathcal{A}_2(D, \mathcal{A}_1(D)) : 2^X \to \mathcal{Y}'$ *is* $(\varepsilon_1 + \varepsilon_2)$-DP.

The proof to Theorem 6.24 can be found in McSherry (2009). Theorem 6.24 indicates that, if an algorithm involves multiple steps of DP algorithms, it is possible to bound the overall privacy budget by bounding the budgets of individual steps.

6.4.5 Beyond the Basics

This section has introduced basic properties regarding the composition of DP. For tighter bounds of DP composition, readers are referred to Dwork et al. (2010) and Kairouz et al. (2015).

6.5 Applications

In this section, we introduce typical application scenarios of differential privacy.

The notion of DP originates from privacy-preserving data analysis. In the early years, data analysis primarily focuses on database applications, such as querying and statistics. In recent years, machine learning, as a class of methods that extract features from data to perform predictive analysis, becomes another popular form of data analysis. In this section, we will introduce applications of DP in both fields.

6.5.1 Querying and Statistics

In this section, we begin with some classical applications in database querying and statistics and show how DP is applied.

Example 6.25 (Query Counting) Query counting is a very common type of database query that inquires how many data samples in the database are with property P.

We introduce an ε-DP algorithm for the query counting problem. The L_1-sensitivity of query counting is 1, in that changing one data sample changes the count by at most 1. Thus, according to Definition 6.16, if $f(P)$ is the exact count for property P, the randomized algorithm $\mathcal{A}_{QC}(P) = f(P) + Y$, where $Y \sim \text{Lap}(1/\varepsilon)$ is ε-DP. The good property of $\mathcal{A}_{QC}$ is that it is DP regardless of the size of the dataset.

We make the following remark on Example 6.25.

Remark 6.26 Example 6.25 holds only for a single query. Suppose we would like to maintain the ε-DP property for m fixed but arbitrary queries $(P_1, \ldots P_m)$; then we would require a noise with scale m/ε, i.e., the noise required scales linearly with the number of queries. It is important to note that the m queries should be fixed, which is often referred to as the "noninteractive" setting.

Example 6.27 (Histogram Counting) One common special case of Example 6.25 is the histogram counting problem, where the queries are disjoint. For example, consider an instructor who divides 0–100 into disjoint bins and queries the number of students whose grades fall into each bin.

Under the problem of histogram counting, we can do better than Remark 6.26. Suppose we have m disjoint histogram queries $P = (P_1, \ldots P_m)$; we note that adding or removing one data sample can only affect at most one of the m queries, instead of m in the case of query counting. Thus, $\text{Lap}(1/\varepsilon)$ would be sufficient for an ε-DP algorithm regardless of m.

Example 6.27 reveals that although we need to support m queries, the property of the problem (disjoint queries) bounds the L_1-sensitivity, which in turn reduces the scale of noise we need. The example suggests that sensitivity is the key concept in designing DP algorithms, and that by bounding the sensitivity, we can design DP algorithms with a tighter privacy budget. A classical example is as follows.

Example 6.28 (Noisy Max) We formulate the noisy max problem as follows. Given m queries $(P_1, \ldots, P_m)$, we would like to know which query returns the highest value, i.e., $\arg\max_i f(P_i), i = \{1, \ldots, m\}$.

A straightforward ε-DP algorithm for the noisy max problem would be that we first return all query results using Example 6.25. Then the data analyst performs postprocessing of taking maximum, which, according to Theorem 6.21, does not affect DP. However, Example 6.25 requires noise with $\text{Lap}(m/\varepsilon)$.

To reduce the noise needed, we rethink the straightforward algorithm introduced earlier. The reason why it needs high noise is that it reveals the query counts to the data analyst, which has sensitivity m. However, the query counts are essentially not required, as the problem is only interested in the index. Thus, by revealing less information to the data analyst, we may do better. One improved ε-DP algorithm is introduced as follows:

- Obtain exact counts x_i of each query P_i.
- Let $\hat{x}_i = x_i + Y_i, Y_i \sim \text{Lap}(1/\varepsilon)$.
- Return $\arg\max_i \hat{x}_i$ but not $\hat{x}_i$. We ignore the possibility of a tie.

The key difference is that by returning only the index but not the noisy query counts, we reduce the sensitivity, and thus the amount of information leaked and the noise needed (from m/ε to $1/\varepsilon$). Readers are referred to Claim 3.9 in Dwork et al. (2014) for a detailed proof.

6.5.2 Machine Learning

Machine learning is a popular class of data-driven algorithms. In this section, we introduce basic DP algorithms for machine learning.

We primarily focus on the problem of empirical risk minimization (ERM) in machine learning, which subsumes a wide range of specific machine learning problems. Formally speaking, given a training dataset $\mathcal{D} = \{\mathbf{x}_i, y_i\}_{i=1}^n$, ERM aims to select a hypothesis h from a hypothesis class $\mathcal{H}$ to minimize the empirical risk:

$$\min_{h \in \mathcal{H}} J(h; \mathcal{D}) = \frac{1}{n} \sum_{i=1}^n l(h(\mathbf{x}_i), y_i) + \lambda \Omega(h), \tag{6.19}$$

where $l(h(\mathbf{x}_i), y_i)$ denotes a loss function, and $\Omega(h)$ is a regularization term to bound the complexity of h. Equation 6.19 subsumes a wide range of specific machine learning problems. For example, let l be the mean squared error and $\mathcal{H} = \{h: h = \mathbf{w}^T\mathbf{x} + b\}$ be the class of linear predictors; then Equation 6.19 corresponds to the linear regression problem. Let $\mathcal{H}$ be neural networks with certain architectures, and l be the cross entropy loss; then Equation 6.19 corresponds to training neural networks.

We then introduce three classes of algorithms that solve Equation 6.19, *output perturbation*, *objective perturbation*, and *gradient perturbation*. Of course, there is a more straightforward way of *input perturbation*, i.e., we simply add noise to the input data to satisfy DP, and postprocessing (learning models) does not compromise the DP property. However, doing so often leads to an excessive amount of noise and poor performance, and thus we omit the method. For simplicity, we assume $h(\mathbf{x}) = \mathbf{w}^T\mathbf{x} + b$.

The discussions in this section will depend on some key concepts, including convexity and Lipschitz property. We refer readers to definitions 1 and 14 in Chaudhuri et al. (2011) for details.

Output Perturbation

Output perturbation is proposed in Chaudhuri et al. (2011) which follows an intuition similar to that of the Laplace mechanism. We solve for the optimal $\mathbf{w}$

and then add noise to it to achieve DP. Formally, the ε-DP algorithm based on output perturbation is defined in Definition 6.29.

Definition 6.29 (Output perturbation) The ε-DP output perturbation method to solve the ERM problem $\mathcal{A}_{OutP}$ contains the following steps:

 (i) Solve $\mathbf{w}^* = \arg\min_{\mathbf{w}} J(h; \mathcal{D})$.
(ii) Return $\tilde{\mathbf{w}} = \mathbf{w}^* + \mathbf{v}$, where $\mathbf{v}$ is sampled i.i.d. from a distribution with probability density function $f_{\mathbf{v}} \propto \exp(-\beta\|\mathbf{v}\|_2), \beta = \frac{\lambda\varepsilon n}{2}$.

Proving that $\mathcal{A}_{OutP}$ is ε-DP requires some assumptions. We formally state the result in Theorem 6.30 (Theorem 6 in Chaudhuri et al. (2011)).

Theorem 6.30 (Output Perturbation is ε-DP) *Assuming that $\Omega(h)$ is differentiable and 1-strongly convex, l is convex and differentiable, and $\forall z, |l'(z)| \leq 1$, then $\mathcal{A}_{OutP}$ is ε-DP.*

A sketch of the proof is as follows. First, we prove that the sensitivity of $J(h; \mathcal{D})$ is at most $\frac{2}{n\lambda}$. (Note that as the range of $J(h; \mathcal{D})$ is $\mathbb{R}$, L_1-sensitivity is equivalent to L_2 sensitivity.) Then, with an argument similar to Theorem 6.13, we prove that $\mathcal{A}_{OutP}$ is ε-DP. We refer readers to theorem 6 in Chaudhuri et al. (2011) for a detailed proof.

Objective Perturbation

Another intuition is that we can optimize a perturbed objective of $J(h; \mathcal{D})$ and thus obtain a perturbed minimizer $\tilde{\mathbf{w}}$. It is also formally described in Chaudhuri et al. (2011).

Definition 6.31 (Objective Perturbation) The ε-DP objective perturbation method $\mathcal{A}_{ObjP}$ to solve the ERM problem involves the following steps:

 (i) Construct a perturbed objective function $\tilde{J}(h; \mathcal{D}) = J(h; \mathcal{D}) + \frac{1}{n}\mathbf{v}^T\mathbf{w} + \frac{1}{2}\Delta\|\mathbf{w}\|^2$, where parameters $\mathbf{v}, \Delta$ are set as follows:
 - First, let $\varepsilon' = \varepsilon - \log\left(1 + \frac{2c}{n\lambda} + \frac{c^2}{n^2\lambda^2}\right)$, where c is an arbitrary constant.
 - Second, if $\varepsilon' > 0$, $\Delta = 0$; otherwise, reset $\varepsilon' = \varepsilon/2$ and $\Delta = \frac{c}{n(\exp(\varepsilon/4)-1)}$.
 - Finally, draw $\mathbf{v}$ i.i.d. from a distribution with probability density function $f_{\mathbf{v}} \propto \exp(-\beta\|\mathbf{v}\|_2)$ where $\beta = \varepsilon'/2$.
(ii) Solve $\tilde{\mathbf{w}} = \arg\min_{\mathbf{w}} \tilde{J}(h; \mathcal{D})$.

Similarly, under some assumptions, the DP property of $\mathcal{A}_{ObjP}$ is stated in Theorem 6.32.

Theorem 6.32 (Objective Perturbation is ε-DP) *Assuming that $\Omega(h)$ is 1-strongly convex and twice differentiable, and l is convex and twice differentiable with $|l'(z)| \leq 1$ and $|l''(z)| \leq c$ for some constant c, then $\mathcal{A}_{ObjP}$ is ε-DP.*

We refer readers to theorem 9 in Chaudhuri et al. (2011) for a detailed proof. In addition to linear regression as we introduce here, section 3.4 and 5 in Chaudhuri et al. (2011) also present object perturbation algorithms for other models, such as logistic regression, support vector machines, and kernel methods. Further, Chaudhuri et al. (2011) experimentally show that in practice, objective perturbation generally performs better than output perturbation.

Gradient Perturbation

As seen in Theorems 6.30 and 6.32, both output and objective perturbation require certain assumptions on models, such as convexity and smoothness. However, for deep neural networks that are in common use, such properties may not hold. On one hand, deep neural networks rely on activation functions such as $\text{ReLU}(x) = \max(x, 0)$ which is not twice differentiable. On the other hand, deep neural networks are known to have highly nonconvex loss surface (Liang et al., 2018; Li et al., 2018a). Thus, another class of DP algorithms should be found to train deep neural networks under DP. Abadi et al. (2016) proposes a solution called *Differentially Private Stochastic Gradient Descent (DPSGD)* to solve the problem, which we introduce in this section.

Before introducing private algorithms, we first briefly introduce backgrounds of deep learning. In the nonprivate setting, training a deep neural network commonly involves iterating the following steps until convergence.

(i) Sample a batch of data uniformly at random $\mathcal{B} = \{\mathbf{x}_{B_i}, y_{B_i}\}_{i=1}^{B}$ from the whole dataset $\mathcal{D}$.

(ii) Run the neural network h and compute the loss function $J(h; B)$ and the gradient of the loss function with respect to network parameters $\nabla_{\mathbf{w}} J(h; \mathcal{B})$.

(iii) Let $\mathbf{w} \leftarrow \mathbf{w} - \alpha \nabla_{\mathbf{w}} J(h; \mathcal{B})$, where α is the step size (also known as the learning rate) of gradient descent.

The algorithm is referred to as *Stochastic Gradient Descent*, as it takes a stochastic batch of data and takes a step in the negative gradient direction to minimize the loss.

Correspondingly, in the private setting, the DPSGD algorithm proposed in Abadi et al. (2016) works as follows:

Definition 6.33 (DPSGD, Abadi et al., 2016) The DPSGD algorithm requires iterating the following steps until convergence:

(i) Sample a batch of data $\mathcal{B}$ with expected size B by sampling each sample $(\mathbf{x}_i, y_i)$ independently with probability $B/|\mathcal{D}|$.
(ii) For each data point $\mathbf{x}_{B_i}, y_{B_i}$, take the gradient $\mathbf{g}_{B_i} = \nabla_{\mathbf{w}} J(h; (\mathbf{x}_{B_i}, y_{B_i}))$.
(iii) Clip all gradients $\mathbf{g}_{B_i}$ such that they have L_2-norm of at most C, i.e., $\tilde{\mathbf{g}}_{B_i} = \frac{\mathbf{g}_{B_i}}{\max(1, \|\mathbf{g}_{B_i}\|/C)}$.
(iv) Compute the average gradient of the batch and add Gaussian noise $\tilde{\mathbf{g}}_B = \frac{1}{B} \sum_{i=1}^{B} \tilde{\mathbf{g}}_{B_i} + N(0, C^2 \sigma^2)$.
(v) Let $\mathbf{w} \leftarrow \mathbf{w} - \alpha \tilde{\mathbf{g}}_B$.

We make the following remark on Definition 6.33.

Remark 6.34 In DPSGD, step (v) is the same as in nonprivate settings. Other differences from the nonprivate settings are stated as follows:

- Step (i) slightly changes the batch sampling method. Intuitively, the difference means that, while in the nonprivate setting we always sample exactly B data samples for each batch, in the private setting we may sample more or less, but in expectation B. This sampling method has a theoretical implication in analyzing the DP property, in that it stresses that any two batches should be independent of each other.
  However, in practice, what people usually do (which is incorrect) is the same as in the nonprivate setting. They randomly permute the whole dataset and iterate them in batches of size B. This is theoretically inadequate (but common in practice), as the batches are not independent of each other.
- Step (ii) takes gradients on each individual sample instead of on the whole batch. Correspondingly, the gradient clipping in step (iii) is essentially bounding the L_2-sensitivity of the model, in that each data point creates a unique gradient that is used to update the model.
  Readers should note that step (iii) is slightly different from the common gradient clipping in deep learning to avoid excessively large gradients. The difference is that step (iii) clips gradients of each individual sample, while in nonprivate settings, it usually suffices to clip the average gradients of a batch.
- Step (iv) adds noise to the gradients, which is similar to the Laplace and Gaussian mechanisms.

Readers may have noticed that there are no DP-related parameters ε, δ in the description of DPSGD. The reason is that, although we can ensure the DP

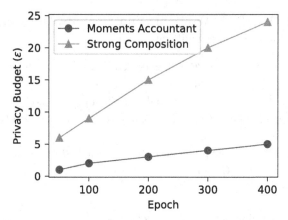

Figure 6.3 Comparison of ε between strong composition theorem and moments accountant method after multiple epochs of training. Figure adapted from Abadi et al. (2016).

property of one DPSGD step, training deep neural networks usually requires thousands of DPSGD steps. Thus, to ensure that the trained network is DP, a tight bound for composition is further required.

Suppose we run T steps of DPSGD, each of which is (ε, δ)-DP. Recalling the theorem of sequential composition (Theorem 6.24), we get $(T\varepsilon, T\delta)$-DP. Even if we use the strong composition theorem in Dwork et al. (2010), we still get $\left(O\left(\varepsilon \sqrt{\log(1/\delta)\,T}\right), T\delta\right)$-DP. By comparison, Abadi et al. (2016) proposes a method called the *moments accountant*, which ensures $\left(O\left(\varepsilon \sqrt{T}\right), \delta\right)$-DP, which saves a $1/\sqrt{\delta}$ factor in the ε part and a T factor in the δ part. For details regarding the moments accountant method, interested readers are referred to section 3.2 in Abadi et al. (2016). Figure 6.3 shows an example of how the moments accountant method compares favorably against the strong composition theorem under multiple epochs of training.

Beyond the Basics

This section introduces some classical methods for solving the general ERM problem. Apart from the general ERM, researchers have also proposed DP algorithms for specific machine learning tasks, such as transfer learning (Papernot et al., 2016), online learning (Jain et al., 2012), clustering (Su et al., 2016), language models (McMahan et al., 2017b), and graph data mining (Xu et al., 2018).

6.6 Advantages and Disadvantages

After the discussions on definitions, algorithms, and applications of DP, in this section we conclude this chapter by analyzing the advantages and disadvantages of DP.

The advantages are as follows:

- **High computation and communication efficiency.** As shown in the randomized response, Laplace, and Gaussian mechanisms, to achieve DP, in general we only need to sample random variables. Thus, DP is highly efficient in both communication and computation. By comparison, cryptographic techniques are often costly. For example, homomorphic encryption requires power and multiplication of large integers, thus being computationally inefficient. Secret sharing requires frequent exchange of intermediate results, thus being communicationally inefficient. Therefore, DP is competitive in terms of efficiency.
- **Flexible privacy-accuracy trade-off.** In DP algorithms, the privacy parameters ε, δ can be manually tuned, which provides practitioners with the flexibility to choose adequate ε, δ depending on the tasks. For example, for financial data with strict privacy requirements, smaller ε, δ should be chosen, while for social media data whose privacy is not strictly required, we can choose larger ε, δ and thus achieve better accuracy.
- **Theoretical guarantee.** Differential Privacy provides a theoretical framework to guarantee and analyze data privacy. Moreover, the guarantee by DP is independent of the computation power owned by adversaries.
- **Versatility.** The randomized response, Laplace mechanism, and Gaussian mechanism do not make specific assumptions on the underlying algorithm. Thus, DP applies to a wide range of tasks. As introduced previously, DP is applicable not only to database applications like queries and statistics, but also to a wide range of machine learning tasks.

However, as there is no free lunch, DP is also limited by the following disadvantages:

- **Compomised accuracy.** Differential Privacy sacrifices accuracy for privacy. As introduced in the Laplace and Gaussian mechanisms, we need to add a larger amount of noise to achieve stricter privacy, which necessarily compromises accuracy. As stated in Abadi et al. (2016), under nonprivate settings, a neural network can achieve 98.3 percent accuracy on the MNIST dataset, but only 97 percent, 95 percent, and 90 percent, under (8, 1e-5), (2, 1e-5), and

(0.5, 1e-5)-DP, respectively. Thus, DP is not applicable in tasks that require high accuracy, such as access control and risk management.

- **Ambiguous meaning of privacy budget.** While the privacy parameters ε, δ provide a theoretical guarantee on the information leaked, these parameters can hardly be interpreted for specific applications. Specifically, given a task, it is hard to determine whether certain ε, δ values are sufficient to achieve a certain level of privacy. Thus, DP does not apply to tasks that require transparency and interpretability of privacy.
- **Vulnerability.** As introduced at the beginning of this chapter, DP primarily protects the privacy of computation results rather than computation processes. Thus, if attackers can obtain intermediate results during the computation process, the privacy of DP no longer holds.

We explained the vulnerability using the example of DPSGD in Definition 6.33. In the setting of DPSGD, the data owner is a trusted curator, and the only risk lies in publishing the trained neural network. In other words, for DPSGD to effectively protect data privacy, the attacker should have access to only the learned model parameters and nothing else. However, if an attacker gains access to other information, such as the gradients during training, DPSGD fails to ensure data privacy. In fact, several works (Geiping et al., 2020; Zhu et al., 2019) have empirically shown that data privacy will be compromised if the attackers can observe the gradients during training. These cases should alert users that DP is vulnerable outside the predefined security model.

7

Trusted Execution Environment

Trusted Execution Environment (TEE) is the solution that implements privacy-preserving computation from the perspective of hardware and architecture. From the system's perspective, TEE provides an isolated operating environment to protect code or data from being stolen or tampered with by the operating system itself or other applications. As commercial operating systems are complex and can only provide weak isolation and weak control for applications, security loopholes are inevitable. Therefore, when applications involving user privacy (such as payment programs) are running alongside other applications on the same operating system, their security, confidentiality, integrity, and availability could be at risk. Trusted Execution Environment is proposed to solve the problem.

7.1 Introduction

The TEE was first defined in 2009 by the Open Mobile Terminal Platform (OMTP) in the *Advanced Trusted Environment OMTP TR1* standard. Trusted Execution Environment was defined as a set of software and hardware combinations that can satisfy two security levels. The first security level is to defend against software attacks. The second security level is to simultaneously defend against software and hardware attacks.

As can be seen, the overall definition for TEE is still quite broad. In short, TEE is to provide a dedicated "operating system" for applications with high security requirements outside the normal operation system, or the Rich Execution Environment (REE). The TEE and REE are isolated from each other over the shared hardware. Therefore, the essence of TEE is isolation.

Up until now, practitioners have not yet reached a consensus on a unified computation model of TEE. However, in general, the following requirements have to be met by TEE implementations:

- **Software/hardware Integrated Isolation.** The isolation provided by TEE should be implemented via both hardware and software. Trusted Execution Environment and conventional operating systems (REE) have independent system resources, including registers, physical memory, and peripherals. Also, data exchange cannot be arbitrarily performed between TEE and REE. The code and resources in TEE are strictly protected under access control policies and cannot be accessed by REE.
- **Shared Computing Power.** Trusted Execution Environment shares the same computing power as the Central Processing Unit (CPU).
- **Openness.** Trusted Execution Environment needs to run in an open environment. It is only necessary to use TEE within a conventional operating system, or an REE.

In the following sections, specific implementations of TEEs that meet the preceding three requirements will be introduced. We will first introduce related terms and concepts of TEE, before introducing several different implementations of TEE and analyzing their strengths and weaknesses. We summarize necessary related terms and concepts in Figure 7.1, including:

- **Trusted Computation Base (TCB).** Trusted Computation Base denotes the necessary components required by applications in TEE, such as operating systems and drivers. In general, the larger the TCB (such as RichOS in conventional operating systems), the less secure it is, because it contains a larger amount of code and is more prone to vulnerabilities.
- **Ring 3 TEE**, which is a class of TEE solutions to protect user-level applications (Ring 3) without trusting Ring 0 (operating system) or lower-level hardware. The most representative Ring 3 TEE implementation is Intel SGX.
- **Ring 0 TEE**, which is a class of TEE solution that can provide isolation from the level of operating systems (Ring 0). The most representative Ring 0 TEE is AEGIS.
- **Ring -1 TEE**, which is implemented at the level of virtualization hypervisors (Ring -1). It ensures isolation and security for applications through a trusted hypervisor. Representative Ring -1 TEE implementations include Bastion and AMD SEV (Secure Encrypted Virtualization). AMD SEV supports encrypting virtual machines and uses a trusted hypervisor to provide TEE for those virtual machines.

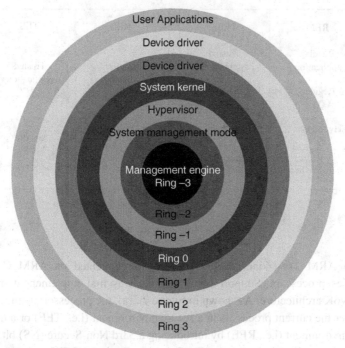

User Applications
Device driver
Device driver
System kernel
Hypervisor
System management mode
Management engine
Ring −3
Ring −2
Ring −1
Ring 0
Ring 1
Ring 2
Ring 3

Figure 7.1 Different Rings in the computer system. Each Ring represents a different set of permissions.

- **Ring -2 TEE**, which is implemented under the hypervisor. One representative implementation is ARM TrustZone.
- **Ring -3 TEE**, which is implemented by coprocessors. The representative implementation is the Trusted Platform Module (TPM).

7.2 Principles and Implementations

7.2.1 ARM TrustZone

Based on the scheme proposed by OMTP, ARM first proposed a hardware-based TEE scheme in 2008, named ARM TrustZone. The ARM TrustZone scheme modifies the hardware architecture of the original processor and introduces two different security levels of protection zones: Trusted Execution Environment (TEE) and Regular Operating System (REE). As shown in Figure 7.2, the two protection zones are completely isolated from the hardware perspective and possess different permissions. Moreover, the processor can only run in one protection zone at a particular time.

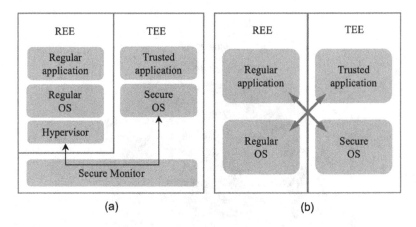

Figure 7.2 TrustZone architecture.

The ARM TrustZone scheme was first implemented on ARM Cortex-A series processors. Support for TrustZone was first implemented by the ARMv6K architecture. As shown in Figure 7.2(a), the processor distinguishes whether the current process is in a secure environment (i.e., TEE) or a nonsecure environment (i.e., REE) by introducing a 33rd Non-Secure (NS) bit. This bit can be read from the Secure Configuration Register (SCR) and was taken into account in designing memory management and buses to control access to memory/IO devices. Meanwhile, TrustZone also introduces a new processor mode, the monitor mode. As shown in Figure 7.2(b), the monitor mode is an intermediate mode between the REE and the TEE when the NS bit is modified. The processor will enter the monitor mode when the processor enters TEE from REE, or vice versa. The state change is mainly achieved by using a set of privileged instructions, called the Secure Monitor Call (SMC). The TEE and REE are completely isolated from each other by hiding registers or posing strict permission controls on registers.

The ARM TrustZone also modified the architecture of the memory system and introduced techniques such as the TrustZone Address Space Controller (TZASC) and the TrustZone Memory Adapter (TZMA). The TZASC is used to translate memory addresses and divide them into two different areas, secure and non-secure. Applications in a secure environment can access nonsecure areas, while the reverse does not hold. The TZMA also provides a similar function but focuses on off-chip memory.

Figure 7.3 shows an example on an ARM Cortex-A processor. The example shows that as ARM TrustZone runs on Ring -2, it is possible to run an operating system in both the TEE and the REE respectively. The operating system running in the TEE is the Trusted OS to host applications that require high security requirements.

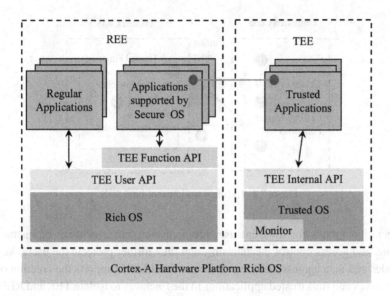

Figure 7.3 Trusted Execution Environment on Cortex-A series processors.

With the rapid development of the mobile Internet, TrustZone has also been introduced to ARM's mobile processor architecture, ARMv8-M. The architecture is designed for ARM's next-generation microprocessor, the Cortex-M. In general, the TrustZone of the Cortex-M series is similar to that of the Cortex-A series. The processor still provides an isolated, secure execution environment for applications through two environments (TEE and REE). However, the TrustZone of the Cortex-M series is restructured from the Cortex-A series, as the Cortex-M series is designed for mobile devices aiming to provide low power consumption and fast context switch. As shown in Figure 7.3, whether the processor runs in a Trusted Environment is determined by the memory of the running code. For example, if we launch the application from secure memory, the processor runs on TEE; if we launch the application from nonsecure memory, the processor runs on REE. This design eliminates the requirement for the monitor mode and the privileged SMC instructions in the Cortex-A series. Therefore, TrustZone on Cortex-M enjoys the advantages of lower latency and lower power consumption.

7.2.2 Intel SGX

In 2013, Intel introduced the Intel Software Guard eXtension (SGX) instruction set for protecting userspace applications. Intel SGX supports isolated

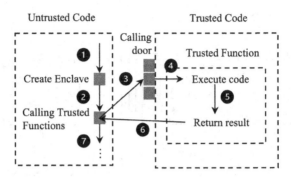

Figure 7.4 The main workflow of Intel SGX.

operation modes for different user programs through a new set of instructions and access control mechanisms, and thus further protects the users' key codes and data against malicious software. Intel SGX supports the creation of Enclaves and runs trusted applications in the Enclaves to isolate TEE and REE.

The main workflow of Intel SGX is shown in Figure 7.4. Users of SGX can create Enclaves with the ECREATE instruction and load data and code with the EADD instruction. Next, SGX users need to initialize the Enclaves with EINIT. EINIT requires an INIT Token to initialize, which is used to indicate whether the developer of the Enclaves program is on Intel's whitelist. The acquisition of the Token requires the program developer to submit identity information to Intel. Through this mechanism, SGX users can quickly distinguish whether the running program is from a trusted developer or not. However, large-scale commercialization of Intel SGX would not be feasible, as Intel is the only manager and controller of trusted applications.

After initialization, SGX users can use the EENTER command to enter the Enclaves and execute protected programs. Only programs located in Ring 3 can use the EENTER command. The EENTER command does not perform a privilege switch, and thus the CPU still executes in the Enclaves mode of Ring 3. Intel SGX uses Thread Control Structure (TCS) to store this type of entry point information.

All Enclave contents reside in the Enclave Page Cache (EPC), which is a protected area of physical memory for storing Enclave contents and SGX data structures. Enclave Page Cache memory is managed in the unit of pages. Page control information is stored in the hardware structure EPCM, where each page corresponds to one EPCM entry, similar to page tables in operating systems. EPCM entries manage basic information of EPC pages, including whether the page has been used, the owner of the page, page type, address mapping, and permission attributes. The memory area of the EPC is encrypted. The encryption/decryption and address translation are performed by the Memory Encryption Engine (MEE) in the CPU.

7.2.3 AMD SEV

Advanced Micro Devices proposed the Secure Encrypted Virtualization (SEV) in 2016 as the first implementation on x86 architectures to isolate virtual machines from the Hypervisor. To better introduce SEV, we first introduce a fundamental technique for SEV – AMD Secure Memory Encryption (SME).

Advanced Micro Devices SME provides a high-performance Advanced Encryption Standard (AES) engine for each memory controller. As shown in Figure 7.5, AMD SME encrypts data when it is written to DRAM and decrypts it when it is accessed. Meanwhile, the key used by the AES engine is randomly generated every time the system is reset and is invisible to the software. The keys are managed by the AMD Secure Processor (AMD-SP) (essentially a 32-bit ARM Cortex A5) integrated into the AMD SOC. The key is generated by the onboard SP 800-90 compliant hardware-based random number generator and stored in a dedicated hardware register that is never exposed outside the SOC.

The host or hypervisor can specify which pages are encrypted. After enabling memory encryption, the 47th bit of the physical memory address (also known as the C-bit, where C stands for enCrypted) is used to mark whether the page is encrypted or not. When the encrypted page is accessed, encryption and decryption are done automatically by the AES engine.

Now, we are ready to introduce the AMD SEV. The main idea of SEV is to encrypt the virtual machine memory to ensure that memory data cannot be directly accessed between different virtual machines or between hosts and virtual machines. The virtual machine memory encryption function provided by SEV can effectively protect virtual machine memory from physical attacks, attacks across virtual machines, or from hypervisors. After enabling the SEV function, bits 43 to 47 of the physical address are used to identify the Address Space ID (ASID) and the C-bit mentioned previously, respectively. When accessing the virtual machine memory through the page table, the physical address of the virtual machine will carry the ASID corresponding to the virtual machine, which is used to determine which virtual machine will be accessed. The ASID of the virtual machine is used during page table traversal to distinguish TLBs. In Cache, C-bit and ASID are used as keys to distinguish different cache lines. In the memory controller, ASIDs are used to distinguish VEKs. Since the ASID in the physical address is automatically added by the hardware and cannot be directly modified by the software, the

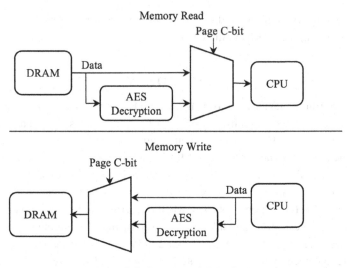

Figure 7.5 Overview of AMD SME.

data read from the memory is encrypted and decrypted directly by the memory controller using the corresponding VEK. To use the AMD SEV technology, the host computer needs to support and enable the AMD SME function.

7.2.4 AEGIS

AEGIS, proposed by MIT in 2003, is regarded as the earliest TEE architecture. AEGIS splits the Operating System (OS) into two parts, one of which runs in a secure environment created by the processor, called the Security Kernel. The Security Kernel manages the TEE and can detect and defend against memory attacks from other applications or the operating system itself. However, all functions of AEGIS can be implemented via hardware, such as the ARM TrustZone and Intel SGX mentioned earlier. Therefore, AEGIS is no longer adopted in real-world applications.

7.2.5 TPM

Trusted Platform Module (TPM) was proposed in 2003 by the Trusted Computing Group (TCG). TPM is an independent chip that securely stores data used to authenticate the platform, such as passwords, certificates, or encryption keys. Trusted Platform Module can also be used to store some measurement information of the platform for verification. In addition to personal computers and servers, TPM can also be used on mobile or network devices.

A major disadvantage of TPM is that it cannot control the software that runs on the devices. In addition, although TPM can provide some parameters and configuration information, Trusted Platform Module is unable to decide whether and how such information is used.

7.3 Advantages and Disadvantages of TEE

Trusted Execution Environment, as a software/hardware integrated solution, has been widely adopted in various applications. Taking Intel SGX as an example, it has been used in cloud computing to prevent leakage of user data privacy and to defend against attacks on the computing platform. However, TEE still suffers from problems, such as security loopholes and reliance upon hardware manufacturers. We will mainly introduce the drawbacks of TEE in the following sections.

7.3.1 Vulnerabilities in Trusted Execution Environment

Since TEE is a software/hardware integrated scheme that does not solely rely on a single cryptographic technique, architectures of TEE are often complex and prone to vulnerabilities. In this section, we take Intel SGX and ARM TrustZone as examples to introduce their fatal vulnerabilities. For example, attacks against Intel SGX mainly fall into three categories: software attacks, micro-architecture attacks, and memory attacks.

Software Attacks

This type of methods aims to attack the software layer of TEE, such as the Intel SGX SDK. In 2019, Jo Van Bulck et al. published the paper *A Tale of Two Worlds: Assessing the Vulnerability of Enclave Shielding Runtimes* (Van Bulck et al., 2019) to analyze the security of Intel SGX from two software levels: Application Binary Interface (ABI) and Application Programming Interface (API) and proposed a series of attacks. Later, in 2020, Mustakimur Rahman Khandaker et al. proposed *COIN Attacks: On Insecurity of Enclave Untrusted Interfaces in SGX* (Khandaker et al., 2020) focusing on the software attacks against TEE. This paper defines the "COIN" attack model against Intel SGX, including Concurrent, Order, Inputs, and Nested attacks. Through these four attack models, the attacker can invoke the interface provided by the Enclave in any sequence and with any input through multiple threads. It also designs and implements an automated testing framework for COIN attacks to detect whether a particular TEE implementation is prone to COIN attacks.

Micro-architectural Attack

Existing micro-architecture attacks primarily follow two ideas. First, attackers can observe the state changes of micro-processors to derive private information. Second, attackers can load elaborately designed backdoor instructions to peek into the contents of buffers. Such attacks can circumvent CPU permission checks and cause privacy leakage.

In 2018, Spectre and Meltdown vulnerabilities were discovered in all series of Intel processors. These vulnerabilities exploit an important feature of the CPU, the Speculative Execution. When a processor processes branch switching instructions (such as if-else), the control flow jumps according to the true/false condition. The jump interrupts the process of instructions in the pipeline, as the processor cannot determine the next instruction to execute until the branch is executed. Thus, the deeper the pipeline, the longer the processor has to stall and wait for the branch. Speculative execution is a technique proposed to solve the problem. It predicts the most likely branch and the next instruction, and fetches and executes the predicted instruction immediately. Contrarily, when exceptions or wrong branch predictions occur in Speculative Execution, the CPU will discard the result of previous executions, restore CPU states to the correct state before predictive execution, and then select the corresponding correct instruction to continue execution. This exception handling mechanism ensures correct program execution. However, the vulnerability is that contents in the CPU cache would not be restored when the CPU states are recovered. Spectre and Meltdown vulnerabilities exploit this design flaw to perform micro-architectural attacks. In 2018, Jo Van Bulck published a paper, *Foreshadow: Extracting the Keys to the Intel SGX Kingdom with Transient Out-of-Order Execution* (Van Bulck et al., 2018), to leverage the preceding vulnerabilities to perform micro-architecture attacks.

Memory Attack

In 2017, Jaehyuk Lee et al. published the first paper on memory attacks on SGX, *Hacking in Darkness: Return-oriented Programming against Secure Enclaves* (Lee et al., 2017). The paper adopts the vulnerabilities in the Enclave caused by memory corruption through Return-Oriented Programming (ROP) attack and proposes Dark-ROP. Dark-ROP differs from traditional ROP attacks by constructing some Oracles to inform the attacker about the state of Enclave, even though the Enclave is strictly protected by SGX hardware. Dark-ROP can cause serious security problems due to its ability to bypass SGX's protection of memory and steal confidential information in memory, such as encryption keys. In 2018, Andrea Biondo et al. proposed *The Guard's Dilemma: Efficient Code-Reuse Attacks against Intel SGX* (Biondo et al., 2018) to further perform memory attacks on SGX, even in the scenario where SGX-Shield is enabled. (SGX-Shield is mainly used to introduce randomization to the memory layout inside SGX to prevent it from being attacked by ROP.)

Similar attacks can also be performed on the ARM TrustZone. Adrian Tang et al. proposed *CLKSCREW: Exposing the Perils of Security – Oblivious Energy Management* (Tang et al., 2017), in which they discover a vulnerability that can use the CPU energy management system: DVFS to take over the mobile device. They also successfully performed such an attack on Android devices equipped with ARM processors. Florida State University and Baidu XLab presented a downgrade attack against ARM TrustZone. After the processor manufacturer finds a vulnerability for TrustZone, they will send an update to the mobile terminal manufacturer to update the relevant firmware, operating system, and software. However, if the TEE lacks version verification, it can be vulnerable to downgrade attacks. Downgrade attacks can roll back TrustZone's firmware and software to a previous and vulnerable version, and then use the vulnerability to attack.

7.3.2 Reliance upon Hardware Vendors

Unlike cryptographic techniques such as Secure Multi-Party Computation (SMPC) and Homomorphic Encryption (HE), the security of TEE does not depend on a specific theory (for example, Homomorphic Encryption relies on lattice encryption theory), but depends on specific hardware vendors. Therefore, the security of TEE becomes difficult to evaluate and verify. In fact, the vulnerabilities described earlier are mainly caused by design flaws made by hardware vendors.

Moreover, commonly used TEE implementations, such as Intel SGX, ARM TrustZone, and AMD SEV, are all developed by corporations in the United States. Therefore, for countries other than the United States, it is still doubtful whether these TEE techniques can be credibly used to protect critical applications related to national security, such as national defense and large-scale financial transactions.

Recently, UC Berkeley's RISELab published a paper, *Keystone: an Open Framework for Architecting Trusted Execution Environments* (Lee et al., 2020). The paper proposes a design and implementation of a customized TEE based on the RISC-V instruction set. Keystone is an open-source project whose code can be maintained and inspected by researchers and practitioners all over the world. Therefore, Keystone has the potential to be widely applied on commodity RISC-V chips and credibly deployed by countries all around the globe.

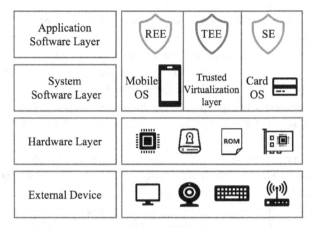

Figure 7.6 Architecture of *Technical Specifications for Mobile Terminal Payment Trusted Environment*.

7.4 Application Scenarios

In this section, we will discuss the application scenarios of TEE from three dimensions: mobile devices, cloud computing, and blockchain.

7.4.1 Mobile Devices

Mobile Payment

An important application of TEE on mobile terminals is mobile payment. The industry standard *Technical Specifications for Mobile Terminal Payment Trusted Environment*, issued by the China Financial Standardization Technical Committee, regulates how applications on mobile terminals can perform mobile payment with TEE. The standard proposes the definition of the trusted environment for mobile device terminals and specifies the overall technical framework, including Trusted Execution Environment, communication security, and data security. As shown in Figure 7.6, similar to the definition in TrustZone, the mobile device payment trusted environment includes:

- Regular Operating System (REE): This is the nonsecure operating system on the mobile terminal. It is responsible for entertainment, communication, and other general applications.
- Trusted Execution Environment (TEE): This environment is used to protect all kinds of sensitive data, ensuring data confidentiality and end-to-end security.

- Secure Element (SE): This is a high-security operating environment on a mobile terminal, which can resist various security attacks from both the hardware and software levels. Applications running on SE are also secured. The private key required for payment is stored in the SE and never leaves the SE. When the user signs a payment transaction, the transaction is confirmed through the Trusted Apps (TA) running in the TEE. It can fully realize the electronic authentication of "what you sign is what you see" without any external devices, leading to both high security and convenience.

Biometric Identification

With the development of mobile devices, biometric information recognition technologies such as face recognition and fingerprint recognition are being applied to mobile terminal applications, such as smartphone unlocking and payment verification. However, in commodity operating systems, face recognition algorithms and biometric data of users are vulnerable to external malicious attacks, resulting in security threats. To address the problem, Apple introduced the fingerprint unlocking system Touch ID in the iPhone 5S and implemented TrustZone in its ARM-based A7 chip. All user fingerprint data and fingerprint identification algorithms are encrypted and stored in the TrustZone. The operating system and other applications cannot access these data completely.

Content Copyright Protection

Nowadays, many Digital Rights Management (DRM) solutions are implemented using TEE, such as Google's Videvine. Digital Rights Management refers to the technology of rights protection, use control, and management for these digital contents, such as audio and video program content, documents, and e-books, in the process of production, dissemination, sales, and use. Digital Rights Management has established a digital program authorization center. The digital content is encrypted and protected with a key, and the header of the encrypted digital content stores the key ID and the URL of the program authorization center. When the user consumes these contents, the DRM system decrypts the content according to the key ID and URL information in the content header. Even if these contents are downloaded and saved by the user, they cannot be used without the verification and authorization of the digital program authorization center, thus strictly protecting the copyright of the program.

In DRM applications, the TEE can protect digital copyrights in the following aspects. First, the TEE has enough computing power to decrypt this encrypted content without affecting applications in the REE. Second, it can be used to run DRM-related trusted programs to prevent these programs from being tampered with by the operating system or other applications. Third, copyright can be strictly protected by policies such as rollback or expiration of keys, and Regular Operating Systems (REE) or applications cannot interfere with the enforcement of these policies.

7.4.2 Cloud Computing

Storage

To protect the security of data stored in the cloud, Intel SGX is widely used by cloud providers for secure storage services. Maurice Bailleu et al. published a paper, *SPEICHER: Securing LSM-based Key-Value Stores using Shielded Execution* (Bailleu et al., 2019), to implement a KV storage system based on Log-Structured Merge Tree (LSM-Tree). The system redesigns the LSM data structure to match the architecture of Intel SGX to ensure the security of data storage. Taehoon Kim et al. proposed *ShieldStore: Shielded In-memory Key-value Storage with SGX* (Kim et al., 2019). The system also uses SGX to provide a secure KV storage system. They mainly solve the performance degradation caused by the data structure used by KV storage exceeding the current EPC (Enclave Page Capacity) of SGX. In the current Intel SGX implementation, the size of EPC is limited to about 128 MB. When the memory usage of the Enclave exceeds the capacity of the EPC, it will cause frequent memory switching, causing high latency. In addition, to protect the data on the memory, memory encryption and decryption will also be performed during switching, leading to further performance degradation. ShieldStore stores the main data structure, i.e., the hash table of KV store, in the unprotected memory. It further encrypts each KV formatted data in the Enclave and stores them in the hash table. When reading data from the KV storage, the data is first obtained from the hash table in the nonencrypted memory and then decrypted in the Enclave to complete the data fetching operation. In addition to KV storage, there is also a series of work aiming to protect databases with SGX. For example, Microsoft published *EnclaveDB: A Secure Database using SGX* (Priebe et al., 2018) to implement a Database Management System (DBMS) based on Intel SGX.

Machine Learning

Machine learning has become an important application in data centers. Machine learning relies on large-scale, high-quality user data to generate accurate models. Therefore, how to protect data privacy during machine learning has become an important issue.

In general, machine learning consists of two phases, training and inference. Training refers to the process of updating the model to fit the data, while inference refers to the process of using the trained model to perform predictive tasks. The paper *Occlumency: Privacy-preserving Remote Deep-learning Inference Using SGX* by Taegyeong Lee et al. (Lee et al., 2019) protects data security throughout the machine learning inference process with the SGX Enclave. When machine learning inference is initiated, users first use a secure tunnel (such as TLS) to transfer the encrypted data into SGX. Then, Occlumency executes the entire machine learning inference in the SGX Enclave and transfers the inference results back to the client again through the secure tunnel.

A more complex scenario than inference is the training scenario because training machine learning models consumes a lot of computing power and requires large-scale input data. For machine learning training, there is also a series of research works that use SGX to protect the training process and the original data. One of the pioneering works is *Oblivious Multi-Party Machine Learning on Trusted Processors* proposed by Olga Ohrimenko et al. (Ohrimenko et al., 2016). The work studies how to implement common machine learning algorithms (e.g., Support Vector Machines, Decision Trees, Matrix Factorization, Neural Networks) efficiently on SGX. At the same time, Roland Kunkel et al. proposed *TensorSCONE: a Secure TensorFlow Framework using Intel SGX* (Kunkel et al., 2019) to further integrate TensorFlow with SGX to achieve a safe, efficient, and general machine learning platform.

Network Middlebox

Network Middlebox is a computer networking device or virtual network device to implement Network Functions (NFs) that support transforming, inspecting, filtering, or other operations over network traffic. A common network middlebox includes the firewall and the Network Address Translator (NAT). The former filters unwanted or malicious traffic, while the latter modifies the source and destination addresses of packets. Middlebox is widely used in cloud computing to improve network security, flexibility, and performance. Due to the complexity of cloud computing networks (such as receiving and sending various types of traffic externally, and accessing sensitive user information internally), how to make cloud computing networks trusted and secure through Middlebox has become an important issue in current cloud computing.

Rishabh Poddar et al. proposed *SafeBricks: Shielding Network Functions in the Cloud* (Poddar et al., 2018) to build a trusted network function by using both SGX and programming language checks. SafeBrick can achieve two goals: (1) It only exposes the encrypted traffic to the cloud computing providers so that users' sensitive information cannot be obtained by the cloud computing providers. (2) When users are developing their networking components,

SafeBrick lowers the trust dependency upon other components and thus facilitates the development of trusted network functions. Huayi Duan et al. proposed *LightBox: Full-Stack Protected Stateful Middlebox at Lightning Speed* (Duan et al., 2019) to solve the performance issues. LightBox can support an I/O rate at 10 Gb/s, which greatly improves the speed of the trusted Middlebox in high-performance networks. Fabian Schwarz et al. (Schwarz and Rossow, 2020) proposed *SENG, the SGX-Enforcing Network Gateway: Authorizing Communication from Shielded Clients*. SENG is a new type of gateway, which can effectively map the firewall to specific applications to achieve fine-grained and precise access control.

7.4.3 Blockchain

Blockchains use a lot of cryptographic algorithms as their underlying technologies. Combining TEE with blockchain is thus a natural approach to further ensure the security of blockchains. In the paper *Proof of Luck: an Efficient Blockchain Consensus Protocol* (Milutinovic et al., 2016), Mitar Milutinovic et al. proposed a novel blockchain consensus scheme – proof of luck. Compared with the traditional consensus scheme – proof of work, the proof of luck algorithm has a smaller delay and lower energy consumption. With proof-of-luck, all participants uniformly generate random numbers r from $[0, 1]$. They then delay r seconds to broadcast consensus. The luckiest participant, i.e., the participant with the smallest r, can become the consensus of the whole chain. Because the entire consensus algorithm runs in TEE, participants are unable to cheat to become the consensus of the entire chain by tampering with random numbers.

8

Federated Learning

Machine learning is widely used in many aspects of our daily life, such as face recognition, speech recognition, and machine translation. However, popular machine learning algorithms, especially deep learning algorithms, require a large amount of data to yield accurate models. In practical applications, these data are often distributed on devices owned by different users or in the databases of different companies. How to jointly use data from multiple parties for model training without compromising the privacy of data owners thus becomes a problem of pressing importance. Federated learning introduced in this chapter is a practical solution to this problem. Due to space limitation, we cannot cover all the details of federated learning in this chapter. We refer interested readers to Yang et al. (2019a).

8.1 Background, Definition, and Categorization

8.1.1 Background of Federated Learning

In the past few years, with advances in computation and data resources, deep learning algorithms have been widely used in various applications of our lives, such as face recognition, object detection, speech recognition, machine translation, and personalized recommendation. An essential factor to the success of deep learning is large-scale labeled data. For example, in academia, the ImageNet dataset (Deng et al., 2009), built by the group led by Professor Fei-Fei Li at Stanford University, contains 14 million high-resolution labeled images, which greatly advanced the development of deep neural networks in the following years (He et al., 2016; Krizhevsky et al., 2012). In industrial applications, the object detection model used by Facebook was pretrained using 350 million Instagram images (Mahajan et al., 2018).

However, in practice, we are often confronted with insufficient data. For example, in the field of medical diagnosis, medical images of patients need to be diagnosed and labeled by medical experts before they can be used to train image recognition models. Such a process often requires a lot of effort from domain experts, and thus, each medical institution may only have a limited number of labeled medical images. Therefore, to leverage large-scale data to train machine learning models, it is necessary to utilize decentralized data distributed among various parties. For example, although a single hospital may only have a limited amount of medical image data, by integrating data from multiple hospitals, the scale of data can be effectively expanded to better support deep learning algorithms.

Meanwhile, as machine learning is applied in an increasing number of applications, users are increasingly concerned about the privacy of their data. To protect personal privacy, users may be reluctant to share their data. For example, disclosure of a user's medical records may lead to discrimination in job seeking and social interactions. To enforce protection over user privacy, more and more laws on data privacy and security have been enacted, such as the General Data Protection Regulation (GDPR) in the European Union (EU) and the Cybersecurity Law of the People's Republic of China. Under increasingly strict laws and regulations, data from multiple parties cannot be directly exchanged or collected centrally due to leakage of private data and violation of regulations. Therefore, how to use data from multiple parties to train machine learning models while complying with data privacy and security regulations is a problem of pressing importance.

To meet the demand, the notion of Federated Learning (FL) was proposed and continually extended by researchers. In 2017, H. Brendan McMahan et al. from Google proposed cross-device FL, which aims to jointly train models using data stored on users' smartphones, such as keyboard input prediction, and sentiment analysis models (Hard et al., 2018; Ramaswamy et al., 2019). In 2019, Professor Qiang Yang et al. of WeBank (Yang et al., 2019d) extended the definition of FL by proposing cross-silo FL, i.e., federated learning that unifies data from different companies. Subsequently, they defined the concepts of horizontal federated learning (HFL), vertical federated learning (VFL), and federated transfer learning (FTL). In the following sections, we will introduce these concepts and definitions.

8.1.2 Definition of Federated Learning

The purpose of federated learning is to train a machine learning model using data distributed among multiple data owners while protecting data privacy.

The obtained model is used for predictive tasks, e.g., classification, forecasting, and recommendation. During the training process, necessary intermediate results are exchanged between the participants, while the data are kept locally. To better protect privacy, we can use privacy-preserving computation techniques, such as homomorphic encryption, to further protect the transmitted information. After the model has converged, the model will be deployed for applications across participants. It is important to note that since each participant in the federation holds only partial data, the models held by each party may also be partial models. Thus, all participants may need to jointly make predictions (also called inference) on new samples. For example, consider a federated learning system that diagnoses patients based on multiple medical information (i.e., medical imaging, test results, vital sign series). To make a diagnosis on a new patient, all related information should be jointly modeled by all parties.

Yang et al. (2019a) define federated learning as a machine learning framework that satisfies the following properties:

- **Multiple participants:** Two or more participants (also referred to as parties or clients) cooperate to train a shared machine learning model. Each participant owns part of the data to train the model.
- **No data exchange:** Raw local data should never leave the corresponding participant.
- **Protected transmission of information:** During the federated learning training process, the exchanged intermediate results need to be protected by privacy-preserving computation techniques.
- **Approximately lossless:** The performance of the federated learning model should be sufficiently close to the performance of the ideal model (i.e., the model trained by collecting data centrally).

This definition states the characteristics that a federated learning algorithm should satisfy. In different application scenarios, researchers have designed different federated learning algorithms to meet specific needs. We introduce the categorization of federated learning in the following section.

8.1.3 Categorization of Federated Learning

In federated learning, each party owns a part of the data. So, it is natural to categorize federated learning according to how data is partitioned.

To formally introduce the categorization of federated learning, we first introduce some necessary notations. We denote N as the number of participants, where each participant is represented by $1, \ldots, N$, respectively. We denote the set of samples owned by participant i as $\mathbb{U}_i$, the feature space as $\mathbb{X}_i$, the label space as $\mathbb{Y}_i$, and the dataset as $\mathbb{D}_i = \{u_i^{(j)}, \boldsymbol{x}_i^{(j)}, y_i^{(j)}\}_{j=1}^{|\mathbb{D}_i|}$, where data point $(u_i^{(j)}, \boldsymbol{x}_i^{(j)}, y_i^{(j)})$ indicates that the ith participant owns the data from sample $u_i^{(j)}$ with features $\boldsymbol{x}_i^{(j)}$ and the label $y_i^{(j)}$. For example, in the field of smart healthcare, $\mathbb{U}$ refers to the set of all patients, $\mathbb{X}$ can refer to features such as medical images, and $\mathbb{Y}$ can represent whether a user is diagnosed with the disease or not. Based on the data partition $(\mathbb{X}, \mathbb{Y}, \mathbb{U})$ among the participants, federated learning can be classified into the following three categories (Yang et al., 2019d).

- **Horizontal Federated Learning (HFL):** In horizontal federated learning, $\mathbb{X}_i = \mathbb{X}_j, \mathbb{Y}_i = \mathbb{Y}_j, \mathbb{U}_i \neq \mathbb{U}_j$, i.e., the participants share the same feature and label space, but have different sample spaces.
- **Vertical Federated Learning (VFL):** In vertical federated learning, $\mathbb{X}_i \neq \mathbb{X}_j, \mathbb{Y}_i \neq \mathbb{Y}_j, \mathbb{U}_i \cap \mathbb{U}_j \neq \emptyset$, i.e., some common data samples are shared among the participants, but the feature and label spaces are different.
- **Federated Transfer Learning (FTL):** In federated transfer learning, we do not impose any restrictions on the sample, feature, and label space, i.e., the sample, feature, and label spaces among the participants can be arbitrarily different. Under such circumstances, we need to effectively use the knowledge (e.g., model parameters) learned from each party's data during the joint training.

Here we give some concrete examples to explain the categorization. If two hospitals want to jointly train a medical image analysis model for the same disease, they have the same feature spaces $\mathbb{X}$, which are medical images; they also share the same label spaces $\mathbb{Y}$, which are the diagnosis results. However, they have different sample spaces, i.e., the set of patients $\mathbb{U}$ are different between different hospitals. Such a scenario complies with the definition of horizontal federated learning. Alternatively, consider two hospitals who want to jointly train a disease diagnosis model using the same set of patients, but Hospital A uses medical image data and Hospital B uses medical record text data. In this case, their feature spaces $\mathbb{X}$ are different but their sample spaces $\mathbb{U}$ are the same, indicating a vertical federated learning scenario. Finally, if two hospitals want to use data from different patients to train medical image analysis models for different diseases, the scenario belongs to federated transfer learning. Taking a scenario with two participants as an example, Figure 8.1, Figure 8.2, and Figure 8.3 show the similarities and differences between the three types of federated learning, respectively. In this chapter, we will introduce federated learning following this categorization.

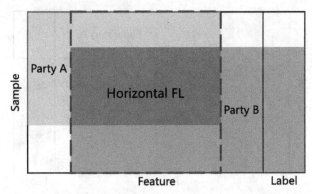

Figure 8.1 Horizontal Federated Learning. From Yang et al. (2019a), reproduced with permission from Springer Nature.

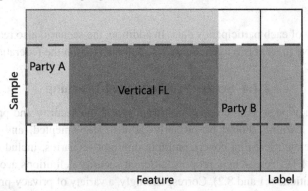

Figure 8.2 Vertical Federated Learning. From Yang et al. (2019a), reproduced with permission from Springer Nature.

Additionally, there are other categorizations of federated learning. For example, based on the different computation and communication capabilities of participants, federated learning can also be categorized as follows (Kairouz et al., 2019).

- **Cross-device FL**, also known as business-to-consumer (B2C) federated learning. It is exemplified by Google's federated learning with users' smartphones. In this scenario, the major challenges are a large number of participants, low computational resources, high transmission overhead, and a small amount of data from a single participant.
- **Cross-silo FL**, also known as business-to-business (B2B) federated learning. In this scenario, each participant is a company or institution, with a relatively small number of participants and stronger communication and computational capacities. However, this scenario often involves the federation of different stakeholders, so it is more important to strictly protect the

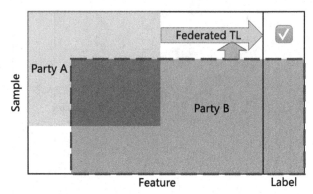

Figure 8.3 Federated Transfer Learning. From Yang et al. (2019a), reproduced with permission from Springer Nature.

privacy of each participant's data. In addition, the scenario also requires an incentive mechanism to encourage participants to join the federation.

8.1.4 Security of Federated Learning

As a privacy-preserving computation framework, the security and privacy of federated learning should be properly defined, implemented, and verified. Since federated learning covers multiple different scenarios, including HFL, VFL, and FTL, researchers propose different security definitions accordingly (see Definitions 8.1 and 8.2). Correspondingly, a variety of privacy-preserving computation techniques are leveraged to implement the security definitions, including HE, SS, and DP. We will provide discussions on the definitions and implementations of privacy in the following sections when we introduce each type of federated learning (see Sections 8.2, 8.3, and 8.4).

8.2 Horizontal Federated Learning

In this section, we introduce horizontal federated learning. Horizontal federated learning, which is shown in Figure 8.1, applies to the case where participants share the same feature space, but have different sample spaces. An intuitive way to understand HFL is to consider a data matrix partitioned in the sample dimension and distributed to different data owners. We will introduce the most commonly used HFL architecture: the client–server architecture. We will then introduce the most general and popular HFL algorithm, Federated Averaging (FedAvg), based on the client–server architecture. Finally, we analyze the privacy risks in HFL and discuss related solutions.

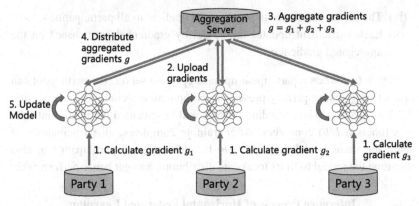

Figure 8.4 Training process of HFL under the client–server architecture. From Yang et al. (2019a), reproduced with permission from Springer Nature.

We first use the same notation as Section 8.1.1 to define the optimization objective of HFL as

$$\min_{\theta} L(\theta) = \sum_{i=1}^{N} L_i(\theta) = \sum_{i=1}^{N} \frac{1}{|\mathbb{D}_i|} \sum_{j=1}^{|\mathbb{D}_i|} l(x_i^{(j)}, y_i^{(j)}; \theta), \qquad (8.1)$$

where θ denotes model parameters; $L(\theta)$ is the global optimization objective; $L_i(\theta) = \frac{1}{|\mathbb{D}_i|} \sum_{j=1}^{|\mathbb{D}_i|} l(x_i^{(j)}, y_i^{(j)}; \theta)$ is the optimization objective of participant i based on its local data; and $l(x, y; \theta)$ is the loss function, such as the cross-entropy loss or the mean squared loss.

8.2.1 Architecture, Training, and Inference Process

The most commonly used architecture for HFL is the client–server architecture, shown in Figure 8.4. We will introduce the training and inference processes of HFL based on this architecture.

Training Process of Horizontal Federated Learning

In the client–server architecture, the stochastic gradient descent (SGD) method is often used to solve the optimization problem in Eq. (8.1). The overall process is as follows:

(i) Each participant samples a batch of data B, and calculates gradients $g_i = \frac{1}{|B|} \nabla_{\theta} \sum_{x,y \in B} l(x, y; \theta)$ based on the batch.

(ii) Each participant uploads g_i to the server.

(iii) The server aggregates the gradients (e.g., averaging $g = \frac{1}{N} \sum_{i=1}^{N} g_i$).

(iv) The server distributes the aggregated gradient to all participants.

(v) Each participant updates the model by gradient descent based on the aggregated gradient g.

In step (ii), when a participant uploads g_i to the server, the participant can protect its g_i using privacy-preserving computation techniques (see Section 8.2.3 for details). The preceding process will be executed iteratively until the loss function $L(\theta)$ converges. After training completes, all participants will share the same model parameters θ. In addition, each participant can also fine-tune the model to fit its local data distribution and get better performance.

Inference Process of Horizontal Federated Learning
In horizontal federated learning, all participants share the same feature space. Thus, each participant has the complete model and can make inferences on new samples independently.

When the model parameters and raw data are held by different participants during the model inference, it is also necessary to ensure the privacy of the data to the model owner, i.e., the model owner should not have access to the raw data (Cheng et al., 2021a; Juvekar et al., 2018; Liu et al., 2020). Therefore, we need to protect the input data with homomorphic encryption and secret sharing, and then perform model inference on the ciphertexts. Also, we can use efficient secure inference algorithms such as GAZELLE (Juvekar et al., 2018). Such algorithms often use a combination of cryptographic techniques such as garbled circuits and homomorphic encryption to achieve fast and private model inference.

8.2.2 The Federated Averaging (FedAvg) Algorithm

A practical problem in HFL is the large communication overhead. For example, in cross-device federated learning, the communication between the server and the participants (smartphones) relies on mobile networks, whose bandwidth may be limited and connections may be unstable. Therefore, the participants may take a long time for gradient uploading and downloading, and may even drop out of the connection. Facing these difficulties, H. Brendan McMahan et al. from Google proposed the Federated Averaging (FedAvg) algorithm (McMahan et al., 2017a) to reduce the communication cost of HFL.

FedAvg optimizes the communication cost of horizontal federated learning based on a simple intuition: the local computation of each participant can be increased to reduce the number of communication rounds required for model convergence. Specifically, instead of transmitting gradients of every batch (in Section 8.2.1), FedAvg transmits gradients every S passes over the local data (often referred to as S *epochs*). Assuming that the current model parameters are $\theta^{(t)}$, the batch size is b, and the learning rate is η, the FedAvg algorithm consists of the following steps:

(i) Each participant divides the local data $\mathbb{D}_i$ into batches of size b.

(ii) For each batch B, the participants perform parameter updates $\theta_i^{(t)} \leftarrow \theta_i^{(t)} - \frac{\eta}{b} \sum_{x,y \in B} \nabla_\theta l(x, y; \theta_i^{(t)})$ until the local dataset $\mathbb{D}_i$ is iterated S times (or S epochs).

(iii) Each participant sends the updated parameters $\theta_i^{(t)}$ to the aggregation server.

(iv) The aggregation server performs a weighted average of the model parameters $\theta^{(t+1)} = \sum_{i=1}^{N} w_i \theta_i^{(t)}$, where w_i is calculated from the size of each local dataset.

(v) The aggregation server distributes $\theta^{(t+1)}$ to the participants.

As shown, FedAvg reduces the communication frequency by $\frac{S|\mathbb{D}_i|}{b}$ times. Experiments in McMahan et al. (2017a) show that although the FedAvg algorithm requires more computation in each round of training, it still improves the overall efficiency by reducing the communication cost, considering that the communication overhead is much larger than the computation overhead.

8.2.3 Privacy Preservation in Horizontal Federated Learning

In this section, we introduce the privacy issue in HFL, including privacy risks, the definition of privacy, privacy-preserving computation techniques, and performance optimization.

In the early stage of HFL research, it is generally assumed that the gradients or model parameters do not reveal information on private data. Thus, keeping data local is considered sufficient to achieve data privacy. Therefore, how to protect the exchanged information, such as gradients, is a generally unexplored topic in the early stages of HFL. However, a series of research works (Geiping et al., 2020; Zhao et al., 2020; Zhu et al., 2019) have shown that it is possible to infer or even accurately reconstruct training data from gradients or model parameters, rendering the assumption invalid.

We take the client–server architecture in Section 8.2.1 as an example to illustrate how exchanging gradients would compromise data privacy. In HFL, we primarily aim to protect data privacy against the aggregation server, as the server is generally more powerful than individual participants. We assume that the server is semihonest, or honest-but-curious, i.e., the server will perform parameter aggregation as per the protocol but may try to steal the private data of the participants.

Based on the preceding assumptions, Zhu et al. (Zhu et al., 2019) propose the Deep Leakage from Gradients (DLG) algorithm, which reconstructs the input data by optimizing the distance between the real and simulated gradients. Specifically, the optimization objective of DLG is

$$\min_{x', y'} \|\nabla_\theta l(x', y'; \theta) - \nabla_\theta l(x, y; \theta)\|^2, \qquad (8.2)$$

where x, y are the real data; θ is the current model parameters; and x', y' are the data features and labels to be optimized. Zhu et al. (2019) demonstrate that the DLG algorithm can accurately reconstruct the input data for a second-order smooth model and single-step gradient updates. Geiping et al. (2020) further improve DLG by optimizing the cosine distance between the simulated gradient and the real gradient instead of the L^2 distance. Furthermore, they experimentally demonstrate that the proposed attack is effective even for multistep gradient updates. Thus, the unprotected transmission of gradients or model parameters in HFL leads to potential privacy risks.

To formally study and further mitigate such privacy risks, under the semihonest assumption, Bonawitz et al. from Google (Bonawitz et al., 2017) define the privacy of HFL as follows:

Definition 8.1 (Semihonest security of HFL (Bonawitz et al., 2017)) Denote the server as S, the set of participants as $\mathcal{U}$, and the input to be aggregated for each participant as g_u. Define the view of any party (including $S, u \in \mathcal{U}$) as the set of all its internal states (e.g., local computation results, random number seeds) and all its received information (e.g., the protected input $[[g_u]]$ sent by other participants). Given a threshold t, during the execution of the aggregation protocol, if the joint view of S and any set of participants $\mathcal{U}' \subset \mathcal{U}$ with $|\mathcal{U}'| < t$ reveals no extra information about the inputs of other participants $g_u, u \in \mathcal{U} - \mathcal{U}'$ besides what can be inferred from the output of the computation, then the aggregation protocol is said to be semihonest secure under threshold t.

We make the following remarks on this definition.

(i) Under the semihonest assumption, the terms "privacy" and "security" can be interchangeably used. We follow the terms used by Bonawitz et al. (2017) and use the term "semihonest security" in this chapter.

(ii) The information exchanged between participants and the aggregation server in HFL can be either gradients or other information. Definition 8.1 does not make assumptions about the exchanged information. Thus, an HFL protocol satisfying Definition 8.1 inherently prevents the leakage from gradients (Geiping et al., 2020; Zhu et al., 2019) because the server cannot even know the gradients from individual participants.

(iii) Definition 8.1 covers the case where the aggregation server colludes with participants, i.e., the aggregation server may have extra access to the internal states of a set of colluding participants (e.g., the real gradient information g_u instead of the protected gradient information). Similarly, Definition 8.1 also covers the case where the server does not collude with participants (by setting $t = 0$).

(iv) One way to prove that an HFL protocol satisfies Definition 8.1 is to prove "indistinguishability" (see Section 3.1), i.e., an arbitrary information jointly computed by S and fewer than t participants $\mathcal{U}'$ can also be computed indistinguishably by $\mathcal{U}'$ (without S). Thus, intuitively, it implies that all information learned by S is already contained by its colluding participants $\mathcal{U}'$, and S learns nothing else.

To satisfy Definition 8.1, a series of works have been proposed to use privacy-preserving computation techniques in HFL. Here, we briefly introduce two approaches: secret sharing and homomorphic encryption. In addition, as a strict implementation of Definition 8.1 often requires significant computation or communication overhead, in practice, people may also weaken Definition 8.1 and achieve privacy protection using differential privacy (DP). We will also cover DP-based approaches in this chapter.

Secret-sharing-based Secure Parameter Aggregation
In the client–server architecture used for HFL, the server is considered to be powerful enough to compromise the privacy of user data. Therefore, to protect privacy against the server, an intuitive idea is that all participants perform a secure aggregation protocol, such that the server will only have access to the aggregated gradient $g = \sum_i g_i$ and cannot learn gradients g_i from individual participants. Intuitively, the aggregated gradients $g = \sum_i g_i$ contain information from all participants, and thus cannot be used to infer the private data of a specific participant. Also, by hiding individual gradients, secure aggregation satisfies Definition 8.1. Thus, the privacy of HFL can be guaranteed by secure aggregation. In this section, we briefly introduce a secure parameter aggregation scheme based on secret sharing proposed by Google (Bonawitz et al., 2017). It provides privacy protection for HFL and also effectively solves the practical challenges.

An important application scenario for HFL is cross-device federated learning. For example, Google uses user data stored in Android smartphones to train machine learning models without collecting user data centrally. In such a scenario, the participants are typically smartphones connected via wireless networks, which poses a series of practical challenges alongside the requirement for privacy protection.

- Since model training requires power consumption, only devices with sufficient power (e.g., connected to the charger) are available for training.
- Since the information is communicated on slow and unstable wireless networks, clients may be slow to respond, or even drop offline completely.

Therefore, whether a client will participate in each round of federated model training is unpredictable and unstable. We cannot assume that there is always a fixed set of participants involved in the secure aggregation. Based on the above constraint, researchers from Google designed a secret-sharing-based protocol (Bonawitz et al., 2017) that is robust to offline and unavailable clients. We provide a brief introduction to the protocol here.

The protocol assumes that there are N participants and one server. Each participant has a parameter vector $x_i \in \mathbb{Z}_R^m, i = 1, \ldots, N$, where $\mathbb{Z}_R$ is a finite field with R (e.g., a large prime number) as the generating element. The purpose of the protocol is to compute $\sum_{i=1}^{N} x_i$ and to guarantee that the server cannot know x_i of any participant i. As we primarily consider privacy threats from the server, we omit the case where clients compromise the privacy of each other. Without loss of generality, we do not consider the weights of parameter aggregation.

The idea of this protocol is very simple, i.e., mutually canceling masks can be designed to mask the values of individual participants without affecting the final sum. Specifically, if $s_{i,j}$ is a random vector negotiated between participants i, j, and we let

$$y_i = x_i + \sum_{j>i} s_{i,j} - \sum_{j<i} s_{j,i} \quad \mod R, \tag{8.3}$$

it follows that

$$\sum_{i=1}^{N} y_i = \sum_{i=1}^{N} \left(x_i + \sum_{j>i} s_{i,j} - \sum_{j<i} s_{j,i} \right). \tag{8.4}$$

As shown, for a particular participant pair i, j with $i < j$, $s_{i,j}$ appears with a positive sign in y_i and with a negative sign in y_j, and thus they cancel each other out, yielding $\sum_{i=1}^{N} y_i = \sum_{i=1}^{N} x_i$. However, this masking scheme cannot handle participant dropouts. Once participant i drops out, $s_{i,j}$ and $s_{j,i}$ cannot be canceled out. To solve this problem, the paper proposes to generate all $s_{i,j}$ by a Pseudo Random Number Generator (PRG) and share the random number seeds among all participants using a threshold secret sharing scheme. With the (t, N) threshold secret sharing scheme, the random number seeds can be recovered as long as at least t of all N participants are online, and thus all $s_{i,j}$ can be recovered. Therefore, as long as over t participants are online, the secure aggregation protocol can be performed. The preceding is a brief description of the protocol proposed in Bonawitz et al. (2017). We refer interested readers to Section 2.4 in this book for the secret sharing protocol involved.

Parameter Aggregation based on Homomorphic Encryption
We can also use homomorphic encryption for parameter aggregation. Given the gradients $g_i, i = 1, \ldots, N$ of each participant, they can be first encrypted and then uploaded to the server. The server aggregates them without decryption and then returns them to the participants, who decrypt them and update local models. Since the server cannot observe the plaintext gradients, as long as the homomorphic encryption scheme is secure, the process satisfies Definition 8.1. However, such methods require strict key management (generation and distribution of public and private keys), and thus cannot be applied in the cross-device scenario where there are numerous participants whose participations are unstable. In contrast, the homomorphic encryption scheme is more suitable for cross-silo federated learning, where the number of participants is relatively small.

However, the cryptographic computation and ciphertext transmission after homomorphic encryption incur significant additional overhead. In HFL with homomorphic encryption, 80 percent of the computation time is spent on encryption and decryption, and the ciphertexts are about 150 times larger than plaintexts (Zhang et al., 2020), causing a large overhead in communication. To alleviate the overhead, the team at the Hong Kong University of Science and Technology led by Professor Wei Wang proposed BatchCrypt (Zhang et al., 2020) as an improvement.

The idea of BatchCrypt is also very intuitive: the model gradients are generally encoded as 32-bit floating point numbers, and after encryption, each floating point number is generally 2048 bits long, which expands by 64 times. However, if k floating-point numbers are compressed into one number and then encrypted, the ciphertext length is also 2048 bits, and a k-time speedup can be achieved. Based on the intuition, BatchCrypt quantizes b floating-point gradient values into low-bit signed integers, packs them into a Batch, encodes them into a long integer, and then encrypts them. To maintain the additivity of the homomorphic encryption during quantization, packing, and encoding, BatchCrypt is designed with a 2-complement-based encoding scheme to encode the signed integers. In addition, to determine the optimal quantization range during quantization, BatchCrypt proposes the distributed analytical cropping method (dACIQ). Empirical experiments demonstrate that BatchCrypt is 23–93 times more efficient and incurs 66–101 times less amount of communication than Paillier in a cross-silo HFL scenario. Meanwhile, the model accuracy drop due to quantization is less than 1 percent. We refer interested readers to the paper (Zhang et al., 2020).

Differential-privacy-based Horizontal Federated Learning

Definition 8.1 is very strong. It can only be implemented by cryptographic tools (e.g., homomorphic encryption, secret sharing), which often require significant overhead. Thus, in practice, for better computational/communication efficiency, we can also implement a relaxation of Definition 8.1 with differential privacy. We provide brief introductions in this section.

Sample-level Differential Privacy An intuitive idea is to apply DP techniques to each sample, such as the DPSGD algorithm introduced in Definition 6.33 and Abadi et al. (2016). Such techniques ensure that no individual samples have a strong influence on the final model, and thus, information of individual samples cannot be inferred. However, DPSGD often requires a high level of noise such that it may compromise the accuracy of the trained model (see Section 6.5.2 for details).

Client-level Differential Privacy As mentioned earlier, sample-level DP can lead to a significant accuracy loss. Therefore, researchers also propose differential privacy at the level of clients. Specifically, differentially private techniques are applied to the gradients g_i uploaded by client i, while in DPSGD, noise is added to gradients computed from each sample. Intuitively, client-level DP ensures that no individual clients have a significant influence on the final model (see Definition 6.11). Consequently, client-level DP makes it difficult for the server to distinguish gradients from different clients and also protects client-side private data. We refer interested readers to papers (Geyer et al., 2017; Hu et al., 2020).

8.3 Vertical Federated Learning

In this section, we introduce vertical federated learning. As shown in Figure 8.2, VFL applies to the case where each participant has the same sample IDs but different feature spaces. For example, through VFL, a bank can work with an e-commerce platform to build a more comprehensive credit assessment model. Leveraging the purchase records of users, banks can more accurately

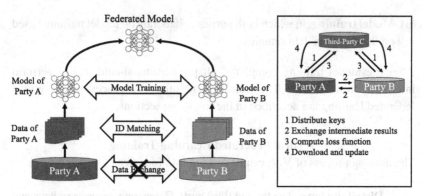

Figure 8.5 Training process of VFL. From Yang et al. (2019a), reproduced with permission from Springer Nature.

evaluate user credits through the users' shopping habits. Vertical Federated Learning can be understood as the case where a data matrix is vertically partitioned and distributed among data owners. In this section, we introduce the common architecture of VFL and briefly introduce a popular VFL algorithm.

8.3.1 Architecture, Training, and Inference

Without loss of generality, we introduce the architecture of VFL with two parties involved. Suppose two companies A and B want to train models with different data features but the same user IDs. However, direct data exchange between A and B is forbidden. Therefore, in VFL, a trusted third party C is often introduced to coordinate the collaboration between A and B. We generally assume that the third party C is honest, i.e., it will accurately execute the VFL algorithm and will not try to infer the private data of participants A and B. Correspondingly, we generally assume that A and B are both semihonest (honest-but-curious), i.e., they may try to infer private information from each other. We make such an assumption for two reasons. On one hand, a trusted third party can either be an authoritative department (e.g., a government agency) or a trusted computing service provider. On the other hand, A and B may not be trustworthy as they may try to infer privacy data from each other for commercial interests.

Given the assumptions on A, B, and C, a common VFL architecture is shown in Figure 8.5, which typically consists of two steps.

(i) **Sample alignment**, in which two parties obtain the common data samples (e.g., users) held by both parties without exchanging raw data. We can use the private set intersection techniques introduced in Section 9.2.2 to achieve this goal (Liang and Chawathe, 2004; Scannapieco et al., 2007).

(ii) **Model training**, in which both parties collaborate on model training based on the common data samples.

After the model training completes, all participants should jointly perform inference on new data. The training and inference processes of vertical federated learning are described in the following sections.

Vertical Federated Learning Training

The training process of VFL can be divided into four steps.

  (i) **Distribute keys**. The trusted third party C generates necessary keys and distributes them to participants A and B.

 (ii) **Exchange intermediate results**. A and B compute and encrypt intermediate results based on the current model. The intermediate results will be used to compute the loss function and update the model.

(iii) **Compute loss function**. A and B upload the intermediate results to C, who computes the loss value and information needed for both parties to perform model updates (e.g., gradients).

(iv) **Download and update**. A and B download the information from C and perform local updates.

Vertical Federated Learning Inference

In VFL, since different participants have different features, each participant only has a partial model corresponding to its features and cannot make predictions independently. Therefore, model inference in VFL relies on all participants. Based on the architecture of Figure 8.5, the inference process of VFL is as follows.

  (i) The third party sends the IDs of the data to be predicted (e.g., user IDs) to participants A and B.

 (ii) Participants A and B make partial inferences about the data given the features available.

(iii) Participants A and B upload the intermediate results to the third party C, who aggregates the intermediate results and returns the inference results.

In the inference process, the data owned by participant A is not exposed to participant B, and vice versa. Similar to training, during the inference process, the intermediate results exchanged should also be protected, such as by homomorphic encryption or secret sharing (Cheng et al., 2021a; Liu et al., 2020).

8.3.2 Vertical Federated Linear Regression

In this section, we introduce a commonly used VFL algorithm, the vertical federated linear regression (VFLR) (Yang et al., 2019a).

We first introduce necessary notations. Suppose participant A has dataset $\mathbb{D}_A = \{x_A^{(j)}\}_{j=1}^N$, and participant B has dataset $\mathbb{D}_B = \{x_B^{(j)}, y^{(j)}\}_{j=1}^N$. Let θ_A, θ_B denote model parameters of participants A and B, and let λ, η denote the regularization rate and learning rate, respectively; the objective function of VFLR can be expressed as

$$\min_{\theta_A,\theta_B} L = \sum_{j=1}^N \|\theta_A^\top x_A^{(j)} + \theta_B^\top x_B^{(j)} - y^{(j)}\|^2 + \frac{\lambda}{2}\left(\|\theta_A\|^2 + \|\theta_B\|^2\right). \tag{8.5}$$

Training Process of Vertical Federated Linear Regression

We further use the following notations to better describe the training process of VFLR:

- Let $u_A^{(j)} = \theta_A^\top x_A, u_B^{(j)} = \theta_B^\top x_B^{(j)}$ denote the intermediate results of the sample $x_A^{(j)}, x_B^{(j)}$ computed by participants A and B.
- Let $d^{(j)} = u_A^{(j)} + u_B^{(j)} - y^{(j)}$ denote the prediction error of the sample $(x_A^{(j)}, x_B^{(j)}, y^{(j)})$.
- Let $L_A = \sum_j (u_A^{(j)})^2 + \frac{\lambda}{2}\|\theta_A\|^2$, $L_B = \sum_j (u_B^{(j)} - y^{(j)})^2 + \frac{\lambda}{2}\|\theta_B\|^2$, $L_{AB} = 2\sum_j u_A^{(j)}(u_B^{(j)} - y^{(j)})$ for the loss values computed independently by participant A, participant B, and jointly by both participants, respectively.

It follows that $L = L_A + L_B + L_{AB}$. Also, the gradients of L on θ_A, θ_B over data sample $x_A^{(j)}, x_B^{(j)}, y^{(j)}$ can be calculated as follows:

$$\frac{\partial L}{\partial \theta_A} = 2\sum_j d^{(j)} x_A^{(j)} + \lambda\theta_A, \tag{8.6}$$

$$\frac{\partial L}{\partial \theta_B} = 2\sum_j d^{(j)} x_B^{(j)} + \lambda\theta_B. \tag{8.7}$$

However, computing $d^{(j)}$ requires collaboration between both participants without exchanging data. Therefore, a trusted third party C is introduced to complete the computation of $d^{(j)}$, and the computations of the loss function and gradient are protected by homomorphic encryption. We use $[[\cdot]]$ to denote homomorphic encryption. Then the training algorithm of VFLR using homomorphic encryption is as follows:

(i) Participants A and B initialize parameters θ_A, θ_B, and the third party C creates public and private keys and distributes public keys to A and B.

(ii) Iterate until the loss L converges.

    (a) A computes $[[u_A^{(j)}]], [[L_A]]$ and sends it to B. ẞB computes $[[u_B^{(j)}]], [[d^{(j)}]] = [[u_A^{(j)}]] + [[u_B^{(j)}]] - [[y^{(j)}]], [[L]]$, and sends $[[L]]$ to third party C and $[[d^{(j)}]]$ to A.

    (b) A computes $[[\frac{\partial L}{\partial \theta_A}]]$, B computes $[[\frac{\partial L}{\partial \theta_B}]]$ and sends $[[\frac{\partial L}{\partial \theta_B}]]$ to the third party C.

    (c) C decrypts $\frac{\partial L}{\partial \theta_A}, \frac{\partial L}{\partial \theta_B}$ and sends them to A and B, respectively; C also decrypts $[[L]]$ and decides whether to continue training.

    (d) A and B update θ_A, θ_B.

Inference Process of Vertical Federated Linear Regression

After training is complete, participants A and B have partial parameters θ_A, θ_B, respectively. When inference is performed on input data x_A, x_B, A and B obtain u_A, u_B, which are uploaded to the third party C. The third party C returns $u_A + u_B$ as the prediction result. Here, there is no need to encrypt u_A, u_B since only the intermediate results are exchanged with third party C, and there is no exchange between participants A and B.

8.3.3 Privacy Preservation for Vertical Federated Learning

Liu et al. (2020) proposed a security definition for VFL with two parties. In this section, we follow this definition to discuss the security of VFLR.

Definition 8.2 (Semihonest security for two-party VFL) Given semihonest participants A and B that do not collude with each other, for any input (I_A, I_B) and a protocol P with $(O_A, O_B) = P(I_A, I_B)$, P is secure against semihonest participant A if and only if there are infinite pairs (I'_B, O'_B) that satisfy $(O_A, O'_B) = P(I_A, I'_B)$. One can similarly define the semihonest security of P for B.

The security of VFLR is analyzed here, based on Definition 8.2:

- By the assumption, the third party C is honest, and thus we do not consider the possibility of information leakage to C; if the third party C is only semi-honest, A and B can apply random masks R_A, R_B, and upload $[[\frac{\partial L}{\partial \theta_A}]] + [[R_A]]$ and $[[\frac{\partial L}{\partial \theta_B}]] + [[R_B]]$ respectively to ensure that C cannot infer private information.

- We analyze the security from the perspective of B. For party B, in each training round, it gets the plaintext gradients $\frac{\partial L}{\partial \theta_B} = (u_A^{(j)} + u_B^{(j)} - y^{(j)})x_B^{(j)}$ (we omit $\lambda\theta_B$ as this term is not related to A). As a result, participant B can compute $u_A^{(j)}$. However, since $u_A^{(j)} = \theta_A^\mathsf{T} x_A^{(j)}$, the right-hand side is an inner product of two unknowns, and we cannot solve for either of them. Therefore, the algorithm is secure against B by Definition 8.2, and similarly against A.

- In the inference process, A can only obtain x_A, and B can only obtain x_B. As there is no additional information exchange, neither party can obtain information about the other.

It should be noted that VFL algorithms, including training, inference, and security analysis, vary with the exact models. Commonly used VFL algorithms also include Gradient Boosting Decision Trees (GBDT), such as SecureBoost and VF2Boost (Cheng et al., 2021a; Fu et al., 2021; Wu et al., 2020). In addition, even VFLR algorithms can be implemented with secret sharing (see Section 2.4 and Du et al. (2004)). Due to space limitations, we are unable to present them in this section. We refer interested readers to corresponding chapters or papers.

8.4 Federated Transfer Learning

In the previous sections, we have introduced HFL and VFL, respectively. However, both of them require aligned feature spaces or user/sample spaces, which are not always satisfied in practical applications. Instead, the datasets owned by participants may have the following properties.

- There are only a few overlapping samples and features.
- The scale of data owned by different participants may vary a lot.
- The data distribution varies significantly from one participant to another. Thus, data from different participants cannot be fit using the same model.

To solve the preceding problems, federated learning can be combined with transfer learning (TL) (Pan and Yang, 2009; Yang et al., 2020a), such that it applies to scenarios with different data distributions or few overlapping samples/features. In this section, we take the paper of Liu et al. (2020) as an example to briefly introduce how federated learning can be combined with transfer learning, and analyze its training and inference processes and its security.

8.4.1 Introduction to Transfer Learning

The core assumption of machine learning is the assumption of Independent and Identically Distributed (I.I.D.) data, which states that the data used for training and testing follow the same distribution. When the assumption is violated, the performance of machine learning models degrades significantly. For example, a text recognition model trained using English characters can achieve good performance on English characters. However, when it is used to classify Chinese characters, it cannot achieve good performance because Chinese characters are much more complex than English characters. Nonetheless, although English and Chinese characters are very different in general, they both consist of common strokes (dots, lines, etc.). Moreover, by common sense, people who know Chinese characters can often learn English characters easily. The above phenomena indicate that English and Chinese characters share many points in common, and that English and Chinese characters can assist each other in training character recognition models.

The preceding example briefly illustrates the concept and intuition of transfer learning. Specifically, the goal of transfer learning is to use knowledge from one domain to help learn a task in another domain. We refer to the former as the source domain and the latter as the target domain. Transfer learning focuses on identifying domain invariant knowledge, i.e., knowledge from the source domain that is generalizable and helpful to the target domain. A typical example described in the book (Yang et al., 2020a) is driving in different countries. In mainland China, drivers sit on the left, while in Hong Kong, drivers sit on the right. Therefore, even experienced drivers from mainland China would be confused at first when they drive in Hong Kong. However, regardless of the country, the driver always stays closer to the center of the road. This serves as a generalizable knowledge that is common in both domains.

Based on the knowledge transferred, transfer learning can be classified as sample-based (instance-based), feature-based, and model-based methods. We refer interested readers to the book on transfer learning (Yang et al., 2020a).

8.4.2 Training and Inference Process of Federated Transfer Learning

As mentioned in Section 8.1.1, FTL does not make any assumptions about either the sample or the feature space of the participants. (Of course, we have to ensure that participants indeed share common knowledge.) This means that FTL algorithms for different settings can be very different. In this section, we take the paper of Liu et al. (2020) as an example to introduce the training, inference process, and privacy protection of FTL.

The paper by Liu et al. (2020) considers the following scenario: participant A is the source domain who holds data $\mathbb{D}_A = \{x_A^{(j)}, y_A^{(j)}\}_{j=1}^{N_A}$, while participant B is the target domain who holds data $\mathbb{D}_B = \{x_B^{(j)}\}$. In addition, we assume that A and B have an overlapping set of samples $\mathbb{D}_{AB} = \{x_A^{(k)}, x_B^{(k)}\}_{k=1}^{N_{AB}}$ which is limited in size and cannot support VFL. We then assume that participant A has some labels corresponding to data held by participant B $\mathbb{D}_c = \{x_B^{(j)}, y_A^{(j)}\}_{j=1}^{N_c}$. Finally, we assume a binary classification problem, i.e., $y \in \{-1, 1\}$. The goal is to learn a classifier that can correctly classify the data of participant B, i.e., the target domain.

Based on the preceding setting, Liu et al. (2020) first design neural network models $\text{Net}_{\theta_A}, \text{Net}_{\theta_B}$ to extract features as follows:

$$u_A^{(i)} = \text{Net}_{\theta_A}(x_A^{(i)}) \in \mathbb{R}^d, u_B^{(i)} = \text{Net}_{\theta_B}(x_B^{(i)}) \in \mathbb{R}^d, \tag{8.8}$$

where d is the feature dimension, and θ_A, θ_B are neural network parameters. In addition, to perform classification, a prediction function φ based on the features u should be designed. The prediction function designed by Liu et al. (2020) takes the form

$$\varphi(u_B^{(i)}) = \frac{1}{N_A} \sum_{j=1}^{N_A} y_A^{(j)} (u_A^{(j)})^\top u_B^{(i)}. \tag{8.9}$$

The preceding function can be understood as a weighted sum of the source domain labels $y_A^{(j)}$ based on the similarity between target domain features $u_B^{(i)}$ and source domain features $u_A^{(j)}$.

The following loss functions are proposed by Liu et al. (2020) for model training.

- First, the classification loss in the target domain is minimized according to the labeled target data $\mathbb{D}_c$:

$$L_1 = \sum_{i=1}^{N_c} l_1\left(y_A^{(i)}, \varphi\left(u_B^{(i)}\right)\right), \tag{8.10}$$

where $l_1(y, \varphi) = \log(1 + \exp(-y\varphi))$ is the binary logistic loss function.
- Second, to extract generalizable features between the source domain A and the target domain B, an alignment loss is designed as

$$L_2 = \sum_{i=1}^{N_{AB}} l_2\left(u_A^{(i)}, u_B^{(i)}\right), \tag{8.11}$$

where l_2 is a distance measure, which can be taken as cosine distance, Euclidean distance, and so on. We take the Euclidean distance $l_2(x, y) = \frac{1}{2}\|x - y\|^2$ as an example.
- Finally, a regularization loss $L_3 = \frac{1}{2}(\|\theta_A\|^2 + \|\theta_B\|^2)$ is applied on neural network parameters θ_A, θ_B.

To summarize, the model parameters will be optimized according to the following objective:

$$\min_{\theta_A, \theta_B} L = L_1 + \gamma L_2 + \lambda L_3. \tag{8.12}$$

Training Process in Federated Transfer Learning

Optimizing Eq. (8.12) by gradient descent requires computing its gradients. However, computing the gradients of the logistic loss $l_1 = \log(1 + \exp(-y\varphi))$ requires exponential and logarithm operations, while techniques such as HE or SS only support additions and multiplications. To address this problem, Liu et al. (2020) proposes a Taylor approximation for l_1:

$$l_1(y, \varphi) \approx l_1(y, 0) + \frac{1}{2}C(y)\varphi + \frac{1}{8}D(y)\varphi^2, \tag{8.13}$$

where $C(y) = -y, D(y) = y^2$. Based on Eq. (8.13), Eq. (8.12) can be approximated as

$$
\begin{aligned}
L = \sum_{i=1}^{N_c} &\left[l_1\left(y_A^{(i)}, 0\right) + \frac{1}{2}C\left(y_A^{(i)}\right)\varphi\left(u_B^{(i)}\right) \right. \\
&\left. + \frac{1}{8}D\left(y_A^{(i)}\right)\varphi\left(u_B^{(i)}\right)^2 \right] \\
&+ \gamma L_2 + \lambda L_3,
\end{aligned}
\tag{8.14}
$$

from which we can derive $\frac{\partial L}{\partial \theta_A}, \frac{\partial L}{\partial \theta_B}$, both of which can be computed by matrix multiplication and addition.

Based on the FTL model and the approximation scheme, Liu et al. (2020) designed two protocols for the FTL model training. The first is based on homomorphic encryption, similar to the protocol in Section 8.3.2. The other is based on secret sharing. Due to the space limitation, we introduce only the HE-based protocol in this chapter. We refer interested readers to Liu et al. (2020) for the SS-based protocol.

Taking participant A as an example, as the loss function $L = L_1 + \gamma L_2 + \lambda L_3$, we have $\frac{\partial L}{\partial \theta_A} = \frac{\partial L_1}{\partial \theta_A} + \gamma \frac{\partial L_2}{\partial \theta_A} + \lambda \frac{\partial L_3}{\partial \theta_A}$, where

- $\frac{\partial L_3}{\partial \theta_A} = \theta_A$ can be computed locally by A.
- $\frac{\partial L_2}{\partial \theta_A} = \sum_{i=1}^{N_{AB}}(u_A^{(i)} - u_B^{(i)})\frac{\partial u_A^{(i)}}{\partial \theta_A}$, where $u_B^{(i)}$ needs to be provided in ciphertexts by party B.
- Computing $\frac{\partial L_1}{\partial \theta_A}$ requires $u_B^{(i)}, \left(u_B^{(i)}\right)^\top u_B^{(i)}$ from B, in the form of ciphertexts.

We omit the analysis for party B, as it is similar to the preceding analysis. Based on the preceding analysis, an FTL training algorithm based on homomorphic encryption is designed as follows.

(i) Participants A and B establish public–private key pairs. We denote encryption operations using the keys from A and B as $[[ ]]_A$, $[[ ]]_B$, respectively.

(ii) Iterate the following steps until convergence.

    (a) A and B run neural networks Net_{θ_A}, Net_{θ_B} locally to obtain features $u_A^{(i)}, u_B^{(i)}$, respectively.

    (b) A and B calculate and encrypt necessary intermediate results for the other party and send them to each other. For example, Party B should calculate and send $[[u_B^{(i)}]]_B$, $\left[\left[\left(u_B^{(i)}\right)^\top u_B^{(i)}\right]\right]_B$ to party A.

    (c) Parties A and B calculate ciphertext gradients based on the obtained intermediate results combined with local plaintext results. For example, Party A calculates the ciphertext gradients $\left[\left[\frac{\partial L}{\partial \theta_A}\right]\right]_B$ based on $[[u_B^{(i)}]]_B$, $\left[\left[\left(u_B^{(i)}\right)^\top u_B^{(i)}\right]\right]_B$.

    (d) A and B generate random masks m_A, m_B respectively, add them with the computed ciphertext gradients, and send them to each other. For example, party A computes $\left[\left[m_A + \frac{\partial L}{\partial \theta_A}\right]\right]_B$.

    (e) A and B decrypt the received ciphertext gradients with masks and send them back to each other.

    (f) A and B subtract the masks locally and perform gradient descent updates.

Here, adding a random mask to the gradients aims to prevent gradient-based attacks (introduced in Section 8.2.3).

Model Inference in Federated Transfer Learning

Given a new data sample x_B, participant B can perform secure inference based on the following protocol:

(i) Party B computes $u_B = \text{Net}_{\theta_B}(x_B)$ and sends $[[u_B]]_B$ to A.

(ii) Party A calculates $[[\varphi(u_B)]]_B$ based on $u_A^{(i)}, y_A^{(i)}$, and adds a random mask m_A to get $[[\varphi(u_B) + m_A]]_B$.

(iii) Party B decrypts to get $\varphi(u_B) + m_A$ and sends it to Party A; Party A subtracts the mask and sends $\varphi(u_B)$ to Party B to complete the inference.

8.4.3 Security of Federated Transfer Learning

In this section, we follow Definition 8.2 and show that as long as the HE schemes are secure, the training and inference processes introduced in Section 8.4.2 comply with Definition 8.2 and are thus secure.

- During the training process, all received ciphertexts and values with random masks (Steps (a)–(e)) can be considered random values and do not reveal private information. The model parameters θ and private data are not revealed to the other party. Taking party A as an example, it obtains plaintext values of $\frac{\partial L}{\partial \theta_A}$, each dimension of which is an equation with $x_B^{(i)}$, θ_B as unknowns. Therefore, as long as there are more unknowns (i.e., $x_B^{(i)}$, θ_B) than equations (i.e., θ_A), it is impossible to uniquely solve for $\theta_B, x_B^{(i)}$. Thus, the training process complies with Definition 8.2.
- In the inference process, we similarly assume that no ciphertexts and values with random masks reveal any private information. Party A gets the information $\varphi(u_B)$, but similar to the analysis of the training process, it is impossible to uniquely solve for θ_B, x_B. Therefore, the inference process also complies with Definition 8.2.

We finally remark that there are many possible algorithms for FTL since there may be infinitely many settings where FTL can be applied (Hong et al., 2021; Kang et al., 2021; Peng et al., 2019). Due to the space limitation, we cannot provide exhaustive discussions. We refer interested readers to the corresponding papers.

8.5 Applications of Federated Learning

In this section, we introduce potential applications of federated learning. Since federated learning covers HFL, VFL, and FTL, it can be applied to a wide range of scenarios. We introduce some representative applications in this section and refer interested readers to chapters 8 and 10 of the book by Yang et al. (2019a).

8.5.1 Natural Language Processing

Deep learning models, especially sequence models represented by Recurrent Neural Network (RNN), are widely used for natural language processing (NLP). Meanwhile, smartphone users enter a large number of texts through keyboards, which can be used to train NLP models for tasks such as sentiment analysis and next word prediction. Since the texts entered by users via smartphones often contain private information, such as geographic location, income status, health conditions, and personal demographics, federated learning can be used to protect the private information of users from being inspected by service providers.

Natural language processing is among the first scenarios where federated learning is applied. Google, as the leading developer of Android, provides services for Android smartphones through the Google Mobile Service (GMS). Google Keyboard (GBoard) is among the most important services in GMS. Using the data logged by GBoard, Google uses federated learning to train and deploy models for a large number of tasks, such as the following.

- **Next word prediction**, which gives suggestions for the next word that a user may type.
- **Out-of-vocabulary word prediction**. Out-of-vocabulary words refer to those not included in the vocabulary, such as names of people, addresses, and acronyms. Out-of-vocabulary words vary from user to user due to different language preferences. Moreover, out-of-vocabulary words of users often contain more private information (e.g., address, name, gender, income level) than in-vocabulary words. Therefore, modeling and prediction of out-of-vocabulary words require the protection of federated learning.
- **Emoji recommendation**. Nowadays, people tend to use a large number of emojis to represent their feelings. Recommending appropriate emojis for a given sentence requires analyzing the sentiment of the current sentence, which may also contain private information about the user (e.g., health status, jobs), which also requires federated learning.

We refer interested readers to papers (Hard et al., 2018; Ramaswamy et al., 2019; Yang et al., 2018).

8.5.2 Smart Healthcare

With the advances in machine learning techniques, it is promising to apply them in medical applications, such as health monitoring and disease diagnosis. For example, through smart devices worn by users such as watches, real-time health data can be obtained, upon which deep learning methods can be applied to give timely alerts to abnormal conditions. As another example, convolutional neural networks can be applied to medical image data for object detection and segmentation, and thus provide advice to doctors.

However, there are two major challenges in applying machine learning to medical data. First, acquiring high-quality medical data with labels is difficult. For example, each labeled medical image needs to be labeled by expert doctors, which is an extremely costly process. In addition, medical data is closely related to the privacy of the patients. If the medical data of a patient is leaked out, the patient is likely to suffer from discrimination in job seeking and social interactions. Thus, federated learning is needed in smart healthcare to combine multiple medical institutions to train high-quality models while protecting the privacy of medical data.

Researchers from NVIDIA, Technical University of Munich, Imperial College London, and German Cancer Research Center published a paper (Rieke et al., 2020) that discusses the potential of applying federated learning in digital healthcare. In the paper, the authors stated that federated learning can help solve the problems of data silo and data privacy faced by traditional machine learning techniques, and can help provide viable solutions for future digital healthcare. The authors also mentioned that several key challenges are still to be addressed for practical federated learning in healthcare, such as data heterogeneity, interpretability, and accountability. Currently, federated learning has been successfully applied in the domain of healthcare for medical record retrieval (Brisimi et al., 2018; Kim et al., 2017; Lee et al., 2018), brain tumor image segmentation (Li et al., 2019; Sheller et al., 2018), and predicting clinical outcomes of COVID-19 patients (Dayan et al., 2021). We refer interested readers to the relevant papers.

8.5.3 Finance

Finance plays an important role in our daily lives. For example, people may invest in various assets to manage their income, or apply for loans for purchasing goods with high prices, such as cars. How to identify the value of an asset or the credit of a user is a crucial challenge for banks and other financial institutions. With the development of machine learning techniques and large-scale data, machine learning models are gradually applied in finance, such as risk control, asset pricing, and fraud identification. However, applying machine learning in finance faces similar problems of data silos and data privacy. On one hand, to accurately evaluate the credit of a user, financial institutions should resort to various data sources, such as shopping records, job records, and financial assets, which are often scattered in different organizations such as companies, e-commerce platforms, and social networks. On the other hand, data regulations for financial institutions are strict, and it may not be feasible for any institution to directly collect user data. Therefore, federated learning is also promising in financial applications.

As a leading company in federated learning, WeBank has applied federated learning in a series of financial applications, such as anti-money laundering, business risk control, and insurance pricing. Interested readers can refer to their technical report (WeBank, 2021). In addition, federated learning has been successfully applied to other applications such as fraud detection for credit cards (Yang et al., 2019e; Zheng et al., 2020). Finally, WeBank open-sources its secure computing platform, FATE, which provides a reliable solution for enterprise-level privacy-preserving computation and federated learning. We will briefly introduce FATE in Section 9.2 of this book.

8.6 Future Prospectives

Since federated learning is only in its infancy, there are still many open problems in federated learning that deserve more research efforts. In this section, from the perspective of privacy-preserving computation, we introduce potential open problems in federated learning. For more general open problems, such as computation, communication, data heterogeneity, and incentive mechanisms, we refer readers to the survey of Kairouz et al. (2019) and the book of Yang et al. (2019a).

8.6.1 Trade-offs between Accuracy and Efficiency under Privacy Protection

In Section 8.2.3, we introduced how the exchanged gradients in HFL can reveal information about the private training data. Thus, the relevant information (e.g., gradients and model parameters) should be protected using privacy-preserving computation techniques. In VFL and FTL algorithms introduced in Sections 8.3 and 8.4, intermediate results are also protected with techniques like homomorphic encryption and secret sharing. However, these efforts provide strict privacy guarantees at the cost of significant additional overhead. For example, experiments in BatchCrypt (Zhang et al., 2020) show that using Paillier to protect gradients in HFL takes about 150 times more computation and communication costs compared to plaintext computation. In addition, if we apply communication optimization schemes to improve efficiency, we would suffer from model performance drops (e.g., accuracy, robustness). Therefore, to achieve data privacy, we are confronted with a trade-off between accuracy and efficiency.

To circumvent the trade-off, existing works can be primarily categorized into three classes.

- First, acceleration schemes on privacy-preserving computation techniques, such as HE and SS, are proposed (Truex et al., 2019; Xu et al., 2019), similar to BatchCrypt (Zhang et al., 2020). However, even with state-of-the-art acceleration schemes, such as BatchCrypt, it still takes about 10 times more computation and communication costs compared to plaintext computation, which is still high in practice.

- Second, some researchers propose to use differential privacy (Chapter 6) for privacy protection in federated learning (Geyer et al., 2017; Hu et al., 2020; Wei et al., 2020). However, while DP is as efficient as plaintexts in terms of both communication and computation, it also introduces new problems. For example, when an insufficient level of noise is added, DP-based federated learning algorithms cannot defend against the DLG attack (Zhu et al., 2019) introduced in Section 8.2.3. On the contrary, with an excessive level of noise, DP adversely affects model performance (e.g., accuracy), as introduced in Section 6.5.2.

- Finally, some researchers propose empirical methods based on data augmentation (Huang et al., 2020a,b) to protect the privacy of training data. Such methods, although simultaneously achieving high efficiency and good performance, cannot provide strict and formal privacy guarantees.

Therefore, how to strike a balance between performance and efficiency under strict data privacy remains an important open problem for researchers around the globe.

8.6.2 Decentralized Federated Learning

Almost all FL algorithms presented in this chapter require trusted (or at least semihonest) third parties to coordinate the training process. For example, HFL requires a semihonest server for parameter aggregation, while VFL (e.g., vertical federated linear regression) requires a trusted third party to coordinate keys and intermediate results. However, in real-world applications, trusted third parties may not always be available. Moreover, if a third party is only semihonest rather than honest, it may become a potential privacy risk and may perform attacks such as gradient-based attacks (Section 8.2.3).

Based on these practical challenges, researchers attempt to remove the reliance on trusted third parties in federated learning. They propose decentralized federated learning, also known as peer-to-peer (P2P) federated learning. For example, based on Bayesian learning, Lalitha et al. (2019) proposes a peer-to-peer federated learning architecture. The paper uses graphs to model peer-to-peer communication patterns among all participants. Each participant maintains a probability distribution of its model parameters, also known as beliefs. In each iteration, each participant aggregates the belief vectors of its first-order neighbors to obtain a more accurate estimate of the global model.

Empirically, on linear regression models and multilayer perceptrons, the proposed architecture suffers from only a small performance loss compared to client–server architectures.

The paper of Roy et al. (2019) presents BrainTorrent, a peer-to-peer federated learning environment. The intuition of the system is similar to that of version control. At each training round, a random participant is selected for model updates. It will aggregate updated models from all other participants and accordingly update its model parameters and versions. Experiments based on medical image segmentation show that BrainTorrent can achieve performance comparable to that of the client–server architectures.

Currently, the state-of-the-art approach for decentralized federated learning is Warnat-Herresthal et al. (2021) published in *Nature*. The proposed approach, coined Swarm Learning, has achieved good results in disease diagnoses such as leukemia, tuberculosis, and COVID-19. In fact, Swarm Learning can be considered as peer-to-peer federated learning using blockchain, and thus can also be called Swarm Federated Learning. The approach uses a blockchain to connect all participants, where all model updates and computations are performed locally by the participants, and parameters are exchanged in a peer-to-peer manner in ciphertexts using blockchain technology. In addition, the framework enables flexible participation by allowing new participants to join the federated learning through Smart Contracts.

Due to its stronger capacity in protecting data privacy, decentralized federated learning is expected to receive greater research attention, and become widely applied in practice.

9

Privacy-preserving Computing Platforms

In the previous chapters, we have introduced various privacy-preserving computing techniques, including their advantages, disadvantages, and applications. To put them in practice under large-scale applications, computing platforms are implemented to provide development and testing tools for various privacy-preserving applications and facilitate large-scale collaboration between enterprises. This chapter introduces several emerging platforms for privacy-preserving computing, including their principles, workflows, and application scenarios.

9.1 Introduction to Privacy-preserving Computing Platforms

In the past decade, with the development of privacy-preserving computing technology and the enactment of related laws, a large number of privacy-preserving computing platforms have been developed worldwide. This chapter selects some representative platforms with different computing techniques to give readers deeper understandings of privacy-preserving techniques in practice.

Table 9.1 summarizes these platforms, their primary privacy-preserving computing techniques, and common application scenarios. We classify the main application scenarios into federated modeling and federated search. Federated modeling refers to multiple participants jointly training machine learning models while preventing original data from leaving their local databases. Federated search refers to performing data queries while preserving the security of the source data and the query information. ·

Despite the fact that privacy-preserving computing platforms have received great attention from the industry, the poor efficiency of privacy-preserving

Table 9.1 *Representative privacy-preserving computing platforms discussed in this chapter.*

Platform	Primary Techniques	Application Scenarios	Open-source?
FATE	Homomorphic Encryption Secret Sharing	Federated Modeling	Yes
CryptDB	Homomorphic Encryption	Federated Search	Yes
PaddleFL	Secret Sharing Oblivious Transfer Garbled Circuit	Federated Modeling	Yes
MesaTEE	TEE	Federated Modeling Federated Search	Yes
Conclave	Secret Sharing, Garbled Circuit	Federated Search	Yes
PrivPy	Secret Sharing, Oblivious Transfer	Federated Search, Federated Modeling	No

computing techniques poses challenges to large-scale deployments of these techniques in the industry. Techniques such as homomorphic encryption (HE) and secure Multi-Party Computation (MPC) protect data privacy at the cost of bringing computational and communication overheads to the whole system. Such overheads become unacceptable for fields requiring timely responses, such as finance, where real-time information feedback is necessary. Therefore, how to optimize the efficiency of these platforms has become an urgent research topic. In Section 9.7, we analyze the efficiency issues in privacy-preserving computing platforms and present some potential solutions to optimize.

9.2 FATE Secure Computing Platform

9.2.1 Introduction to FATE

Federated AI Technology Enabler (FATE) (WeBank, 2019) is an open-source project launched by WeBank in 2019. It provides a distributed secure computing platform to support the Federated Learning Ecosystem. Federated AI Technology Enabler implements various security protocols such as secret sharing, homomorphic encryption, and hash functions to enable collaboration between multiple parties in compliance with privacy and security regulations. It also

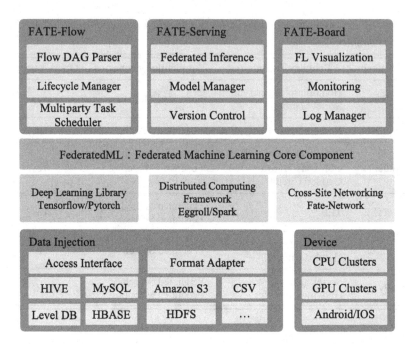

Figure 9.1 Architecture overview of FATE.

implements various federated machine learning algorithms such as logistic regression, tree algorithms, deep learning, and transfer learning. The FATE platform is user-friendly due to its clear visual interface and flexible scheduling system. It also provides a convenient data privacy protection solution for various industrial applications, especially finance. Recently, KubeFATE has been proposed, which implements Docker and Kubernetes-based deployment approaches. Thus, FATE supports containerized and cloud deployment, which further reduces operation and maintenance difficulties.

The framework of FATE is shown in Figure 9.1. The FATE-Serving component is responsible for high-performance commercial online modeling services, which supports efficient federated online inference and model management. The FATE-Board visualization tool provides tracking and statistics of the model training process. It presents graphical information about data transfer, training logs, and model output in a user-friendly manner.

The FederatedML component of FATE implements security protocols and common federated learning algorithms. All functions are developed in a modular and extensible manner. Developers can easily call existing federated learning algorithms and can also easily develop new federated learning algorithms. The component contains the following elements:

- **Federated Machine Learning Algorithms,** including learning algorithms such as logistic regression, SecureBoost, neural networks, and transfer learning. In addition, data preprocessing methods such as feature selection, and secure protocols such as private set intersection are also included.
- **Multiparty Security Protocols,** including homomorphic encryption, secret sharing, RSA, and Diffie–Hellman key exchange.
- **Tools.** The FATE platform also includes modular federated learning tools such as encryption tools, statistics modules, and transfer variable autogenerator.
- **Extensible Framework.** To facilitate the development of new federated learning modules, FATE provides standardized modules that can be reused to keep user modules neat.

The FATE-Flow component is the task scheduling system for federated modeling, which is responsible for parsing the modeling process based on user-defined DSL files and for executing federated modeling tasks with multiparty scheduling. It also manages the task lifecycle and tracks the input and output information such as data, parameters, models, and performance in real time. It is worth mentioning that FATE-Flow supports two distributed computing frameworks, Eggroll and Spark, to implement computing and storage in clusters. Eggroll is a distributed computing and storage framework developed by Webank, which is suitable for many federated learning application scenarios.

Based on this architecture, the basic workflow of FATE tasks is as follows. First, users submit federated learning tasks to the system. Then, the system receives the tasks, schedules them through FATE-Flow, and invokes FederatedML to implement privacy-preserving computation. Data communication between multiple parties is implemented via FATE-Network. In addition, users can view the task status and monitor the log information in real-time through FATE-Board.

In the next section, we describe the privacy-preserving computing techniques used in FATE.

9.2.2 Privacy-preserving Computing Techniques in FATE

Hash Tables

Hash functions are algorithms that map a message with arbitrary length to an n-bit large integer. It plays an important role in digital signature and password protection. The data encoded by hash functions (one-way hash functions in general) is almost irreversible, making hash functions not suitable for data encryption. The FATE platform supports various hash functions, including

MD5, SHA-1, SHA-2, and SM3. Generally, the SHA-256 algorithm is used by default.

Private Set Intersection (PSI) operations are often implemented with hash functions (Chen et al., 2004) in FATE. For example, in vertical federated learning, the feature spaces of the datasets possessed by different participants differ from each other while the sample spaces are relatively similar. Therefore, participants can jointly build a model by training over the shared samples. Before training, they need to compute the intersection of samples without exposing their original data. By performing hash functions on the original sample ID and introducing obfuscation with the RSA encryption algorithm, all participants can only get their shared sample IDs without getting other information.

Secret Sharing

Secret sharing is an important technique for splitting and storing information among multiple participants, which can be used in key management, identity authentication, and data security protection. Secret sharing ensures that original data can only be recovered when the shares held by multiple participants are combined. Verifiable secret sharing is now commonly used to prevent unsuccessful information reconstruction and data tampering caused by untrusted participants. By introducing commitment and verification, secret sharing guarantees that participants can verify the data security and accuracy.

The FATE platform uses the Feldman verifiable secret exchange (Feldman, 1987). In addition to data partitioning and storage, the additive homomorphism of the algorithm further enables secure multiparty data summation. Each participant generates a random homomorphic function to encrypt the data and computes the corresponding commitment information. The receiver confirms the correctness of the data by passing the encrypted data and the commitment information, and decrypts the data using Lagrangian interpolation to obtain the sum. The summation operation based on secret sharing can be applied to scenarios such as multiparty feature aggregation.

Homomorphic Encryption

The most frequently used privacy-preserving technique in FATE is homomorphic encryption. Due to the huge computational overhead of fully homomorphic encryption, FATE adopts a partially homomorphic encryption, Paillier Encryption (Paillier, 1999), to encrypt the transferred intermediate results and further perform addition between ciphertexts. For example, in federated model training, the participants need to calculate the gradients and loss to update the local model and check for convergence. Since different participants possess different data, they usually need to perform calculations based on the local

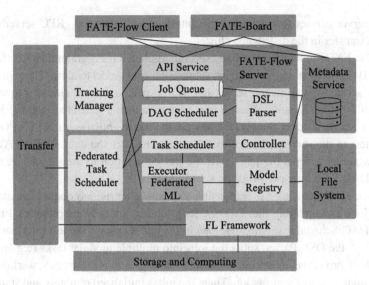

Figure 9.2 Workflow of FATE-Flow.

parameters first, and then aggregate the results and execute further calculations to obtain the joint results. To ensure the privacy of intermediate results, each party needs to encrypt their own data before aggregation. With homomorphic encryption, the receiver cannot recover the information carried in the ciphertext, but can still perform computation on the ciphertext to achieve the purpose of joint modeling.

9.2.3 Workflow of FATE

Based on the privacy-preserving computing technology, FATE has designed FATE-Flow, which guarantees a secure task workflow. As the scheduling system on the FATE platform, FATE-Flow is the core component to execute and manage tasks. This section introduces the workflow and architecture of FATE-Flow.

The workflow of FATE-Flow is shown in Figure 9.2. The FATE-Flow platform consists of two separate components: the FATE-Flow server, which is a server-side process that needs to run continuously, and the FATE-Flow user, which is a client-side process that helps users submit tasks to the server.

Before starting a task, the FATE-Flow server should be launched. During the startup process, the server initializes the resource management module, task scheduling module, and the database. Then, it creates an HTTP server that supports multithreaded access and continuously listens on its port. In addition, the server defines the gRPC service interface and starts the gRPC server for data transfer in the distributed cluster.

The FATE-Flow server defines several Application Programming Interface (API) services for data upload, job submission, and model loading. These interface services listen to the server-side HTTP port and route clients' requests to different URL paths. When a user tries to launch a federated learning job, he or she first starts the FATE-Flow client, which initiates an HTTP POST request to the server interface to submit and register the dataset. The FATE-Flow server accepts the job, sends the job information to the job queue, and the DAG Scheduler performs job scheduling.

The DAG Scheduler is responsible for managing the job queue, i.e., starting jobs and updating the status of each job according to its progress. First, the DAG Scheduler submits the jobs in the queue, parses the job information through the DSL Parser, splits the jobs into multiple modular tasks (e.g., data reading, private set intersection, model training), obtains the specific workflow, and updates it as a waiting job. Then, the job is initialized remotely and started at each site by the federated scheduler (including allocating computational resources, obtaining information on the dataset, etc.). The job status is updated to running job and the job flow is sent to the Task Scheduler for scheduling. At the end of the job, the DAG Scheduler calls the Federated Scheduler to remotely save the training results and terminate the training.

The Task Scheduler is the module that schedules the subtasks in a single job. It is responsible for starting the tasks at the specified step based on the workflow, monitoring the progress of each task in real-time, and returning the progress to the DAG scheduler. The status of all tasks in all sites is set to wait for tasks initially. The Task Scheduler synchronizes the progress of tasks at each site with the Federated Scheduler. For each waiting task, Task Scheduler checks whether all its dependent predecessors are completed, and if so, it updates the task status to the running task and invokes the Federated Scheduler again to synchronize the task status with the corresponding site and starts the task.

The Federated Scheduler is a remote task scheduling module that provides several remote jobs or task scheduling interfaces (e.g., create a job, start a job, start a task, stop a task). The DAG scheduler and task scheduler implement cross-site task management by calling these interfaces. After receiving instructions from other modules, the Federated Scheduler constructs gRPC packets, creates gRPC clients, and initiates a one-way Remote Procedure Call (RPC) to send data to the local communication component. As FATE supports different distributed computing frameworks, the implementation of communication can be different with variant frameworks. If Eggroll is chosen, the cross-site communication component is Roll Site, and if Spark is chosen as the distributed computing framework, the cross-site communication component is Nginx. The packets are forwarded between different sites and finally received by the FATE-Flow server at the target site to achieve cross-domain communication.

The remotely sent packets are routed to the receiver's controller (Job Controller or Task Controller). Job Controller is the module responsible for executing job scheduling at the current site, and can execute job creation, start and stop. It also saves training results according to remote instructions. Task Controller is used to manage the tasks at the current site. On the one hand, it can be invoked by the Job Controller to create tasks; on the other hand, it can be requested to start or stop tasks at this site based on remote instructions. Task Controller calls Task Executor to start a task by creating a child process. At the end of the task, Task Controller updates the task status and invokes the Federated Scheduler to send the task status to the initiator of the job.

Task Executor is the lowest-level executor in FATE-Flow, which invokes the function modules in FederatedML to perform the corresponding read/write or computation operations. All function modules in FederatedML are inherited from the ModelBase class. Task Executor calls ModelBase to execute specific functions (e.g., vertical logistic regression, horizontal SecureBoost), and ModelBase identifies which operations (e.g., fitting, cross-validation, model loading, prediction) need to be performed under the current function based on the task information, constructs a list of operations, and executes the operations in the list in order.

The preceding is an introduction to the workflow of FATE-Flow, which goes from user submission to system initiation of the specific operations. With the support of this flow, it is easy to get started with the FATE platform. With the guidance of the official documentation, users can easily execute federated learning jobs. As a result, FATE has already been used in many industrial applications. Next, we discuss the application scenarios of the FATE platform.

9.2.4 Applications of FATE

Federated Car Insurance Pricing

In traditional car insurance pricing, the quality of the vehicle itself is often used as the criterion for pricing. However, in reality, factors such as the driving environment and driving habits of the vehicle owner should also be considered. Unlike the simple "car-based pricing," "driver-based pricing" requires a lot of user information to assist the decision-making process. However, user information, including driving records, vehicle maintenance records, and previous insurance records, is owned by different companies and government departments and unable to be gathered centrally. Through federated learning, multiple data owners can jointly build more accurate user evaluation systems that improve car insurance pricing and reduce business risks. Meanwhile, privacy of user records is maintained during modeling.

Federated Credit Risk Management

Banks and other financial institutions need to conduct credit reviews when they audit loan applications from small enterprises. Auditing loan applications is difficult and time-consuming for several reasons. First, banks may not have access to sufficient information on business records and credit status. Second, credit qualifications of enterprises may vary significantly. The long credit review process thus creates problems, especially for small enterprises, such as slow asset turnover. By combining multiple sources of data and obtaining multidimensional credit profiles, banks can jointly build a federated model with richer features to better depict credit profiles of enterprises, and thus accelerate the process of loan audition for banks.

Federated Disease Diagnosis

Medical care is highly related to the well-being of citizens. With the advances in electronic medical information, such as medical images, healthcare services based on data-driven machine learning is a promising solution. However, medical information such as diagnostic data is generally considered private information of patients, and thus cannot be shared directly. Consequently, as small medical institutions cannot gain access to large-scale medical data, they are unable to learn trustworthy machine learning models for diagnosis and are thus considered less attractive to patients. This essentially enlarges the gap between large medical institutions and smaller ones and makes it more costly for patients to seek medical care. With the advent of federated learning, joint modeling of diseases between different medical institutions are enabled, which can improve the quality of disease diagnoses for all participating institutions, especially small ones with less data. By improving healthcare services provided by small medical institutions, federated learning makes high-quality medical care more accessible to a wider range of citizens.

9.3 CryptDB Encrypted Database System

9.3.1 Introduction to CryptDB

With the rapid development of cloud computing, data security issues are gaining more attention. In real-world scenarios, sensitive information in online

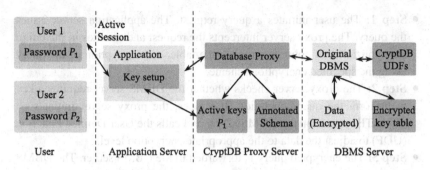

Figure 9.3 Framework of CryptDB.

applications can be easily stolen because attackers can exploit software vulnerabilities to get access to private data, and curious or malicious database administrators can also capture or disclose data. To solve this problem, an effective way is to use storage encryption, where data is encrypted using either symmetric or asymmetric encryption algorithms before it is stored on cloud servers. After nearly two decades of development, many solutions have been proposed. Massachusetts Institute of Technology's Computer Science and Artificial Intelligence Laboratory (CSAIL) proposed the open-source cryptographic database system CryptDB (CSAIL, 2011) in 2011. The CryptDB system uses MySQL as its back-end database management system to store encrypted data. The system implements homomorphic encryption on the database, which allows the DBMS server to execute cryptographic queries just like plaintext queries.

The framework of CryptDB is shown in Figure 9.3. The system consists of a trusted user, an application server, a proxy server, and an untrusted DBMS server. The user is the owner of the data and stores the data in the database server. The proxy server is the middleware in CryptDB. When the user queries or updates the ciphertext stored in the database, the proxy server needs to rewrite the original query statement so that it can be executed directly on the ciphertext. When the database returns the query result to the user, the proxy server needs to decrypt the ciphertext result and finally sends the decrypted results back to the user. The database management system server (DBMS server), as a database service provider, is responsible for helping users to store and manage private data. However, it is not necessarily trustworthy from the user's viewpoint and may snoop on the user's private data.

Based on this system framework, a typical CryptDB data query process is shown in what follows.

- **Step 1:** The user initiates a query request. The application server issues the query. The proxy server intercepts the request and rewrites it, including anonymization of column names in the table, and encryption of the query using the specified encryption scheme.
- **Step 2:** The proxy server checks whether the DBMS server requires a key to perform the query operation. If it does, the proxy server initiates an UPDATE request on the DBMS server and calls the User Defined Function (UDF) to adjust the data to the appropriate encryption level.
- **Step 3:** The encrypted query is forwarded to the DBMS server. The DBMS server uses standard SQL statements to execute the query.
- **Step 4:** The DBMS server sends the query result back to the proxy server, who decrypts the ciphertext and further returns it to the user.

9.3.2 Privacy-preserving Computing in CryptDB: SQL-aware Encryption

In order to execute standard SQL statements directly on ciphertexts, CryptDB uses various cryptographic schemes as listed in what follows.

Random (RND)

Random encryption provides the highest security. The results of RND encryption are probabilistic, i.e. two independent encryptions over the same value lead to different results. However, RND does not support any homomorphic computation on ciphertexts.

Deterministic (DET)

Unlike RND, DET guarantees identical encryption results for the same plaintexts, leading to two outcomes. On one hand, DET is less secure than RND. On the other hand, DET encryption can be used to compare two ciphertexts to see if their corresponding plaintexts are the same. This also indicates that RND can be used to execute equality predicates.

Order-preserving Encryption (OPE)

The OPE scheme is an order-preserving encryption without revealing the underlying values, i.e., $OPE_K(x) < OPE_K(y), \forall x < y$, and key K. Therefore, OPE enables order-related operations on ciphertexts, such as sorting. However, the security of OPE is lower than that of DET due to the leakage of the data ordering. Therefore, the proxy server sends the OPE encryption result to the DBMS server only when the user initiates an order-related request.

Homomorphic Encryption (HOM)

Technical details of homomorphic encryption can be found in Chapter 3. Homomorphic encryption allows the DBMS server to directly perform calculations on the ciphertext. However, CryptDB only supports homomorphic addition based on Paillier encryption while homomorphic multiplication is complex and inefficient. Based on homomorphic addition, homomorphic encryption can be used to implement operations such as SUM and average.

Join (JOIN and OPE-JOIN)

Join encryption can be combined with DET encryption and OPE encryption to execute equality and range join on ciphertexts respectively. Obviously, the two columns of data to be joined should be encrypted by the same key; otherwise, there is no valid relationship for the join operation. To solve this problem, CryptDB introduces the JOIN-ADJ encryption scheme to switch the key during runtime. When the same key is used, the result of JOIN-ADJ encryption of plaintexts is deterministic and it is almost impossible to get the same ciphertext from different plaintexts. Initially, the JOIN-ADJ encryption is performed with different keys for each column of data, so that no Join operation can be performed between any two columns of data. When the proxy server receives a JOIN request, it sends a new key to the DBMS server to adjust the encryption value of one or more columns so that their JOIN-ADJ keys are the same as the key of another column of data, and the Join operation can thus be performed between columns with the same key.

Word Search (SEARCH)

To implement the keyword search function (LIKE), CryptDB uses the encryption strategy described in Song et al. (2000). The security of SEARCH encryption is the same as RND encryption. The SEARCH encryption scheme does not disclose to the DBMS server whether a keyword occurs multiple times in the database. However, the number of encrypted keywords is known to the DMBS server. The DBMS server can infer the number of different or repeated keywords by comparing the data volume of SEARCH ciphertexts with RND ciphertexts.

9.3.3 Queries Over Encrypted Data

Onion Encryption Layers: Queries-based Adaptive Encryption

The core design of CryptDB is an adjustable encryption module that dynamically determines the level of encryption exposed to the server. Section 9.3.2

Table 9.2 *Data layout of plaintexts and ciphertexts in CryptDB.*

Employees		Table1							
ID	Name	$C1$-IV	$C1$-Eq	$C1$-Ord	$C1$-Add	$C2$-IV	$C2$-Eq	$C2$-Ord	$C2$-Search
23	Alice	x27c3	x2b82	xcb94	xc2e4	x8a13	xd1e3	x7eb1	x29b0

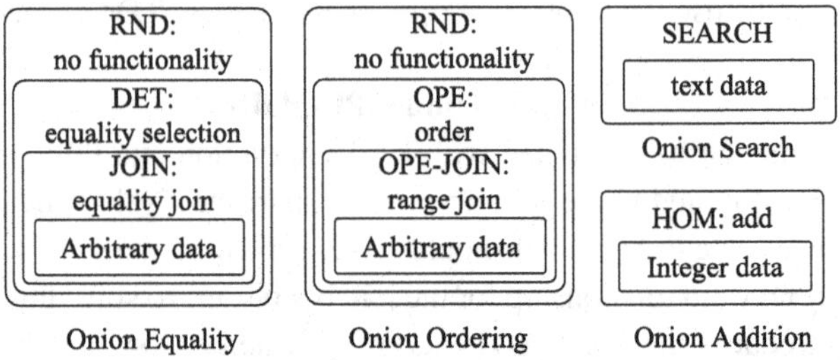

RND: no functionality DET: equality selection JOIN: equality join Arbitrary data	RND: no functionality OPE: order OPE-JOIN: range join Arbitrary data	SEARCH text data Onion Search HOM: add Integer data
Onion Equality	Onion Ordering	Onion Addition

Figure 9.4 Onion Encryption Layers.

describes various encryption algorithms used in CryptDB. Each of these algorithms can perform some cryptographic operations independently, such as size comparison and addition. If multiple cryptographic operations need to be executed at the same time, the preceding algorithms should be combined. However, the system cannot predict what the next operation is. CryptDB uses Onion Encryption Layers as shown in Figure 9.4. For the same column of data, different levels of encryption results are obtained by combining different algorithms. Onion names represent the allowed operations over the ciphertexts at their layers.

The multilayered structure in the Onion Encryption Layers is designed to ensure the security of the data and the support of cryptographic algorithms at the same time. In this model, each encryption scheme is an onion, and each layer of the onion performs a corresponding encryption algorithm on the data. Each layer of encryption serves a different purpose: the outermost encryption algorithm has the highest security and is almost free of information leakage; the inner algorithm is relatively secure but supports more homomorphic operations. In addition to data encryption, CryptDB also anonymizes table and column names. Table 9.2 shows an example of plaintext in database and corresponding ciphertext in CryptDB. The associated values of $C1$ and $C2$ represent different encryption results for ID and Name, respectively. In the same encryption layer of each onion, CryptDB uses the same key to encrypt data of the same column, but different keys are used for different columns, different encryption layers, and different onions. This ensures that the proxy server does not need to change keys repeatedly when operating on the same column of data, thus preventing the DBMS server from inferring additional information from the data while improving the working efficiency.

9.3.4 Application Scenarios of CryptDB

Management of Open-source Forums

In a forum software (e.g., phpBB), the system needs to accept or deny a user's browsing request based on the user's permissions. For example, the system wants to ensure that private messages sent by one user to another are not seen by others, the posts in a forum can only be accessed by users in certain groups, and the name of a forum can only be displayed to users who belong to groups with access to it. The CryptDB system can provide these guarantees and reduce the damage caused by attacks.

First, CryptDB requires forum developers to annotate their database schema to specify user roles and the data each role can access, allowing CryptDB to capture access control over shared data at the level of SQL queries. In addition, in the event of an attack, CryptDB limits the damage caused by a destroyed application or proxy server to data accessible only to users who are logged in during the attack. In particular, an attacker cannot access the data of users who were not logged in during the attack. However, the leakage of the data belonging to active users is inevitable; given that it is impractical to perform arbitrary computations on encrypted data, some data of active users must be decrypted by the application.

In CryptDB, each user has a key that allows them to access their own data, and CryptDB encrypts different data items with different keys, and uses a key chain starting from the user's password to the encryption key of the SQL data item in order to achieve access control. When a user logs in, they provides their password to the proxy server. The proxy server uses this password to obtain the onion key to process queries on the encrypted data and decrypt the results. According to the access control, the proxy server can only decrypt data that the user can access. When a user logs out, the proxy server also deletes the user's key.

Management of Conference Review Software

In many international conferences, conference management software is used to ensure the security and reliability of the paper submissions and review process, such as HotCRP and Microsoft CMT. However, some management software does not prevent the committee chair from logging into the server and seeing who is involved in the review of the paper with which he is associated. This essentially breaks double-blind review for conference chairs. To address the problem, conferences previously had to set up a second server to review papers co-authored by chairs. When the system is deployed in CryptDB, even if the chair logs into the application or database, he cannot know who has reviewed his paper because there is no decryption key.

Privilege Management of Admissions System

In a common university admission system, information submitted by applicants and feedback from schools is managed according to access privileges. CryptDB allows an applicant's folder to be accessed only by the applicant himself/herself and reviewers. An applicant can see data in their folder other than letters of recommendation. Any additional access requests will be denied by CryptDB.

9.4 MesaTEE Secure Computing Platform (Teaclave)

9.4.1 PaddlePaddle R&D Deep Learning Platform

An industry-level open-source deep learning platform, PaddlePaddle (Baidu, 2020b), which stands for PArallel Distributed Deep LEarning, was launched by Baidu with a widely distributed product chain. With the growing demand for data security, Baidu has built two secure computation solutions based on the PaddlePaddle ecosystem: one is the PaddleFL software solution based on secure multiparty computation, and the other is the MesaTEE hardware solution based on a trusted execution environment. The remaining part of this section will give a brief introduction to PaddleFL and a detailed introduction to MesaTEE.

9.4.2 PaddleFL Federated Learning Framework

The PaddleFL (Baidu, 2020a) system is an open-source federated learning framework based on PaddlePaddle. It supports many popular machine learning algorithms and their federated implementations, including traditional machine learning methods, computer vision algorithms, natural language processing algorithms, recommendation algorithms, and transfer learning. Figure 9.5 shows its framework. This section briefly describes the privacy-preserving computing techniques used by PaddleFL.

The PaddleFL system uses the ABY[3] (Mohassel and Rindal, 2018) secure computing framework for federated neural networks and the PrivC (He et al.,

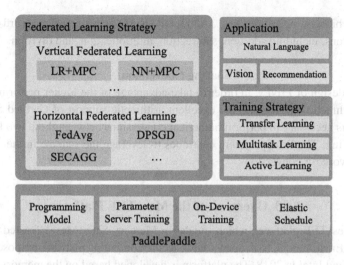

Figure 9.5 Framework of PaddleFL.

2019) framework for federated logistic regression. The PrivC framework is a two-party secure computing framework implemented in C++ based on protocols such as secret sharing, 1-out-of-2 oblivious transfer, and garbled circuits. PrivC basically follows the security principle of the ABY (Demmler et al., 2015b) secret sharing framework and uses two secret sharing schemes: Arithmetic Sharing, and Garbled Sharing.

Arithmetic Sharing

The method of generating Arithmetic Sharings in PrivC is conventional: Party A generates a random number r, calculates $x_a = x - r$, and sends r to Party B, who sets $x_b = r$. When the source data x needs to be recovered, Party A and Party B send their local shares to each other and calculate addition respectively, i.e., $x = x_a + x_b$. To implement multiplication operations, PrivC generates multiplication triples using oblivious transfer. The detailed algorithm is described in Section 4.3.

Garbled Sharing

In Section 5.2, we describe two optimization schemes for garbled circuits, namely, ciphertext random ordering and single decryption, as well as costless XOR circuits. Based on these principles, secret sharing based on garbled circuits, namely Garbled Sharing, is applied in PrivC, whose concrete implementation is described in Chapter 5. Bit-wise XOR and AND operations can be efficiently performed over Garbled Sharing. Therefore, PrivPy supports most secure bit-wise operations (e.g., AND, OR, NOT) as well as some word-wise operations, including addition, subtraction, multiplication, and division.

Sharing Conversion

In the design of PrivPy, in order to take advantage of the higher performance of Arithmetic Sharing and the excellent arithmetic support of Garbled Sharing, it is necessary to perform numerical conversions between these two kinds of sharing. The PrivPy system continues to leverage the scheme in the ABY framework for conversions.

9.4.3 Overview of the MesaTEE Platform

The MesaTEE platform, which stands for Memory Safe (Mesa) Trusted Execution Environment, is an open-source secure computing platform proposed by Baidu and Intel in 2018. The platform is developed based on the memory-safe programming language Rust and uses Intel SGX technology to build a trusted execution environment which provides strong protection for data privacy. The MesaTEE platform provides "Functions as a Service" (FaaS) to users, with a large number of built-in functions in the fields of machine learning and federated computing to simplify the computing and programming processes. Meanwhile, MesaTEE is extremely flexible, allowing developers to build new SGX applications through development tool kits. In late 2019, the platform entered the Apache Incubator. In 2020, Teaclave, the open-source community version of MesaTEE (The Apache Software Foundation, 2020), was proposed.

Figure 9.6 shows the framework of the MesaTEE platform, which consists of the trusted execution environment, the FaaS service, and the executor.

9.4.4 Trusted Execution Environment in MesaTEE

The MesaTEE supports a variety of trusted execution environment systems as its back-ends, including Intel SGX, AMD SEV, and ARM TrustZone. Next, we take Intel SGX as an example and introduce the framework of MesaTEE.

As a software extension to common X86 architectures, Intel SGX helps users run applications in enclaves and protects private data with trusted executable environments. Intel SGX SDK helps programmers control the security of applications without relying on any system software. An introduction to Intel SGX can be found in Section 7.2.2.

However, Intel SGX, which is implemented via C/C++, may suffer from memory corruption and is not sufficiently resistant to memory attacks. The leverage of the memory-safe language Rust can eliminate related problems

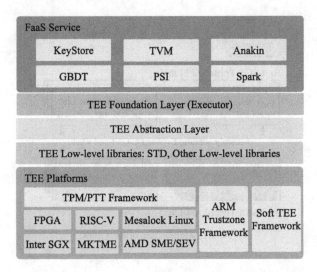

Figure 9.6 Structure of the MesaTEE platform.

and ensure memory security. However, if Intel SGX is completely discarded and only Rust is used, a large number of missing features will arise, leading to a significant decrease in functionality. Therefore, combining Rust and Intel SGX becomes a better solution.

Rust SGX (Wang et al., 2019) is a wrapper for the Intel SGX using Rust at the bottom of MesaTEE and provides a set of Rust-based APIs to the upper layer. Following Rust's memory-safe features, Rust SGX ensures that any interaction with the Intel SGX SDK is memory-safe. It has been shown that Rust SGX does not cause significant performance degradation. Currently, the system is renamed Teaclave SGX SDK. The system framework is shown in Figure 9.7.

The system structure is divided into three main layers. The bottom layer is the Intel SGX library. The middle layer is the language binding between Rust and C/C++, and the top layer is the Rust SGX library. The core part is the middle layer that implements the secure binding between two languages. The idea of the middle layer is to regulate the behavior of nonsecure C/C++ codes through a secure memory management mechanism and a high-level type system that supports secure operations over pointers. The secure memory management mechanism mainly aims to encapsulate the data types that are created by C/C++ and exposed to Rust and ensure that heap objects generated by Rust calls to C/C++ can only be automatically freed by Rust at the end of the program life cycle. In this way, memory security is guaranteed based on

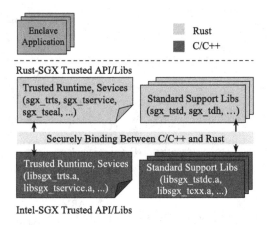

Figure 9.7   Architecture of Rust SGX.

Rust's stable memory management. The high-level type system implements the representation of complex C/C++ data types in Rust (e.g., encapsulating address and data length information of C/C++ data types), and enables users to construct complex C/C++ data types and call the Intel SGX library through the Rust SGX API by giving the corresponding structure definition and initialization functions.

9.4.5 FaaS Service

As a FaaS platform, MesaTEE provides API to users, receives Remote Procedure Call (RPC) requests initiated by users, and provides corresponding services. Its basic processing flow is shown in Figure 9.8.

The FaaS platform provides several services that operate within a trusted execution environment, including the following:

Authentication Service: Authentication Service provides a user authentication mechanism implemented with the JSON Web Token (JWT) standard. Users need to obtain a valid token to interact with the platform.

Front-end Service: Front-end Service is the entry point for all user requests. The front-end verifies the user's identity or token and forwards the request to corresponding service.

Management Service: Management service is the central service of the FaaS platform. It handles almost all requests, such as function or data registration, creating or invoking tasks, and access control.

Storage Service: Storage service is responsible for storing functions, execution data, and task information. This database system is implemented based

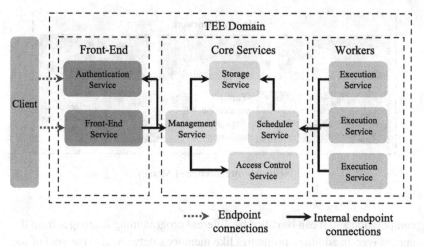

Figure 9.8 Workflow of MesaTEE service.

on LevelDB, which provides persistent protection of data in trusted execution environment.

Access Control Service: Access Control Service provides flexible management control of data access according to the access rights to data in multiparty federated computing.

Scheduling Service: Scheduling Service assigns tasks to work nodes with computational capabilities for execution.

Execution Service: Execution Service interacts with the scheduler, receives the task, and invokes the executor to complete the job. On a single cloud device, multiple nodes with different computational capabilities may exist simultaneously.

The services in MesaTEE basically consist of two parts of operations: untrusted application and trusted enclave. The application part is responsible for managing the services, initiating and terminating the enclave part of the operation, while the enclave part provides secure services for user RPC requests through trusted channels and performs data processing in a trusted execution environment.

9.4.6 Executor MesaPy

The executor is one of the core components of the FaaS platform and is responsible for running the built-in functions according to user requests. In MesaTEE, the executor needs to guarantee the confidentiality of private data during the

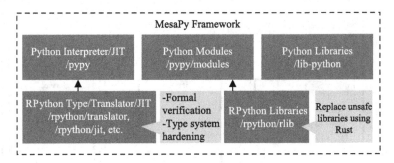

Figure 9.9 Architecture of MesaPy.

computation and it can be called by different programming languages from the upper layer. In addition, properties like memory safety are also the goal of the executor. Two kinds of executors are designed in MesaTEE.

- **Built-in executor**: In MesaTEE, there are many statistically compiled built-in functions. To ensure memory safety, these built-in functions are implemented with Rust. The built-in executor assigns user requests to the corresponding built-in function for execution.
- **MesaPy executor**: The MesaPy executor is equivalent to a Python interpreter. User-defined Python functions can be executed in the MesaPy executor. The executor also provides an interface to fetch and store data during runtime. Next, we give a brief introduction to the MesaPy executor.

Nowadays, Python is an integral part of data-driven applications such as machine learning. However, Python encapsulates a large amount of C code, which is known to be memory insecure. Thus, there are rising security concerns on Python and Python-based data-driven systems in privacy-preserving computing. Although a more advanced interpreter, PyPy, rewrites the Python interpreter and some libraries based on RPython, there remain some compiler libraries and third-party libraries written in C. To solve the security challenges caused by C, Baidu proposed the MesaPy (Wang et al., 2020) interpreter. This interpreter is based on PyPy and fixes some security issues by rewriting third-party libraries using Rust language and adding security guarantees such as out-of-bounds check for arrays. For inevitable dependencies on C language in the interpreter, MesaPy uses formal verification tools to check memory issues, including buffer overflow, null pointer dereference, and memory leakage issues. Meanwhile, MesaPy supports using Intel SGX to complete the interpretation of Python code, allowing developers to implement secure

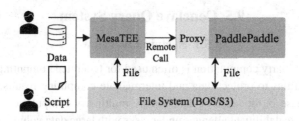

Figure 9.10   Interaction between MesaTEE and PaddlePaddle.

operations running in a trusted execution environment with Python. Figure 9.9 gives the basic framework of MesaPy.

9.4.7 Application Scenarios – MesaTEE and PaddlePaddle

With the development of the Teaclave open-source community, numerous system implementations based on MesaTEE have gradually emerged. The combination of MesaTEE and PaddlePaddle is one of the typical examples.

MesaTEE supports multiparty collaborative task processing. When multiple participants perform federated computing, MesaTEE schedules the works and transfers the workflow to the TEE, including data upload, task execution, and result acquisition, thus ensuring data security. Therefore, in scenarios such as secure multiparty computation, PaddlePaddle can use MesaTEE to achieve privacy-preserving computation. The interaction between MesaTEE and the PaddlePaddle is shown in Figure 9.10. In this system, MesaTEE acts as a scheduler for multiparty collaboration, treats the PaddlePaddle as an execution environment, and sends tasks to the trusted execution environment of PaddlePaddle for execution through RPC remote calls. The files are all stored as ciphertext, so that computation contents are protected from the outside of the trusted execution environment. In order to execute operations in the trusted execution environment without changing the way PaddlePaddle is used, the system uses a special file management system and modifies back-end runtime library of PaddlePaddle.

Compared with platforms based on secure multiparty computation, Mesa TEE-based hardware data security protection avoids a large number of remote data exchanges between different parties, thus reducing the risk of system crashes caused by remote interaction problems such as network failures. Similar to other privacy-preserving computing platforms (Section 9.2.4), the system combining PaddlePaddle and MesaTEE can be applied to finance, medical, and other fields to achieve the maximum utilization of isolated data.

9.5 Conclave Query System

9.5.1 System Overview

Secure multiparty computation is often used for federated computing between multiple parties to protect data and intermediate computing results. With the rapid increase in the scale of data, secure multiparty computation inevitably encounters scalability challenges under tasks with large data volume. Common secure multiparty computation systems would take an extremely long time to complete tasks with large data volumes, such as in multiparty database queries. One practical solution to optimize the scalability of secure multiparty computation systems is to reduce the use of MPC as much as possible while still preserving the security of the system. However, it requires users to identify and remove redundant MPC operations, which is unrealistic for most data analysts. Therefore, a practical and user-friendly system is needed to help implement the conversion from database queries to efficient MPC operations.

To address these issues, the SAIL Lab at Boston University led the development of the Conclave (Volgushev et al., 2019) open-source query compilation system in 2018. The system achieves acceleration of secure data queries based on MPC by combining data parallelism, plaintext computation, and MPC instructions. There are two kinds of back-ends integrated in Conclave: one containing Python and Spark (Zaharia et al., 2012), which is used to execute plaintext computations; the other, leveraging Sharemind (Bogdanov et al., 2008) and Obliv-C (Zahur and Evans, 2015), is used to execute MPC operations. The design of Conclave is based on three ideas.

(i) Conclave conducts analysis over query requests to distinguish instructions that must be executed under the MPC from those removable from MPC to achieve high performance. Without sacrificing data security, Conclave performs query transformation. Although the workload of some participants may increase, the end-to-end workload of the whole task is optimized and the overall running time is reduced.

(ii) Based on the analysis of the query, Conclave adds coarse-grained annotations on the input relations and achieves speed-up on instructions that are slow to process, such as join and aggregation, by combining MPC instructions and plaintext computation.

(iii) By generating codes, Conclave combines scalable but insecure data processing systems such as Spark with secure but computationally inefficient MPC systems such as Sharemind or Obliv-C.

Conclave minimizes the computation overhead of MPC with a lightweight computation workflow. Computations which only use local data or public data can be executed directly with plaintext. Conclave ensures that end-to-end security is guaranteed even if part of the computations are performed outside MPC. Since Conclave uses existing secure multiparty computing systems as its back-end, it provides the same security guarantees as common MPC algorithms. For example, all private data in the process and the frequency of different values are hidden in Conclave. At the same time, Conclave provides hybrid protocols that combine plaintext and MPC computations. Users can choose to sacrifice some security in exchange for better performance. By adding corresponding annotations to the input data, the user gives Conclave the permission to execute plaintext computation over the data.

Similar to other query compilers, Conclave compiles relational queries into Directed Acyclic Graphs (DAGs) consisting of basic relational operations and executes DAGs on multiple back-end systems. Conclave assumes that users participate in federated computation under certain conditions. First, the data held by each party matches the requirements of the query. Second, each party needs to run a Conclave agent to communicate with the other parties and manage the local computation. Third, each party should run an MPC computing endpoint (e.g., an Obliv-C or Sharemind node). In addition, the parties can choose a parallel data processing system (e.g., Spark) to perform the plaintext computation. If such a system is missing, Conclave uses Python to perform sequential computations.

Query operations in Conclave are almost identical to ordinary queries on a single trusted database. The only difference is that the user needs to specify the ownership of the data by adding an annotation to help Conclave locate the data and identify the required participants for the query. Users can even create relational models across participants and use them in the process of query commands. In addition, users can specify the recipients of the output by giving output annotations. Finally, Conclave sends the query results in plaintext to the specified participants after recognizing corresponding instructions.

As mentioned earlier, Conclave allows users to sacrifice some security for better performance, which is done by adding trust annotations. The user uses these annotations to specify which participants have access to specific columns of data. For example, a company may hold information about its own subsidiaries, such as business turnovers. However, the company may be willing to disclose this information to a trusted party, such as regulators or cooperative enterprises. By using such an approach, Conclave avoids redundant MPC operations, thereby significantly improving performance.

To manage such a trust relationship, Conclave defines a trust set that contains several parties for each column, in which any party can access the plaintext data of that column and perform plaintext operations locally with other accessible data like public data. Obviously, the owner of the data is in the trust set of the data naturally.

9.5.2 Privacy-preserving Computing Techniques in Conclave

As described in Section 9.5.1, Conclave supports both Sharemind and Obliv-C back-ends. We will take Sharemind as an example to introduce how privacy-preserving computing techniques are applied in Conclave.

Sharemind (Bogdanov et al., 2008) is a secure computing framework introduced by the Estonian company Cybernetica. The security is based on privacy-preserving computing techniques such as homomorphic encryption, secret sharing, and trusted execution environment. Currently, Sharemind consists of two products, Sharemind MPC and Sharemind HI. The Sharemind MPC platform enables privacy protection through secret sharing and supports a variety of secure multiparty computation solutions. One of the main schemes is the 3-out-of-3 secret sharing scheme based on additive secret sharing, which splits a private value s into $s_1 = \text{random}(), s_2 = \text{random}(), s_3 = s - s_1 - s_2$. Depending on the type of data to be processed, all operations under this scheme require the corresponding modulo operations. For example, for 64-bit integers, all operations are reduced modulo 2^{64}. The Sharemind solution accepts the existence of a semitrustworthy party among the three parties, but information leakage is still inevitable in the case of a joint attack by two parties.

As mentioned in the introduction of Shamir's secret sharing in Chapter 2, this scheme satisfies additive homomorphism. For example, there exist two secrets u and v that are split into sharings $u_1, u_2, \ldots, u_n$ and $v_1, v_2, \ldots, v_n$. The sharings are sent to different parties. If each party performs addition on local sharing u_i and v_i, the sum of the results of all parties is still equal to $u + v$. But the implementation of multiplicative homomorphism is not so straightforward. Sharemind constructs a new sharing strategy based on the Du–Atallah protocol (Du and Atallah, 2001). In this strategy, the secrets u and v are split and sent to three parties. $\mathcal{P}_1$ holds u_1 and v_1, $\mathcal{P}_2$ holds u_2 and v_2, and $\mathcal{P}_3$ holds u_3 and v_3. According to $u = \sum_{i=1}^{3} u_i, v = \sum_{i=1}^{3} v_i$, we can get $uv = \sum_{i=1}^{3} \sum_{j=1}^{3} u_i v_j = \sum_{i=1}^{3} u_i v_i + \sum_{i \neq j} u_i v_j$. In order to implement such an operation, the following steps are required.

(i) First, $\mathcal{P}_1$ locally computes the multiplication $u_1 v_1$. $\mathcal{P}_2$ locally computes the multiplication $u_2 v_2$. $\mathcal{P}_3$ locally computes the multiplication $u_3 v_3$.

(ii) Then, there are six different groups of i, j, k which satisfy $i, j, k \in \{1, 2, 3\}$ and any two numbers in the group are different from each other. To compute $\sum_{i \neq j} u_i v_j$, the following operations are performed for each group $\{i, j, k\}$ separately.

- $\mathcal{P}_k$ generates random numbers α_i and α_j, which are respectively sent to $\mathcal{P}_i$ and $\mathcal{P}_j$.
- $\mathcal{P}_i$ computes $u_i + \alpha_i$ and sends the addition result to $\mathcal{P}_j$. Conversely, $\mathcal{P}_j$ computes $v_j + \alpha_j$ and sends the result to $\mathcal{P}_i$.
- $\mathcal{P}_i$ computes local secret sharing $w_i = -(u_i + \alpha_i)(v_j + \alpha_j) + u_i(v_j + \alpha_j)$. $\mathcal{P}_j$ computes the local secret sharing $w_j = -(u_i + \alpha_i)v_j$. $\mathcal{P}_k$ computes the local secret sharing $w_k = \alpha_i\alpha_j$. Then we have $w_1 + w_2 + w_3 = u_iv_j$.

(iii) Finally, the results of the preceding steps are aggregated to a trusted third party to perform the addition operation, which yields the multiplication result uv. Then this result is split and shared again, which completes the homomorphic multiplication under secret sharing.

Based on the homomorphic addition and homomorphic multiplication operations introduced earlier, most secure computations can be implemented.

9.5.3 Conclave Query Compilation

Based on the privacy computing techniques described in Section 9.5.2, Conclave needs to implement multiparty secure queries based on query instructions. Query compilation is the process of converting query instructions into secure computations. As described in Section 9.5.1, the key optimization of Conclave is to accelerate the system performance by reducing unnecessary MPC operations.

Combined with annotations in input-output relations, Conclave can automatically determine which parts of a query must run under MPC. To achieve the goal of minimizing MPC operations while maintaining security guarantees, Conclave combines static analysis and query rewriting transformations. Figure 9.11 shows how Conclave minimizes MPC operations. Overall, Conclave completes query compilation in four steps as follows.

(i) In the initial state, all operations are under MPC. First, Conclave propagates ownership annotations from the input relations to the intermediate relations. It also propagates ownership annotations from the output relations to the intermediate relations in reverse, thus determining where the MPC frontier is located. Then, with this information, Conclave replaces the query with an equivalent one with fewer MPC operations across multiple parties. The DAG ends up containing some inner MPC operations, as well as efficient plaintext operations near the root and leaf nodes.

(ii) Conclave propagates the trust annotations from the input relations along the DAG and combines them to determine which part of the operations can be run outside MPC. Conclave then replaces the operations that can

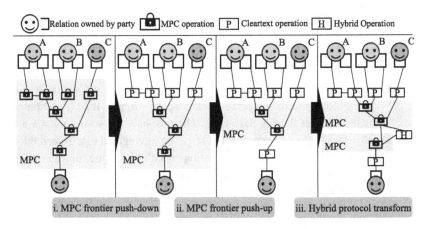

Figure 9.11 Workflow of Conclave query compilation.

be run outside MPC with hybrid operators based on the information obtained from the trust annotations, dividing the original single MPC operation into a number of smaller MPC computation operations and local plaintext operations.

(iii) In order to further reduce the number of overhead in secure computations (e.g., sorting, etc.), Conclave replaces them with lighter but equivalent plaintext operations when possible.

(iv) Finally, Conclave slices the DAG at the frontier of MPC to generate sub-DAGs to split queries. Conclave generates codes for the sub-DAGs and executes them on the back-end.

The specific implementations of these steps are described next.

Annotation Propagation

The annotations in the input and output relationships, including owner annotations and trust annotations, provide information about the root and leaf nodes of the DAG. Conclave performs two passes of this information along the DAG.

The first pass is the pass of ownership annotation. Conclave passes down the ownership of the input relations (root node) in topological order, and passes up the final output relation (leaf node) ownership in reverse topological order. For each intermediate operation, the ownership of the output relation depends on the ownership of the input relation. If all its input relations come from the same party, its output relations belong to that party as well. If the operation's input relations come from different parties, the output relations are considered to have no owner and corresponding operations must be executed under MPC.

The second pass is the pass of trust annotation. Since the trust set of each input column has been defined by trust annotations, Conclave passes these trust annotations in topological order. Similarly, Conclave defines the trust set for intermediate relations. A party is trusted by an intermediate relational column if, for that column, it is in the trust set of all input relational columns of the operation (i.e., has access to the plaintext data of all columns). Trust annotation propagation enables Conclave to compute intermediate relations using hybrid operators to ensure that no information other than user-annotated publishable information is leaked.

By passing annotations, Conclave reduces MPC operations while strictly guaranteeing that parties only have access to specific input-output relations and the intermediate relations derived from such relations.

Determining MPC Frontier

After annotation propagation introduced in Section 9.5.3, Conclave basically identifies which operations can be converted to plaintext. Next, it replaces such operations with local plaintext operations and splits other operations into two parts, i.e., preprocessed local operations and MPC operations. Through these transformations, the local operations gradually increase. The frontier between MPC and the local plaintext computation gradually moves toward the interior of the original DAG, which only contains MPC operations.

Hybrid Operator

When rewriting operations, Conclave uses hybrid operators that include both plaintext and MPC operations to replace the original MPC operations with high computational complexity. Three hybrid operators are supported in Conclave, which are Hybrid Join, Public Join, and Hybrid Aggregation. The implementations of these three operations are based on the premise that a party is in the trust set of all input data. First, the preprocessing operations such as data shuffle are run under MPC, and then relevant information is revealed to the trusted party. Second, the trusted party performs complex operations such as concatenation and aggregation in plaintext based on the input data and returns the computation results to different parties by secret sharing. Finally, Conclave integrates the results obtained from the plaintext computation back into the MPC framework through a number of select and shuffle operations.

Reducing Oblivious Operations

In MPC, in order to remain control-flow agnostic, oblivious operations such as sorting are time-consuming. To reduce such overhead, two methods are used in Conclave for optimization.

Tracking and reducing redundant sorts: Conclave traverses the DAG to track whether there are some operations after which the data is already in order, and removes redundant sorting operations accordingly. Similarly, Conclave checks whether there are operations that shuffle the data and destroy the ordering. The results of such operations are marked as unsorted.

Move sorts to plaintext processing whenever possible: Similar to moving the MPC frontier, if a party has access to all input data for the sort, the operation can be executed by plaintext processing. In particular, suppose that a concatenation operation is performed on a number of ordered data and the result of concatenation needs to be sorted. Although concatenation is not order-preserving, Conclave can achieve ordering by introducing a merge operation after concatenation. Compared to an oblivious sort on all data, an oblivious merge over several ordered partitions of data has a much lower overhead. The basic idea of such optimization is to introduce more plaintext operations to reduce the amount of MPC operations, thus significantly improving the overall performance.

9.5.4 Applications of Conclave

Market Concentration: To prevent monopoly, the government needs to investigate the market shares held by each company. In general, the Herfindahl–Hirschman Index (HHI, the sum of the squares of the market shares of all companies in a particular market) can be used to measure market concentration and monitor changes in market shares. The calculation of HHI requires knowing the market size, which can be obtained by analyzing a large number of transaction records for each company. Such large-scale data requires high computation performance. In addition, corporations are generally reluctant to share the transaction records to governments as they expose private information about the corporations. Therefore, a Conclave query system can be introduced between the government and companies, allowing the government to perform market regulation without compromising the privacy of corporations.

9.6 PrivPy Privacy-preserving Computing Platform

9.6.1 Platform Overview

The PrivPy platform (Li et al., 2018b) is a multiparty computation platform developed by Hua Kong Tsingjiao, with general scalability, high parallelism, and hybrid computing capabilities between plaintext and ciphertext. The

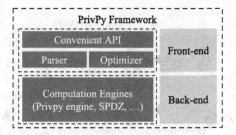

Figure 9.12 Framework of PrivPy.

PrivPy platform integrates privacy-preserving computing methods such as MPC, federated learning, and differential privacy. It satisfies the data security and computing correctness under the semihonest assumption. The PrivPy platform supports both federated query and federated modeling and provides an easy-to-use front-end interface of privacy-preserving computing to lower the barrier of development.

The framework of the PrivPy platform, shown in Figure 9.12, consists of a front-end that provides programming interfaces and code-checking optimizations, and a back-end that provides computational acceleration and privacy protection.

The PrivPy platform is user-friendly in that it provides users with simple Python programming interfaces to implement common privacy-preserving computing operations. These interfaces support processing over ndarray data types and broadcast operations, which is similar to the Numpy library in machine learning. All operations provided by the interfaces support computations over scalars, vectors, and matrices. This allows users to easily migrate machine learning projects to PrivPy to achieve privacy-preserving computation. In addition, the front-end can perform automatic detection and optimization of user code to avoid performance loss due to inappropriate user operations. This function is mainly implemented by operation simplification or data batching operations such as extraction of common factors, loop vectorization, and expression vectorization. At the same time, the front-end can also process large-scale data simultaneously according to the requirements of practical applications, such as computation operations on a $1,00,000 \times 5,048$ matrix.

The PrivPy platform's back-end integrates a library with about 400 secure computation functions, including various logic functions and federated learning. The back-end implements are based on the 2-out-of-4 secret sharing protocol, with hierarchical management of operators and rich computational functionality. A detailed introduction to the protocol is in Section 9.6.2.

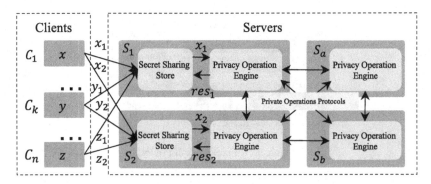

Figure 9.13 Structure of the PrivPy back-end.

The PrivPy platform introduces a generic private operation layer between the front-end and back-end to decouple them. To reduce the interaction overhead between the front-ends and back-ends, the back-end on each server functions as a library. In the design, Python is the common programming choice for big-data-related industries. Therefore, the front-end interface of PrivPy is implemented in Python. To ensure efficiency, the back-end of PrivPy is implemented in C++. However, users can use the same front-end programming interface to connect different computing back-ends by evaluating and optimizing performance. Currently, three kinds of back-ends are supported in PrivPy: SPDZ back-end, ABY^3 back-end, and PrivPy back-end. Among them, we focus on the PrivPy back-end in this book. The specific implementation of privacy computing techniques in the PrivPy back-end is described next.

9.6.2 Privacy-preserving Computing Techniques in PrivPy

2-out-of-4 Secret Sharing

The 2-out-of-4 secret sharing protocol combines two secure three-party computing architectures, SecureML (Mohassel and Zhang, 2017) and ABY^3 (Mohassel and Rindal, 2018). It builds a trusted computing system by using four semihonest servers S_1, S_2, S_a, and S_b. The system framework is shown in Figure 9.13.

We assume that all data in the system falls in $\mathbb{Z}_{2^n}$. When user C_1 wants to share the digit x, the process of data sharing is as follows.

- C_1 generates the numbers x_1 and x_2, where x_1 is a random number within $\mathbb{Z}_{2^n}$ and $x_2 = x - x_1$. C_1 sends x_1 and x_2 to the server S_1 and S_2, respectively.
- S_1 forwards x_1 to S_b and S_2 forwards x_2 to S_a.

- S_1 and S_2 generate the same random number r using the same random seed and compute $x_1' = x_1 - r$ and $x_2' = x_2 + r$ respectively. S_1 sends x_1' to S_a and S_2 sends x_2' to S_b.
- At this time, S_1 and S_2 respectively hold $\{x_1, x_1'\}$ and $\{x_2, x_2'\}$. S_a holds $\{x_2, x_1'\}$, denoted as $\{x_a, x_a'\}$. S_b holds $\{x_1, x_2'\}$, denoted as $\{x_b, x_b'\}$.

After the sharing is complete, the original data x is encoded into $[[x]] = (x_1, x_1', x_2, x_2', x_a, x_a', x_b, x_b')$. Each of the four servers holds two numbers randomly distributed within $\mathbb{Z}_{2^n}$. None of them can reconstruct the original data x alone. Clearly, 2-out-of-4 sharing satisfies additive homomorphism, i.e., $[[x]] + [[y]] = [[x + y]]$. In practice, since the original data is usually a decimal floating-point number, shift and intercept operations are often needed to map the original data to a large integer in $\mathbb{Z}_{2^n}$, i.e., $\widetilde{x} = \lfloor 2^d x \rfloor$. Additive homomorphism is still satisfied if we ignore the precision loss.

Compared to ABY^3, the 2-out-of-4 secret sharing protocol saves the overhead of data precomputation by introducing a fourth server and maintains the original communication complexity. The proofs of its security and correctness follow those in SecretML and ABY^3.

Fixed-point Number Multiplication

In the previous section, we illustrated the additive homomorphism in the 2-out-of-4 secret sharing protocol. In this section, we will describe the implementation of multiplication in this protocol. The main idea of fixed-point multiplication in PrivPy follows SecureML and ABY^3. However, different from these frameworks, PrivPy omits the process of precomputation.

Assume there are two fixed point numbers x and y shared among the servers S_1, S_2, S_a, and S_b according to the protocol in Section 9.6.2. Among them, S_1 holds $\{x_1, x_1', y_1, y_1'\}$, S_2 holds $\{x_2, x_2', y_2, y_2'\}$, S_a holds $\{x_a, x_a', y_a, y_a'\}$, and S_b holds $\{x_b, x_b', y_b, y_b'\}$. The following computational operations are executed:

- S_1 generates random numbers r_{12} and r_{12}', and computes $t_1 = x_1 y_1' - r_{12}$ and $t_1' = x_1' y_1 - r_{12}'$. After the computation, S_1 sends t_1 and t_1' to S_b and S_a, respectively.
- S_2 uses the same random seed as S_1 to generate the same random numbers r_{12} and r_{12}', and computes $t_2 = x_2 y_2' + r_{12}$ and $t_2' = x_2' y_2 + r_{12}'$. After the computation, S_2 sends t_2 and t_2' to S_a and S_b, respectively.
- S_a generates random numbers r_{ab} and r_{ab}', and calculates $t_a = x_a y_a' - r_{ab}$ and $t_a' = x_a' y_a - r_{ab}'$. After the computation, S_a sends t_a and t_a' to S_2 and S_1, respectively.

- S_b uses the same random seed as S_a to generate the same random numbers r_{ab} and r'_{ab}, and computes $t_b = x_b y'_b + r_{ab}$ and $t'_b = x'_b y_b + r'_{ab}$. After the computation, S_b sends t_b and t'_b to S_1 and S_2, respectively.
- S_1 stores $z_1 = (t_1 + t_b)/2^d$ and $z'_1 = (t'_1 + t'_a)/2^d$. S_2 stores $z_2 = (t_2 + t_a)/2^d$ and $z'_2 = (t'_2 + t'_b)/2^d$. S_a stores $z_a = (t_a + t_2)/2^d$ and $z'_a = (t'_a + t'_1)/2^d$. S_b stores $z_b = (t_b + t_1)/2^d$ and $z'_b = (t'_b + t'_2)/2^d$.

After the computation, the final values stored by each party are checked. We take z_1 and z_2 as examples.

$$\begin{aligned} 2^d(z_1 + z_2) &= t_1 + t_b + t_2 + t_a \\ &= x_1 y'_1 - r_{12} + x_b y'_b + r_{ab} + x_2 y'_2 + r_{12} + x_a y'_a - r_{ab} \\ &= x_1 y'_1 + x_b y'_b + x_2 y'_2 + x_a y'_a \qquad\qquad (9.1) \\ &= x_1 y'_1 + x_1 y'_2 + x_2 y'_2 + x_2 y'_1 \\ &= (x_1 + x_2)(y'_1 + y'_2). \end{aligned}$$

It can be inferred that z_1 and z_2 stored on S_1 and S_2 are a group of secret shares of $xy/2^d$. The final result is divided by 2^d to ensure that data scale remains unchanged after the multiplication is completed, so that data overflow caused by too many multiplications can be prevented. Similarly, z'_1 and z'_2 are also a group of secret sharings of $xy/2^d$. Since $z_1 = z_b$, $z_2 = z_a$, $z'_1 = z'_a$, and $z'_2 = z'_b$, the 2-out-of-4 secret sharing protocol is still satisfied, thus proving that the method achieves secure multiplication.

9.6.3 User Programming Interface

In the overview of the PrivPy in Section 9.6.1, we mentioned that PrivPy provides a set of Python programming interfaces, and developers can import the PrivPy library directly in Python to implement secure computation. Secure computations based on PrivPy differ very little from the ordinary computations in Python in terms of code implementations. The developer only needs to declare the private variables before the computation and call the reveal method on the result to recover the plaintext from secret sharings after the computation. Such an easy programming approach hides the complex multiparty secure computation process, enabling the developers to easily implement privacy-preserving computation.

In general, the interface of PrivPy is similar to that of the Numpy toolkit and supports various operations on ndarray data structures, including vector calculations and broadcast operations. Therefore, when performing machine learning training, users can simply replace ndarray with PrivPy to ensure the security of scalars and vectors. On receiving the input data, PrivPy automatically identifies the data type and converts the scalars and vectors to the custom private data types SNum and SArr respectively. For these two specific data types, PrivPy overloads the common operators +, −, *, ¿, =, etc. When performing operations on privacy data types, the overloaded operators execute the corresponding privacy-preserving computation methods based on the data types in order to maintain the difference between secure computation operations and ordinary operations.

9.6.4 Applications of PrivPy

Government Regulations: For the government, in order to regulate enterprises in the continuous developments of the market and the economy, efficient data analysis must be executed based on large-scale data, such as enterprise operation logs. However, enterprise data usually contains private information, making organizations reluctant to share core secrets. In addition, the problem of data interception and theft by malicious third parties is inevitable during large-scale data transmission and storage. To achieve effective regulation under data security, the use of privacy-preserving computing technology such as secret sharing through PrivPy can be effective.

Federated Data Mining: To investigate the status of the industry and optimize strategic decisions, enterprises are motivated to share data with partners in related industries and discover potential opportunities. However, affected by the risk of data leakage, enterprises are commonly divided into independent data silos, making data sharing essentially impossible. The PrivPy platform enables such federated data mining across enterprises. Participants are thus relieved of data security concerns and can benefit from a reliable joint credit assessment system. This is of great significance in promoting cross-industry integration and optimizing the industry structure.

AI secure prediction: Constrained by limited computing power, some enterprises cannot afford to train and predict over their own data locally. Alternatively, they rent cloud servers to perform computing tasks, which inevitably risks exposing local data. By providing secure cloud computing through PrivPy, enterprises can send their secret data to the cloud to perform computation with guaranteed data security. Meanwhile, with the help of MPC, combining data from partners can further improve the accuracy of the trained models, bringing further benefits to participating companies.

9.7 Efficiency Issues and Acceleration Strategies

Currently, a variety of privacy computing techniques are widely used in secure computing platforms, such homomorphic encryption, secret sharing, differential privacy, and trusted execution environments. Although these techniques have rigorously ensured data privacy, it also leads to a significant drop in computation and communication efficiency. In an attempt to achieve both data security and high efficiency, researchers at Clustar provide a series of secure acceleration schemes based on theoretical analysis and practical applications. The paper of Jing et al. (2019) provides a comprehensive discussion of the performance issues in training federated learning models, based on which diverse solutions are proposed in following works (Cheng et al., 2021b; Yang et al., 2020b; Zhang et al., 2021). Next, we present a detailed description of the efficiency issues of privacy-preserving computing and the corresponding solutions.

9.7.1 Efficiency Issues in Privacy-preserving Computing Techniques

Homomomorphic Encryption

Homomorphic encryption and decryption of data require mathematical operations on long integers. The computational complexity of these operations is related to both the encryption algorithm and the selected key length. In general, longer keys lead to higher security and lower computational efficiency. In order to ensure a sufficient level of security, keys with a length over 1024 bits are generally used. Homomorphic encryption is costly not only in the encryption/decryption processes, but also in operations between ciphertexts. For example, the addition and multiplication of ciphertexts require modular multiplication and modular exponentiation, which are computationally more complex than plaintext operations. Further, ciphertexts of homomorphic encryption also create communication overhead. Taking Paillier homomorphic encryption as an example, after the data is homomorphically encrypted, it will expand in size from 32 or 64 bits to a long integer with the same length as the public key (e.g., 1024 or 2048 bits), which creates burdens to communication.

Secret Sharing

In secret sharing, both the splitting and recovery of secrets compromise efficiency. In the secret splitting process, the secret needs to be divided into n sharings by certain mathematical calculations and then distributed to n participants. In the secret recovery process, it is necessary to collect k different sharings ($k \leqslant n$) and then recover the secret by mathematical computation specified by the algorithm. For example, Shamir algorithm requires recovering the secret by solving a congruence equation. Therefore, secret splitting and recovery require additional computation and communication overheads.

Differential Privacy

Differential privacy requires adding a certain amount of noise to each query result (e.g., with the Laplace mechanism or the exponential mechanism), thus introducing enough randomness to guarantee user privacy. Adding noise to the query results requires some additional computation, which causes a slight decrease in efficiency.

Oblivious Transfer

To ensure that the sender does not know which of the multiple optional messages the receiver has received, oblivious transfer requires encrypting the message data and the random numbers using an encryption algorithm (e.g., RSA algorithm). In addition, multiple data transfers between the sender and the receiver (including the public and private keys) are required according to the algorithm. Therefore, oblivious transfer causes additional overhead in both computations (encryption) and communication (transmission).

Garbled Circuit

Similar to oblivious transfer, garbled circuits involve a large number of encryption and decryption operations and various transformations of the ciphertext. Furthermore, many additional data transfers between the participants are introduced.

The computational efficiency problem caused by privacy-preserving computing techniques can be solved by heterogeneous computing. The problem of communication efficiency, on the other hand, can be solved by applying network optimization techniques.

9.7.2 Heterogeneous Acceleration of Privacy-preserving Computing

Definition of Heterogeneous Computing

Heterogeneous computing refers to using processors of different types of instruction sets and architectures to form a computing system. Common processors include CPU (X86, ARM, RISC-V, etc.), GPU, FPGA, and ASIC. Next, we provide an introduction to the four types of processors.

Central Processing Unit (CPU)

The CPU is one of the core components of a computer system, whose main function is to read, decode, and execute instructions. The CPU mainly consists of the arithmetic and logical unit (ALU), control unit (CU), register, cache, and the data bus that keeps them interconnected. We can classify CPUs into Reduced Instruction Set Computing (RISC) and Complex Instruction Set Computing (CISC) according to the instruction sets they support. In general, the length and execution time of instructions in RISC is relatively fixed compared to CISC. Reduced Instruction Set Computing instructions have better parallelism and the corresponding compilers are more efficient, while CISC instructions are optimized for different tasks, at the cost of more complex circuits and a lower level of parallelism. The classical CISC instruction set is X86, and typical RISC instruction sets include ARM and MIPS.

Graphics Processing Unit (GPU)

A GPU is a microprocessor originally designed to execute image or graphics processing tasks on personal computers, game consoles, and mobile devices such as smartphones. In recent years, due to their extremely good performance in floating-point calculations and parallel computing, GPUs have been widely used in scenarios where large amounts of computing power are required, such as big data processing, large-scale scientific research calculations, and artificial intelligence. Architecturally, GPUs contain tens to hundreds of small processors. Compared to CPUs, these individual processors are weak in terms of performance, but they can perform parallel operations very efficiently, which leads to considerable execution efficiency when the same processing is performed on large batches of data. Due to their advantage in parallelism, GPUs have been increasingly used in general-purpose computing in recent years. Specifically, using GPUs to do parallel computing on batched data has become increasingly common.

Field Programmable Gate Array (FPGA)

Field Programmable Gate Array is a product developed on the basis of PAL, GAL, EPLD, and other programmable devices. This device adopts the concept of Logic Cell Array (LCA), which consists of three internal parts: Configurable Logic Block (CLB), Input Output Block (IOB), and Interconnect. Field Programmable Gate Arrays are programmable devices with a different structure compared to traditional logic circuits and gate arrays (such as PAL, GAL, and CPLD devices). Combinational logic can be implemented by combining look-up tables in FPGA. The look-up tables can be connected to D flip-flops, which can be further used to drive other combinational circuits or I/O ports.

This constitutes a basic logic unit module that can realize both combinational and sequential logic functions. The logic of FPGA is implemented by programming data into the internal static storage cell. The value in the storage cell determines the logic function of the cells and the way the modules are connected to each other. Ultimately, the functions of FPGA can be determined. Field Programmable Gate Arrays allow unlimited times of programming. As a semicustom circuit, FPGA addresses the shortcomings of static circuits while overcoming the shortcomings of the limited number of gates in the original programmable devices.

Application-Specific Integrated Circuit (ASIC)

The term ASIC is a generic one for an integrated circuit that is specially designed and manufactured for a specific purpose. An integrated circuit is a miniature electronic device or component that uses a certain process to interconnect the digital components including transistors, resistors, capacitors, inductors, and wiring. The components are placed on one or several small semiconductor wafers or dielectric substrates, and then packaged in a housing and become a microstructure with the required circuit function. The larger the size of the integrated circuit, the more difficult it is to build for specific requirements. To solve these problems, ASICs have emerged. Application-Specific Integrated Circuits are classified as full custom or semicustom. Full custom requires the designer to design all the circuits, requiring a lot of manpower and resources. It is flexible but inefficient to develop. Semicustom uses standard logic cells, and the designer can select the required logic cells or even system-level modules (e.g., multipliers, microcontrollers) and IP cores from the library. These logic units are already designed to be reliable so that designers can complete the system more easily. Application-Specific Integrated Circuits have the characteristics of high variety as well as short design and production cycles. Compared to general-purpose integrated circuits, ASICs have the advantages of smaller size, lighter weight, lower power consumption, increased reliability, improved performance, enhanced confidentiality, and lower cost.

Solving the computational challenges in privacy-preserving computing through heterogeneous computing has become a popular research direction in academia and industry recently. An example of how to accelerate privacy-preserving computing through heterogeneous computing in the FATE platform is introduced the following discussion. Specifically, the computational bottleneck of privacy-preserving computing in FATE is mainly based on the encryption of data with the Paillier algorithm and the computation of ciphertext.

Feasibility Analysis

- In the cryptographic operations of FATE, the computation of different data does not affect each other, enabling massive parallelism. Heterogeneous computing is suitable for accelerating such computational tasks.
- Computational formulas involved in federated learning are not complex but come at enormous quantities. Heterogeneous computing is suitable for accelerating such repetitive lightweight computations.
- Federated learning is a computation-intensive task, as the time of data I/O takes less than 0.1 percent of the total time. Heterogeneous computing is well-suited for accelerating such computation-intensive tasks.
- Data in federated learning are generated in a large number of batches, satisfying the characteristics of huge data volume.

Combining the four preceding observations, federated learning is well suited for heterogeneous acceleration.

Challenges in Heterogeneous Acceleration

Although federated learning has many features suitable for heterogeneous acceleration, it also faces the following challenges:

- Operations among large integers need to be executed in federated learning, while heterogeneous devices do not directly support large integer operations.
- Computation in federated learning involves a lot of modular exponentiation operations, which are costly for heterogeneous devices.
- A large number of intermediate computation results need to be cached in federated learning, while heterogeneous devices have limited storage space due to constraints over cost and energy.

Acceleration Scheme

(i) **Element-level Parallelism via Divide-and-conquer** If the N-bit large integers a and b are decomposed into multiple parts, then the addition and multiplication operations among large integers can be decomposed into many small integer operations that can be computed in parallel. In this way, the heterogeneous devices can efficiently perform complex computations on large integers.

(ii) **Optimization Algorithm Combining Exponentiation by Squaring and Montgomery Multiplication** The Paillier encryption algorithm used in the FATE platform makes extensive use of modular exponentiation operations ($a^b \bmod c$). How to compute them efficiently by heterogeneous computation is the core of improving computational efficiency. We make the following observations regarding exponentiation operations.

First, the computational complexity can be optimized through exponentiation by squaring algorithm. The main idea is that, to compute the value of a^k, it is not necessary to multiply a by k times. Instead, $a^{k/2}$ can be computed first and then squared. By continuously squaring the result, only $\log k$ times of multiplication are needed to obtain a^k. Based on this idea, b can be expressed in binary and the result can be obtained by $O(N)$ multiplications and modulo operations. The advantage of exponentiation by squaring is that it can reduce the complexity to $O(N)$ and the intermediate computation results do not exceed c. The disadvantage is that $2N$ modulo operations, which are costly for GPUs, are required. To overcome this problem, FATE introduces the Montgomery multiplication algorithm to perform modular multiplication efficiently. The advantage of the Montgomery algorithm is that no modulo operation is needed, thus greatly increasing the overall performance.

(iii) **Chinese Remainder Theorem to Reduce the Size of Intermediate Results** We first show the decryption algorithm of Paillier as follows:

$$m = \frac{L(c^\lambda \bmod n^2)}{L(g^\lambda \bmod n^2)}, \text{ where } n = pq, \ L(x) = \frac{x-1}{n}. \tag{9.2}$$

It is not difficult to find that bit-width of the final computation result of Paillier Decryption Algorithm (9.2) is N, where N is the bit-width of n. However, the bit-width of intermediate result is $2N$, requiring more memory for storage. Since the storage of heterogeneous devices is limited, the computational performance is greatly affected.

$$m_p = \frac{L(c^{p-1} \bmod p^2)}{L(g^{p-1} \bmod p^2)} \bmod p, \tag{9.3}$$

$$m_q = \frac{L(c^{q-1} \bmod q^2)}{L(g^{q-1} \bmod q^2)} \bmod q \tag{9.4}$$

$$\begin{cases} x \equiv m_p \ (\bmod \ p), \\ x \equiv m_q \ (\bmod \ q). \end{cases} \tag{9.5}$$

The Chinese Remainder Theorem (CRT) can decompose the modulo operations, thus reducing the size of intermediate results. We use two subterms m_p and m_q (Eq. (9.3) and Eq. (9.4)) to construct a system of congruence equations (Eq. (9.5)) satisfying CRT. The solution of this system is denoted by $\text{CRT}(m_p, m_q)$. It can be shown that the decryption result is equivalent to $\text{CRT}(m_p, m_q) \bmod pq$, so that the value of m can be obtained by CRT. We have two observations on Eq. (9.3), Eq. (9.4), and Eq. (9.5). First, none of the bit-widths of results of the three equations exceeds N bits, thus reducing the size of the required memory. Second, the original equation is simplified from a $2N$-bit operation to an N-bit operation, which reduces the computational complexity significantly.

Extensive implementations and evaluations show that a 50~70× overall acceleration can be achieved for federated learning with the preceding three optimization schemes.

9.7.3 Network Optimization for Data Transmission

Common optimizations for network mainly include network infrastructure upgrade, transport layer protocol optimization, network traffic scheduling, private network construction, and application layer optimization.

Network Infrastructure Upgrade

By upgrading network hardware devices, the efficiency of network data transmission can be significantly improved. For data center networks (where all participants of privacy-preserving computing are in the same cluster), the efficiency of data transmission can be improved by upgrading the network bandwidth (e.g., from a 10 Gbps network to a 100 Gbps network). This requires purchasing switches, routers, NICs, and network cables for the data center that support higher bandwidths. Furthermore, network latency can also be significantly reduced by purchasing network equipments that support the Remote Direct Memory Access (RDMA) technology, thereby reducing the time required for each round of data transfer. For communication across data centers, the efficiency of data transfer can be improved by purchasing higher network bandwidth from telecom carriers as well as adapted NICs and cables.

Transport Layer Protocol Optimization

To improve the performance of data transmission, researchers have been working on designing efficient transport layer protocols. Optimizations in this area fall into two main categories. The first category involves several optimizations of the widely adopted TCP protocols, such as (1) TCP Cubic replaces congestion window changes in the original TCP with a cubic function. The growth of the window depends on the time of two packet losses, which is independent of Round Trip Time (RTT) and has the feature of RTT fairness. (2) Based on the fact that network switches commonly support Explicit Congestion Notification

(ECN), Data Center TCP (DCTCP) determines the size of the congestion window based on the proportion of packets that are marked with ECN within an RTT. (3) TCP BBR uses the estimated bandwidth and delay to directly infer the degree of congestion and thus calculate the sliding window, instead of depending on packet loss (congestion) information feedback as in the traditional TCP algorithm. The second category includes the design of a new transport layer protocol to replace TCP. For example, Google proposed Quick UDP Internet Connections (QUIC) protocol with five innovative designs to significantly improve the performance of data transmission: (1) Reduce connection establishment time by using caching. (2) Migrate congestion control from kernel space to user space. (3) Apply multiplexing without head-of-line blocking. (4) Use forward error correction to reduce retransmissions. (5) Smooth migration of connections.

Network Traffic Scheduling

In recent years, traffic scheduling has become a hot topic in networking. Network traffic scheduling mainly refers to deciding when and at what rate to transmit each data stream in the network, which has a very important impact on the performance of data transmission. By setting scheduling goals and designing corresponding traffic scheduling algorithms, it is possible to plan how data will be transmitted in the network and thus significantly reduce transmission time. Common scheduling goals include providing bandwidth and deadline guarantees for data transmission of computational tasks, minimizing the average completion time of all data transmission tasks, minimizing the overall completion time of a group of data transmissions belonging to the same computational task, minimizing traffic transmission costs, and sharing bandwidth fairly. The common scheduling management methods are divided into three main categories: distributed scheduling, centralized scheduling, and hybrid scheduling. According to different communication scenarios, the existing solutions can be further divided into three types: intradata center traffic scheduling, interdata center traffic scheduling, and traffic scheduling between individual terminals and data centers. In terms of the granularity of scheduling, there are four main types: flow group-based scheduling, single flow-based scheduling, flow-slice-based scheduling, and individual packet-based scheduling. The key to improving transmission efficiency of privacy computing through network traffic scheduling is to clarify the communication scenario and scheduling target, select the appropriate scheduling method and scheduling granularity, and design an effective scheduling algorithm.

Private Network Construction

For network data transmission across data centers, the time required for data transmission can be optimized by building/purchasing a private network to avoid competing for bandwidth with other users' network traffic. Compared with public network transmission, private networks have two main advantages.

(i) Lower latency. Because cross-datacenter private networks are generally used for communication between cross-city data centers with long distances, if data is transmitted through a public network, it will pass through more hopping nodes and has a relatively larger delay. For example, the transmission delay of cross-territory communication between Beijing data and Shanghai data center can reach 1000 ms under the optimal situation using public network transmission. But if it is replaced by a cross-datacenter private network, the speed will be much higher, and the delay can be reduced to within 50 ms.

(ii) Strong stability. Transmission through the public network will be affected by the performance of various backbone nodes, resulting in great instability. On the contrary, after the establishment of a private network, it can realize the direct interconnection between two (or more) data centers, thus avoiding network failure and packet loss caused by a single failure point, and maximizing the stability of transmission without being affected by the public network.

Application Layer Optimization

The application layer can also be optimized for network transmission. The first one is DNS optimization, using HTTP DNS instead of Local DNS. Most standard DNS interacts with DNS servers based on UDP. HTTP DNS uses the HTTP protocol to interact with DNS servers, thus bypassing the operator's Local DNS service, effectively preventing domain name hijacking and improving the efficiency of domain name resolution. The second one is connection reuse, which avoids repeated handshakes. For two servers that need to communicate frequently, connections can be maintained for a long time, thus avoiding the overhead of re-establishing network connections. The third optimization is data compression and encryption. The amount of data transmitted can be reduced. There are already many mature algorithms to compress the transmitted data, such as Gzip, Google's Brotli, and FaceBook's Z-standard. In addition to the compression algorithms, the characteristics of the application can be used to only transfer part of the data. For example, in some distributed AI model training, it is not necessary to synchronize all the computational data on different servers. In this case, only part of the data is transmitted.

Experimental results show that the preceding five optimization schemes can greatly strengthen the distributed cluster communication efficiency. Specifically, the network latency is reduced by 75 percent, and task performances are improved by an average of 200 percent (and in extreme cases by 450 percent). Therefore, these optimization schemes can significantly improve the communication efficiency of privacy-preserving computing in practice.

10

Case Studies of Privacy-preserving Computing

10.1 Financial Marketing and Risk Control

Background

Marketing and risk control are critical tasks in finance. Machine learning models have been applied to these tasks to improve the performance. For example, in risk control, when a bank processes the loan application, it checks the background of the customer such as the customer's income and history of loans. Machine learning models could help to score the customer and gives an initial risk score on the customer. As for marketing, machine learning models help the company to find potential customers from a large population so that the cost of customer filtering is reduced.

However, the data features in a single bank or company may be not enough to train a machine learning model. The bank or company may only have the records in their own database. To get a larger dataset for training, the bank or company has to collaborate with other entities, which may be illegal. In order to ensure the performance of machine learning model and legality, the machine learning training has to adopt privacy-preserving machine learning technologies.

Case Study

The dataset outside of a bank could improve the accuracy of the user portrait. The outsourcing database may come from websites or government, and the datasets of the bank and other entities have the following features:

- Distributed dataset: the dataset cannot be exchanged between these entities to ensure legality.
- Complicated computation: machine learning training on these datasets involves huge computation.

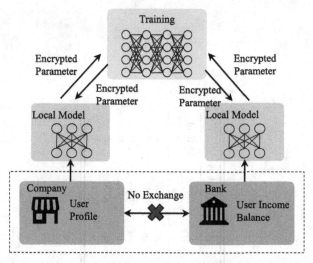

Figure 10.1 Collaborated risk control workflow.

Figure 10.1 shows the architecture of a collaborated risk control between a bank and a company. The machine learning task is based on vertical federated learning. Table 10.1 shows an example of data entries in these datasets. The company has the information of users such as the user's job, birth place, loans, and investments. The bank has the user's income and the label which indicates breach of contract. The bank is unable to get an accurate user portrait only on the customer's income and it needs the oursourcing dataset.

The collaborative risk control is divided into three steps:

- Private Set Intersection.
- Model Training.
- Inference.

We elaborate these steps in detail.

Private Set Intersection

As shown in Table 10.1, user ids are different in different entities and the training has to be conducted in their intersection. This process is called Private Set Intersection, or PSI. Here we introduce a PSI algorithm based on hashing and RSA encryption, as shown in Figure 10.2.

Assume that company A has user set $u_A = \{u_1, u_2, u_3, u_4, u_5, u_6\}$ and the bank B has user set $u_B = \{u_1, u_2, u_3, u_4, u_7, u_8\}$.

First, bank B generates public key (n, e) and private key (n, d) with the RSA scheme and sends the public key to the company A.

Table 10.1 *Collaborative Risk Control.*

	Company A					Bank B		
ID	Job x_1	Birth Place x_2	Work Place x_3	Loans x_4	Investments x_5	ID	Income x_6	Default y
u_1	Engineer	Beijing	Beijing	4	4	u_1	6000	1
u_2	Officer	Beijing	Shanghai	2	3	u_2	8000	0
u_3	Driver	Shanghai	Shanghai	4	3	u_3	6000	0
u_4	Teacher	Guangzhou	Beijing	2	1	u_4	7000	0
u_5	Bank Employee	Shenzhen	Beijing	5	7	u_7	9000	0
u_6	Engineer	Shenzhen	Shenzhen	5	6	u_8	9000	1

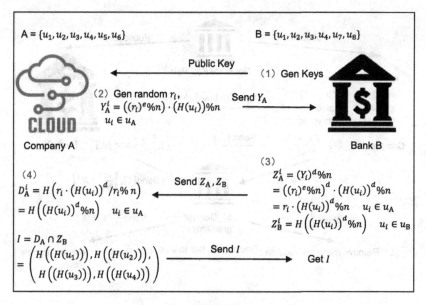

Figure 10.2 Private Set Intersection.

Then, company A generates random number r_i for every element in u_A and encrypts r_i with the public key. The ciphertexts are then multiplied with the hashed user ids and the result is noted as Y_A and is expressed as

$$Y_A^i = ((r_i)^e \% n) \cdot (H(u_i)) \% n, \quad u_i \in u_A. \tag{10.1}$$

Note that the mapping from u_i, r_i to Y_A^i is known to the company A. Y_A is sent to bank B.

Next, bank B decrypts Y_A with the private key and the result is noted as Z_A:

$$Z_A^i = (Y_i)^d \% n = ((r_i)^e \% n)^d \cdot (H(u_i))^d \% n = r_i \cdot (H(u_i))^d \% n, \ u_i \in u_A. \tag{10.2}$$

Similarly, bank B generates hashed user ids from u_B and encrypts with the private key. The ciphertexts are hashed again with the same function and the result is noted as Z_B:

$$Z_B^i = H((H(u_i))^d \% n), \ u_i \in u_B. \tag{10.3}$$

Bank B sends Z_A and Z_B to company A, who will perform division on the element of Z_A to eliminate the random number. The result is hashed again with the same hash function. The result is noted as D_A:

$$D_A^i = H\left(r_i \cdot \frac{(H(u_i))^d}{r_i \% n}\right) = H((H(u_i))^d \% n), \ u_i \in u_A. \tag{10.4}$$

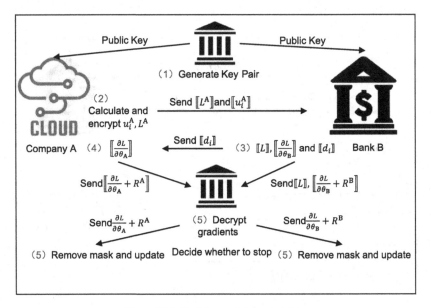

Figure 10.3 Training on intersected data.

Company A calculates the intersection of D_A and Z_B, and the result can be expressed as

$$I = D_A \cap Z_B = (H(H(u_1)), H(H(u_2)), H(H(u_3)), H(H(u_4))). \qquad (10.5)$$

Now, both parties get the intersection on their private set without revealing the set to the other party.

Model Training

After getting the intersection on their dataset, the parties are able to train a machine learning model on their intersected dataset. During the training, the parties will not exchange private data directly; instead, they send encrypted result to each other for training. We introduce a scheme based on homomorphic encryption with the help of a third party (Yang et al., 2019c). The process is illustrated in Figure 10.3.

First, the third party generates a key pair for homomorphic encryption and sends the public key to the parties.

Then, company A calculates:

$$u_i^A = \theta_A x_i^A,$$

$$L^A = \sum_{i \in I} (u_i^A)^2 + \frac{\lambda}{2}\theta_A^2. \qquad (10.6)$$

The local feature is x_i^A and θ_A is the parameter of model. The intersection is I and $\sum_{i \in I}$ means to iterate through the intersection and sum the results. These two expressions are the intermediate results in the training.

Next, company A encrypts the results and sends them to bank B. We use $[\![.]\!]$ to express the encrypted results. Bank B calculates the loss and gradient, which can be expressed as:

$$u_i^B = \theta_B x_i^B,$$

$$[\![d_i]\!] = [\![u_i^A]\!] + [\![u_i^B - y_i]\!],$$

$$[\![L]\!] = [\![L^A]\!] + [\![\sum_{i \in I}(u_i^B - y_i)^2 + \frac{\lambda}{2}\theta_B^2]\!] + 2\sum_{i \in I}[\![u_i^A]\!](u_i^B - y_i),$$

$$[\![\frac{\partial L}{\partial \theta_B}]\!] = \sum_{i \in I}[\![d_i]\!]x_i^B + [\![\lambda\theta_B]\!]. \tag{10.7}$$

Bank B adds random mask R^B to the gradient and loss and sends it to the third party for decryption. Also, $[\![d_i]\!]$ is sent to company A who calculates the gradient with

$$[\![\frac{\partial L}{\partial \theta_A}]\!] = \sum_{i \in I}[\![d_i]\!]x_i^A. \tag{10.8}$$

Party A also adds random mask R^A to the gradient and sends it to the third party for decryption.

Finally, the third party returns the decrypted results to parties A and B, who remove the random mask and update their model parameters. The loss is also decrypted and the third party may decide whether to stop training.

The training is repeated until the model has converged.

Note that the training protocol is designed for linear regression, not for other machine learning models such as logistic regression.

Inference

After training, both parties are online for inference service. Figure 10.4 shows the process of inference.

The inference task is conducted with the following steps:

First, bank B calculates the hash of data id and sends it to company A. If company A does not have the data id, it replies with a message indicating failure and stops inference; otherwise, company A replies with

$$u^A = \theta_A x^A. \tag{10.9}$$

Then, bank B produces the inference result with

$$\hat{y} = u^A + \theta_B x^B, \tag{10.10}$$

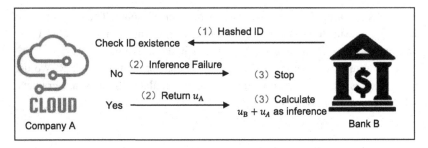

Figure 10.4 Inference on trained model.

where $\hat{y}$ is the inference result, θ_B is the model in bank B, and x^B is the data in the bank B.

In practice, when Area Under the Curve (AUC) plays as the metric, the collaborative machine learning model improves the performance by 10 to 20 percent.

Current federated learning platforms such as FATE offer end-to-end federated learning service for parties with heterogenerous datasets. The parties can provide meta information about their datasets and the platform will perform PSI, training, and inference automatically.

Summary

In this section, we introduced how the entities such as banks or companies can collaboratively train machine learning models for marketing and risk control. Federated learning enables training without exchanging the datasets and all messages are encrypted. In the example, the bank gets the risk score for the customer with the machine learning model that conducts inference on both its local dataset and outsourcing dataset. It is an important case in risk control, considering the bank often lacks extra information on the customers.

10.2 Advertising Billing

10.2.1 Scenario

Advertisers want to know the number of click-throughs from different channels to track their marketing and strategies in advertising. A simple and widely used practice is to add the click source to the URL address of the page that pops up after clicking on the ad, e.g., "Source=Twitter" means the click is from Twitter. In this way, the advertisements placed on different platforms are directed to the same page. Advertisers can easily understand the source of each click and use standard network traffic analysis tools to get statistical results.

Therefore, they can understand the advertisements' effectiveness on different platforms easily. Such statistics also correspond to a common charging way for online advertising – "Cost Per Click" (CPC). The number of clicks on different platforms is a direct business metric of interest to advertisers and a basis for payment to advertising platforms.

There is another charging model for online advertising – Cost Per Mile (CPM), which is based on the advertisement's exposure. CPM has also become a mainstream advertising charging model. On the one hand, people's behavior (i.e., potential customers who view ads) is complex. Customers may be impressed and purchase the item after viewing its advertisements several times, but they may not click on the ad to make a purchase. Therefore, the purchase cannot be covered only by statistics on the number of clicks and the source of clicks. On the other hand, because of the complexity of advertising, a significant percentage of advertisements do not directly promote products but rather focus on promoting brand image and building consumer awareness. Such advertising does not seek direct clicks from viewers, so it is difficult to price ads with click-through indicators.

For online advertising platforms, it makes more sense to charge for exposure, as they can more accurately control the number of times an ad is exposed. In contrast, the advertising content largely influences clicks and even purchases. However, advertising platforms should help advertisers understand the effectiveness of their advertisements after exposure; i.e., what is the conversion rate from exposure to clicks and even purchases? How many consumers who have purchased an item have seen the advertisement on the platform?

In an exposure-based advertising billing process, it is necessary to know how many advertisements placed on the platform are seen by users. It is essential to decide how much to charge the advertisers based on the purchases made by users who have seen the advertisements (i.e., customer conversion). Take the example of a brand's product A. The online shopping platform where the consumer bought the product records all the orders of product A and knows who has purchased the product. The advertising platform has the advertising exposure data and knows which users have seen the advertising for product A provided by the platform. If both platforms check their data and find the users who appear in the data of both platforms, they can accurately trace the users who have purchased products that have seen the ads on the advertising platform. Then, they can calculate the advertising exposure effect. If the set of users who have seen the ads is U_1 and the set of new customers of advertisers is U_2, then it is possible to calculate:

$$P = U_1 \cap U_2.$$

Based on the information of P, platforms can decide how much they need to charge advertisers for advertising. For example, an advertising platform may charge for the number of elements of P, which reflects how many new customers have seen the advertisement. The advertising platform can also charge for the percentage of elements of P in U_2, which reflects the rate of new customers reached by the advertising.

However, the preceding process requires advertisers and advertising platforms to exchange the corresponding data for intersection calculation. Such computation can reveal the user's activity in viewing advertisements and the advertiser's customer list. Such a privacy leakage is unacceptable to both users and advertisers restricted under legal rules. Firstly, it is because the two platforms are often different companies and cannot directly disclose information due to the protection of trade secrets. Next, this information includes consumers' personal information and cannot be disclosed or used to identify consumers. Therefore, we need an ad delivery algorithm that does not compromise privacy.

10.2.2 Case Study

How can we compute the overlapped data between two parties, i.e., find the data intersection, while keeping both parties' data privacy? This problem is called private set intersection (PSI) in the research field. One idea is to encrypt each piece of data in the dataset with some cryptographic function so that another party cannot read or decrypt the encrypted data. Suppose the encryption functions of the online shopping platform and the advertising platform are $f(x)$ and $g(y)$, respectively. To implement the data intersection computation under the encryption condition, we design $f(x)$ and $g(y)$ in such a way that they satisfy the interchange encryption; that is, when the data entry $x = y$ in the database has the following equation:

$$f(g(y)) = g(f(x)).$$

In this way, both parties only need to encrypt their data and send them to each other. While receiving the encrypted data from the other side, both parties will encrypt it again to obtain the result of two different encryption sequences. The encrypted results do not reveal the original data and can be used for direct comparison so that the intersection of the two databases can be known, thus completing the traceability of the advertising exposure effect.

For example, suppose the advertiser has six customers $U_2 = \{u_1, u_2, u_3, u_4, u_5, u_6\}$, and the advertising platform has eight users who have seen the ad recorded as the set $U_1 = \{u_1, u_2, u_3, u_7, u_8, u_9, u_{10}, u_{11}\}$. Note that we can already see the intersection of $\{u_1, u_2, u_3\}$ by the notation here, which is made for demonstration purposes and does not show the exact contents of the set to any of the participants in the actual run. The advertiser has the following encrypted set:

$$E(U_2) = \{f(u_1), f(u_2), f(u_3), f(u_4), f(u_5), f(u_6)\}.$$

Now, both sides randomize the elements in their datasets and exchange the encrypted datasets for another layer of encryption. In this example, on the advertiser's side, the computation is

$$E(E(U_1)) = \{f(g(u_1)), f(g(u_2)), f(g(u_3)), f(g(u_7)), f(g(u_8)),$$
$$f(g(u_9)), f(g(u_{10})), f(g(u_{11}))\}.$$

Note that here, the order of these ciphertexts is randomized, so the advertiser platform cannot determine the user information by order of the ciphertexts. Similarly, on the platform side, there are

$$E(E(U_2)) = \{g(f(u_1)), g(f(u_2)), g(f(u_3)), g(f(u_4)), g(f(u_5)), g(f(u_6))\}.$$

Next, both parties agree to compare the set of ciphertexts of the secondary encryption of either party. Suppose they made the comparison on the advertising platform, i.e., to compare $E(E(U_2))$ and $E(E(U_1))$. By the properties of f and g, we have

$$f(g(u_1)) = g(f(u_1)),$$
$$f(g(u_2)) = g(f(u_2)),$$
$$f(g(u_3)) = g(f(u_3)).$$

The number of identical ciphertexts is the number of elements in the intersection. Here we get three intersection elements; however, due to the random sorting and iterative encryption, we cannot determine the exact intersection of user from these ciphertexts.

10.2.3 Lessons Learned

In this case study, we present a case where an advertising delivery platform and an advertiser use privacy-preserving computing techniques (i.e., private set intersection intersection) for accurate billing of ads. Private set intersection intersection has many applications in privacy-preserving computing. For example, the first step in vertical federated learning is private set intersection, where multiple parties need to find common users. The advertising billing presented in this section is a clever application of private set intersection, where advertisers and ad delivery platforms perform accurate billing of ad delivery under the premise of privacy protection. In addition to this scenario, there are several other applications for private set intersection. For example, in a securities company's product marketing, the sales department needs to determine whether the new users in the business department were brought in by the sales department's marketing. Using private set intersection, they can determine which of the customers were brought in by advertising.

10.3　Advertisement Recommendation

10.3.1　Background

Internet advertising is an important part of modern media marketing, which uses websites, applications, and other media to promote various brands of goods through texts, images, audios, and videos. With the booming development of the Internet, Internet advertising has touched every aspect of people's life, and traditional advertising is gradually being replaced. The mainstream model of the Internet advertising system is RTA (Real-Time API), in which users, brands, and media are the three main participants. As shown in Figure 10.5(a), when there is an advertisement space vacancy on the user side, the advertising platform on the media side asks the brand through the API whether to participate in the competition for advertisement placement, and then combines the decision returned from the brand side for the next placement of advertisement to improve the effectiveness of brand commodity advertising. This requires the brand side to have the ability to judge whether to place an advertisement or not. Some brands have an advertisement placement history or an accumulation of user portrait data; but in reality, most brands do not have the ability to collect, analyze, and model data, and individual brands do not have a comprehensive user portrait, which will lead to bad performance and a large cost of advertisement placement.

In the traditional RTA advertising mode, the brand side will buy a large amount of user data from third-party data providers to help the training of decision models. However, with the increasing concern of society about data privacy and the gradual improvement of relevant laws and regulations, it has become very difficult for the brand side to purchase third-party data, which has seriously harmed the profits of brands. Therefore, privacy-preserving computing empowering traditional Internet advertising is also slowly gaining the attention of researchers and advertising practitioners.

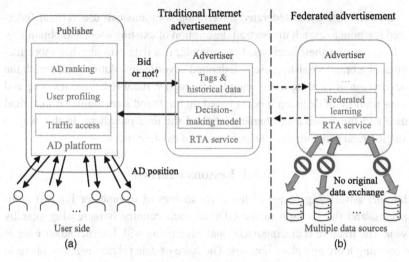

Figure 10.5 Illustration of federated advertisement.

10.3.2 Case Study

As one of the concrete forms of privacy-preserving computing, the federated advertising solution is a practical application of privacy-preserving computing empowering traditional Internet advertising. As shown in Figure 10.5(b), federated advertising solution uses the technology of federated learning to fuse the knowledge of multiple data sources without the exchange of raw data to help the training of decision models in RTA placement services. Auxiliary data is introduced compliantly and legally. The reason is that, in federated learning, only intermediate results are exchanged between participants, and the intermediate results are encrypted before being transmitted. The federated advertising solution applies the idea of "data does not move, the model moves" to the traditional Internet advertising field, solving the problem of lack of data on the brand side, thus reducing advertising costs and increasing business benefits.

On the one hand, the federated advertising solution can use horizontal federated learning to increase the sample size of brand parties, which enables media to know the interest points of unknown users and then obtain new users. For example, if multiple brands have different user groups, the federated advertising solution could use horizontal federated learning to jointly train the RTA decision model on the data of multiple brands to integrate the interests of different user groups. In this way, a single brand can complete its advertising to new users.

On the other hand, federated advertising solutions can use vertical federated learning to enrich the portrait description of existing users and obtain new information on their interests. For example, if a data provider has more features of a brand's existing users, federated advertising solutions can enrich the description of existing users' interests through vertical federated learning and joint training of decision models based on the brand's accumulated historical data and the richer user characteristics of the data providers. In this way, a single brand can complete the promotion of existing users.

10.3.3 Lessons Learned

Internet advertising is one of the main sources of income for Internet companies, and the its ratio in the GDP of each country is increasing year by year. The trend of replacing traditional advertising with Internet advertising is becoming more and more obvious. The issue of data privacy is a new obstacle to the development of Internet advertising at present. With the improvement of relevant laws and regulations, it is increasingly difficult for brands that want to place advertisements to complete accurate customer acquisition, and the cost of customer acquisition is getting higher and higher. The federated advertising solution gives us a way out, so privacy-preserving computing to empower the Internet advertising industry is now becoming more practical and feasible. In addition to federated learning, other privacy-preserving protection technologies will also be gradually applied in this field in the future.

10.4 Data Query

10.4.1 Scenario

Besides machine learning modeling, another practical application area of privacy-preserving computing is relational querying. Compared with federated learning, the characteristics of relational query are its simple logic and lack of complex computation such as model training. Take "three-factor query" as an example. A customer needs to provide his name, cell phone number, and social security number when opening an account at a bank. Then the bank needs to check whether the customer's cell phone number and social security number are consistent. If they are, the bank can process the next step of information approval. Otherwise, the customer needs to correct his personal information. In this querying process, the information is stored at multiple institutions under privacy protections; the calculation is relatively simple and does not involve complex analyses (e.g., training models). We categorize such applications as union queries.

In most existing query scenarios, a table merge operation based on the foreign keys in the tables should be complete if a query involves multiple tables in a database (such as a joint query between the SSN-Name or SSN-Phone Number tables). We need to merge the two tables based on the SSN and perform our example's name-mobile phone number query and matching operation. However, if the two tables belong to different companies or institutions, the table merge operation will expose the name-mobile phone number relationship of the user. Such a privacy leakage could result in theft of the user's cell phone number by a malicious organization. We want to complete the user information query and matching operation without privacy leakage, so we need a relational query scheme based on privacy-preserving computing.

Here is a general definition of a relational query. Suppose there is a querying party A and a data holder B. Party A has the query condition f, and B has the data D. After completing the federated query, A wants to obtain the query result $f(D)$. During the query process, it is crucial to ensure that A's query conditions are not known by B and that A cannot obtain any information about B's data other than the query results. The following part describes the differences in the types of computations and operators in the query process and introduces three different federal query scenarios: IV-value query (statistics); three-factor (or four-factor) verification (matching); and secure face matching (model inference).

- **IV value query** In privacy-based data collaboration, the user cannot see the provider's data features and distribution due to privacy requirements, which poses a significant challenge for privacy-preserving joint modeling, e.g., how the user can evaluate which features the provider uses for modeling. This problem is especially significant when the provider has a great number of features. In practice, the relational query can be used to query the IV value of each feature under the features of the data provider using the tag value of the tag holder (i.e., the data application) under privacy protection. Then, it can rank the importance of the features based on the IV value and select only the features with a solid ability to distinguish the tag value for modeling.
- **Three-factor/four-factor verification** In banks or payment institutions, it is common to check whether the personal information provided by customers matches, such as name, SSN, phone number, and bank card number. This information is often stored in multiple parties and cannot be verified by a single party. For example, Bank A may need to go to Carrier B to check if the cell phone number matches the ID number. In this process, it is necessary to ensure that Operator B is not informed of Bank A's query information and query results, while Bank A can only get "match" or "no-match" results. At

the same time, both parties need to agree on a query agreement and conduct an audit to protect the privacy of the data source. For example, if Bank A repeats a query more than ten times for a particular ID number, it is considered cheating. In this way, there is no more risk of information being stolen from Bank A.

- **Secure face matching**. In offline stores, when a customer enters a store, face recognition using a camera is employed to obtain the customer's identity information to provide better service to the customer. However, general stores cannot build face recognition systems, so they need the help of external organizations to build models and face feature libraries. The collected faces of customers are private information. They cannot be directly uploaded to the cloud for model inference or comparison with the samples in the face feature database. Therefore, privacy-preserving computing techniques are needed to protect the user's image information in this scenario. One solution of secure face matching is to use homomorphic encryption to upload the collected user images to the cloud for subcryptographic computation and return the results. The private key is used offline to decrypt the user information.

10.4.2 Case Study

Moving back to the user's name-mobile phone number verification service, we want to verify a user's submitted information without compromising the user's privacy, i.e., SNN-name-mobile phone number verification. After the user provides the encrypted information, the service provider will only get a successful or unsuccessful match result and will not see the user's ID number or cell phone number in plain text.

Here, this book provides a very similar solution to the private set intersection technique. Assume that the encryption functions of the bank and the operator are $f(x)$ and $g(y)$, respectively, and that they are designed in such a way that $f(x)$ and $g(y)$ satisfy the exchange encryption, i.e., $f(g(y)) = g(f(x))$ when the data entry $x = y$ in the database.

Suppose the user submits the triad of ID number, name, and phone number as (id, name, phone). Then, after encryption, we get

$$(f(id), f(name), f(phone)).$$

The bank sends this information to the operator, who uses the encryption function g to calculate

$$(g(f(id)), g(f(name)), g(f(phone))).$$

Then, the operator sends the twice-encrypted data back to the bank. At the bank, this ciphertext is compared with the bank's precalculated encrypted database of the operator, and if the comparison is successful, the corresponding user exists, which means that the information submitted by the user is valid, and if it is not, the information submitted by the user is incorrect. In this process, the bank does not know the plaintext of the ID number, name, or cell phone number submitted by the user, but only the corresponding ciphertext to complete the comparison.

10.4.3 Summary

In this subsection, we introduced an example of privacy data query. Compared to the model training scenario of federation learning, privacy data query is characterized by simple computational tasks and is usually done based on statistical methods. In the implementation of privacy-preserving computing, we tend to focus on more complex computational scenarios such as machine learning model training. However, in traditional data cooperation, such as three-factor verification, a large number of computational tasks are relatively simple query tasks and less difficult to implement, while their application scenarios and applications are relatively wide, and the demand for privacy protection is also great. It is very important to deal with this kind of relational query problem well, which will be of great help to the future development and implementation of privacy-preserving computing. From the perspective of privacy security, one of the main problems of joint query applications is to ensure that an attacker cannot use the results of multiple queries to infer privacy information; e.g., if the value of $A + B + C$ is queried for the first time and the value of $A + B + C + D$ is queried for the second time, the value of D can be inferred using the results of both queries. A straightforward solution is to add noise to the data using differential privacy, but the noise has some impact on the query results.

10.5 Genetic Research

Introduction

With the development of genetic testing technology, the cost of gene sequencing is getting lower and lower, which has accumulated a large amount of DNA, RNA, and genotype data. Making good use of this data can bring many benefits to society and human health. For example, we can use genetic testing to detect potential diseases in advance. In the research and application of genetic data, data cooperation is essential, and millions of data samples are needed to predict the genetic predisposition of a complex trait in a statistical sense. However, data privacy in the field of genetics is extremely important. By analyzing the genome sequences of individuals and their families, it is possible to predict the disease risk for individuals. The leakage and abuse of genetic data will lead to the leakage of personal privacy information and cause genetic discrimination in various fields of society such as insurance, employment, and education. Therefore, the safe sharing and analysis of genetic data between different institutions through privacy-preserving technology has become the key feature to enable cooperation between different institutions carrying out genetic research.

Case Study

Here, we take genome-wide association study (GWAS), a commonly used analysis method in the field of genetic research, as an example to discuss the practical method of using private computing to integrate and analyze genetic data in a safe and reliable way.

Genome refers to all the genetic information in an organism including DNA and RNA. A DNA molecule is a macromolecular polymer composed of a series of nucleotides. The DNA nucleotide sequence consists of four types of nucleotides: adenine, cytosine, guanine, and thymine, denoted as A, C, G, and T, respectively. The sequence of these nucleotides in DNA is the carrier of genetic information. Through transcription and translation, cells in organisms can generate corresponding proteins according to specific DNA sequences, thereby showing different individual phenotypic traits. We refer to the basic unit of heredity that controls biological traits as genes. Through the DNA replication mechanism, genes can be passed from one cell to another new cell, and the genetic information carried can be transmitted to the organism's offspring. Therefore, we can often see similar traits between parents and children, such as skin color, hair color, and double eyelids. Finding the relationship between genes and phenotypic traits can help us predict their traits based on gene sequences, and in the future, gene editing technology can be used to treat genetic diseases.

Genome-wide association study (GWAS) refers to a research approach identifying the relationship between genomic variants and phenotypic traits at the genome-wide level. Genome-wide association study analysis can comprehensively reveal the genomic variants related to the occurrence, development, and treatment of diseases by analyzing genome-wide, high-density genetic markers on DNA sequences of a large-scale population. Due to genetic variation, different human individuals exhibit different genotypes and phenotypes. Among them, the most common genetic variation is single-nucleotide polymorphism

(SNP), which mainly refers to the polymorphism of the DNA sequence caused by the variation of a single nucleotide. Single-nucleotide polymorphisms account for approximately 90 percent of known genetic variations.

By analyzing the statistical association between SNPs and phenotypes, GWAS can mine the impact of individual gene loci on phenotypic traits. For example, GWAS can analyze a large number of data samples to find that, when the SNP at a certain locus is changed from adenine A to guanine G, the probability of occurrence of a certain disease is greatly increased. Therefore, it can establish an association between the SNP and occurrence of the disease.

A typical GWAS analysis can be divided into two steps: first, it uses principal components analysis (PCA) to correct for population stratification; then, it uses the principal components of PCA as covariates and employs linear regression, logistic regression, and other models to extract the relationship between SNPs and the population. To validate discovered relationships between gene markers and phenotypes, GWAS uses hypothesis testing to assess the significance of associations in a statistical sense. For example, we can calculate the p-values of tests and extract the associations that have small p-values. Genome-wide association study analysis requires two main conditions: first, the population stratification of the data should be considered and controlled to reduce the influence of irrelevant SNPs; second, in order to mine significant associations between genes and phenotypes, GWAS requires the calculation to be performed on large-scale genetic data to ensure that the phenotype considered has a sufficient number of various genotype samples. At present, many practical applications require millions of DNA samples.

Genetic data is important private data for individuals. Using simple anonymization methods cannot completely resist attacks specifically designed based on genetic data characteristics. Several commonly used attack methods in the field of genetics are as follows:

- Attacks with meta data: In addition to DNA and RNA data, genetic data generally includes height, weight, and other trait information of individuals, which is called meta information. Existing research has shown that using meta information such as gender, age, and surname can map DNA sequence samples to individuals, resulting in genetic data leakage.
- Attack with Y chromosome: for male individuals, attackers can use the Y chromosome for genetic tracking and building a genetic family tree to map anonymous DNA data to specific individuals.
- Attack with genotype: after the attacker obtains the DNA data, he can predict the phenotypic traits of individuals and thus link the DNA data to specific individuals with similar traits.

- Attack with SNPs: studies have shown that we can uniquely identify a person with 75~100 SNPs.

Therefore, when using genetic data, it is necessary to carefully assess the risk of privacy leakage and propose private-preserving solutions. In order to conduct secure GWAS analysis, researchers have tried to use privacy-preserving computing technology to perform principal component analysis of genetic data, conduct multiparty linear modeling, and calculate p-values under the premise of privacy protection. This privacy-preserving solution faces the following two challenges:

- Efficiency: The genetic data sample often has an excessively large number of dimensions, e.g., more than a million. Therefore, the efficiency of privacy-preserving computing becomes a great challenge. Specifically, how to perform private PCA and linear modeling in an acceptable time has become a hard problem.
- Security: The security requirements of genetic data are high. Researchers need to design a solution to ensure the security of genetic data.

In practical implementations, researchers often need to consider the trade-off between efficiency and privacy. At present, the mainstream privacy-preserving computing technologies that can achieve secure and reliable GWAS analysis are based on either secure multiparty computation or homomorphic encryption. Secure multiparty computation is based on garbled circuits, requiring multiparty servers holding their respective genetic data to communicate successively during the analysis process, so it is difficult to put into practical use. Homomorphic encryption allows all parties to encrypt their genetic data for centralized analysis and processing without breaching the privacy of each party's genetic data. However, its ciphertext computational overhead is high and needs to be optimized for the specific computational needs and characteristics of GWAS analysis. In order to explore the potential of homomorphic encryption in GWAS analysis tasks, in 2018, the fifth iDASH secure genome analysis competition was jointly held by the University of California, San Diego, the University of Texas Health Science Center, and Indiana University Bloomington, which aims to use homomorphic encryption to realize efficient and secure GWAS analysis. Among the competitors, research teams from the University of California, San Diego and Duality Technology jointly won first place. Here is a brief introduction to Duality's research team's implementation of GWAS analysis using homomorphic encryption (Blatt et al., 2020a,b).

The overview framework of their scheme for GWAS analysis based on homomorphic encryption is shown in Figure 10.6. First, the participants

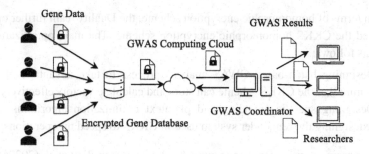

Figure 10.6 GWAS analysis solution based on homomorphic encryption.

obtain the public key from the GWAS coordinator. Each participant encrypts their genetic data held using the public key and sends the encrypted data to the encrypted genetic data bank. The encrypted genetic data bank stores all encrypted personal genetic data from participants. When researchers have new GWAS analysis requirements, initiated by the GWAS coordinator, the encrypted genetic data in the data bank is sent to the homomorphic encryption computing cloud for GWAS analysis and calculation with homomorphic operations. Due to the noninteractive feature of homomorphic encryption, the entire computing process does not require repeated communication with participants. After the analysis is finished, it sends the output in the form of ciphertext to the GWAS coordinator, which then decrypts and sends the GWAS analysis results to the requested researchers.

Current fully homomorphic encryption schemes are inefficient and can hardly support the analysis on large-scale genetic data. In order to solve the problem of high computation overhead of homomorphic encryption, Duality's research team made improvements in two aspects: the GWAS analysis algorithm and the underlying homomorphic encryption scheme. In terms of the analysis algorithm of GWAS, Duality's research team made several approximations of the algorithm of the results as follows:

- Using a relatively simple gradient descent method to update the model parameters of the logistic regression model. The researchers found that the relevant SNPs can be extracted by only one step of descent with sufficient accuracy.
- Using a simple polynomial function (i.e., $0.5 + 0.15625x$) containing only addition and multiplication to approximate the logistic function, thereby reducing the complexity of homomorphic operations while ensuring accuracy performance.
- Delaying the calculation of the p-values to the client side, thereby delaying the complex testing calculation to the plaintext calculation part, which greatly reduces the computational burden on the homomorphic encryption computing cloud.

In terms of homomorphic encryption scheme, the Duality team further optimized the CKKS homomorphic encryption scheme. The main optimizations are as follows:

- Designing batch-based GWAS analysis process to take advantage of the feature that the CKKS scheme can store and calculate vectors effectively.
- Designing specific encoding and plaintext optimization algorithms, and redesigning the remainder system used in CKKS to speed up operations.

For more optimization details, we refer the readers to Blatt et al. (2020a).

Discussion

The preceding genetic analysis case is a typical federated learning scenario where modeling is performed with data held by each party. Possible further optimization solutions include (i) using advanced hardware solutions to accelerate homomorphic operations. For example, Clustar has designed a heterogeneous solution combining FPGA and GPU for the federated learning framework FATE, which significantly improves the calculation speed under the homomorphic ciphertext; (ii) designing new homomorphic encryption algorithms, which is often difficult due to its complex mathematical theory; (iii) using the Trusted Execution Environment (TEE) to protect data against the server. However, its security is guaranteed by hardware, which is difficult to apply in some restricted scenarios.

In this section, we have introduced an application of private computing for federated genetic data. Although the proper use of genetic data brings us many benefits, genetic data analysis often requires a large amount of data, which calls for the cooperative sharing of genetic data between institutions. At the same time, the privacy of genetic data significantly matters in individuals' lives. Thus, data collaboration must be carried out under strict protection of privacy. There are many challenges in privacy-preserving data collaboration in the field of genetics, mainly focusing on efficiency and security level, and these two issues often conflict with each other. Improving the trade-off between efficiency and privacy will open a lot of possibilities to genetic data cooperation and research.

10.6 Pharmaceutical Research

10.6.1 Scenario

Predicting and prioritizing the properties of a great number of compounds is an essential step in the early stages of drug discovery when exploring the design of new drugs. Machine learning can be used in this stage to process large amounts of experimental data and accelerate the analysis of compound properties, such as the compound's affinity for a target and the absorption, distribution, metabolism, excretion (ADME) of this compound. In general, more abundant and higher-quality data results in a better performance of machine learning. In pharmaceutical engineering, increasing the amount of data means more expenditure and more time in experiments. Moreover, several pharmaceutical organizations cannot publish the experimental data before the drug is officially introduced into the market. Therefore, how to solve the problem of data silos among pharmaceutical organizations has become a research priority.

10.6.2 Case Study

Quantitative Structure-Activity Relationship (QSAR) is a classical model in pharmaceutical design. It can be used for modeling and predicting the relationship between the structure and activity of pharmaceutical molecules. There are several attempts in life sciences to share and model biological and pharmaceutical data through classical cryptographic computational means. However, as the regulations (e.g., GDPR in the EU, CCPA in the US) proposed worldwide aim at protecting data privacy and requiring that data cannot be exported locally or across domains, traditional data sharing methods are challenged.

Transversal Federated Learning provides a privacy-preserving computing version of the QSAR process (Chen et al., 2020), enabling the training of models between multiple healthcare organizations without revealing any information. The commonly used QSAR is a two-dimensional quantitative conformational relationship, which takes the overall structural properties of a molecule as parameters and performs a regression analysis on the physiological activity of the molecule to model the correlation between chemical structure and physiological activity. Two major elements are required to form a QSAR, namely activity parameters and structural parameters, and a linear regression model is usually used to establish the mathematical relationship between them. Assuming a multipharmaceutical organization scenario, each organization has a dataset containing different activity and structural parameters, they would like to jointly build the linear regression model to reduce the delay cost. This process can be easily achieved through cross-sectional federation learning, which proceeds as follows.

Each pharmaceutical organization uses its own data for model training. After training, it encrypts the model parameters using secure multiparty computation technology and sends the encrypted results to the service provider.

- The service provider performs secure aggregation of the parameters without obtaining any information about the pharmaceutical organization.
- The service provider returns the aggregation results to each pharmaceutical organization.
- The pharmaceutical organization decrypts the aggregation results and updates the local model.

Experiments on the QSAR process using horizontal federated learning show that the result of multiuser collaborative QSAR modeling with FL-QSAR is significantly better than single-user QSAR modeling using only their private data. With specific model optimization, FL-QSAR can achieve the same or similar results as direct integration of multiuser small molecule data for QSAR modeling while protecting the privacy of pharmaceutical molecule structures. With specific model optimization, FL-QSAR can achieve the same or similar model prediction results as QSAR modeling by directly integrating multi-user molecule data while protecting the privacy of pharmaceutical molecule structures.

10.6.3 Lessons Learned

The privacy-preserving computing technology introduced in this section breaks the barrier of data not being shared directly between different pharmaceutical organizations. It provides an effective solution for collaborative drug discovery, which facilitates collaborative drug discovery under the prerequisite of privacy protection and is suitable for extension and application to other related fields of biomedical privacy-preserving computing.

10.7 Speech Recognition

Backgrounds

Speech recognition technology is an important achievement in the development of modern technology, which enables computers to recognize human speech and convert it into text. Speech recognition technology is also known as Automatic Speech Recognition (ASR), Computer Speech Recognition, or Speech-to-Text (STT). From the technical aspect, with the rapid development of deep learning and big data technologies, the technical path of speech recognition began to gradually develop from the traditional signal processing processes (e.g., filtering and coding) to machine learning processes (e.g., neural networks and deep learning). During the training of the machine learning model, a large amount of user speech data is required to obtain an accurate model. In commercial speech recognition scenarios, in order to ensure the accuracy of speech recognition, users need to provide user speech data to get customized speech recognition models.

However, speech data is extremely sensitive personal private data. Similar to facial information, voice is also immutable and non-impersonal in nature. This means that the leakage of personal voice information would be a permanent and irreversible information leakage. As a result, some data protection laws, such as the EU General Data Protection Regulation (GDPR), mandate that data cannot go out of local or cross-domain. This means that speech recognition models can no longer be trained using traditional methods (i.e., centralized training). Therefore, how to legally use user speech data to implement ASR is a very important topic. Privacy-preserving computing provides a solution to this problem.

Case Study

ASR systems usually contain two important components: Acoustic Model (AM) and Language Model (LM). Acoustic Model is responsible for establishing a one-to-one correlation between speech signals and phonemes, and LM gives a way to search for grammatically correct word sequences. In ASR services, the service provider provides a generic ASR system to the subscriber. This is a typical "centralized" training model, i.e., the user needs to deliver the data to the service provider to retrain the model. Obviously, the user's voice data is accessed by the service provider during this process, and there is a risk of data leakage.

The TFE system provides a secure ASR solution (Jiang et al., 2021), which is illustrated in Figure 10.7. The service provider maintains a set of global ASR models, and users can transform the global ASR models into customized ASR models that meet their needs by transfer learning techniques. The user data is only stored locally and could not be accessed by the service provider, thus protecting user privacy.

To enable service providers to continuously update the global ASR model, the TFE system introduces federation learning and evolutionary learning techniques. When a user computes a customized AM, it is homomorphically encrypted and passed to the service provider, which constructs a pool of customized AMs. Finally, the user gets a customized ASR model and the service provider completes an optimization iteration of the global model, achieving a "win-win" situation.

Summary

The immutable nature of personal biometric information such as face information, voice information, and fingerprint information at this stage means that the

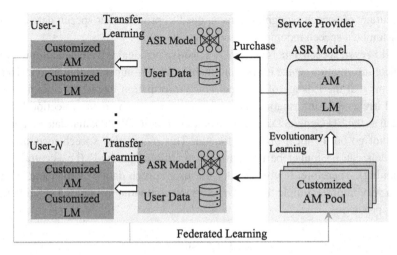

Figure 10.7 System framework of TFE.

processing of biometric information needs to be secured at the technical level. In the field of speech recognition, privacy-preserving computing provides a technical means to protect personal speech data without causing significant loss of speech recognition performance, while taking a key step toward the goal of legal and secure usage of the data.

10.8 Privacy-preserving Computing in Governments

Background

Governments are significant customers of privacy-preserving computing techniques because they possess much sensitive data. With the increasing concerns about privacy protection, the flow of data between different regions is becoming increasingly restricted. Therefore, securing the normal functioning of government affairs on the assumption that sensitive data is safeguarded has become an important topic. Sharing data between government departments helps governments break down data silos, improve data utility, and increase their service capability, resulting in more practical and effective decision-making. Several policies have been published. The State Council of China promulgated the Interim Measures for the Administration of Government Information and Resource Sharing in September 2016 and the Implementation Scheme for Integration and Sharing of Government Information Systems in May 2017, both of which emphasize the need to formulate and improve laws and regulations to ensure that personal privacy is not disclosed or infringed.

```
┌─────────────────────────────────────────────────┐
│  Faculty Profile:                                │
│    ID:                    Name:                  │
│    Gender:                Nationality:           │
│    Birthday:              Birthplace:            │
│    Affiliation:           Affiliation Type:      │
│    Work Address:          Zip Code:              │
│    Job:                   Job Level:             │
│    Qualification:         Mobile Phone:          │
│    Office Phone:          E-mail:                │
│    ID Card Type:          ID Card No.:           │
│    Bank Name:             Bank Account:          │
│    Emergency Contact:     Emergency Number:      │
│    School:                Political Status:      │
└─────────────────────────────────────────────────┘
```

Figure 10.8   A faculty profile sample in education departments.

Case Study

Government data is not only large in quantity, but also consists of various types of data, has high potential value, and contains a great deal of sensitive information. Additionally, every government department has its respective duty. Exchanging data between departments is restricted. Therefore, it is possible to build a secure data sharing platform with the aid of privacy-preserving computing techniques to realize the multidepartment applications of private data and improve government efficiency.

In reality, it is feasible that one department A needs data owned by another department B. For example, in order to avoid tax evasion, the revenue department may require statistics from the real estate department possessing citizens' real estate and basic information such as names, ages, and housing situations for tax regulation. Apparently, the real estate department's data contains sensitive information. Sending it to the revenue department directly runs the danger of leaking raw data during transmission. Another scenario is when departments at different levels need to share data. For example, a county education department owns all faculty information in the county, including education experience, annual incomes, and families, which can be used for faculty evaluation. The information is accessible to municipal and provincial education departments but not to others. Figure 10.8 illustrates a faculty profile sample.

As discussed earlier, using the aforementioned privacy-preserving computing techniques to solve a series of problems, such as sharing data between government departments or regions, has become a new trend today.

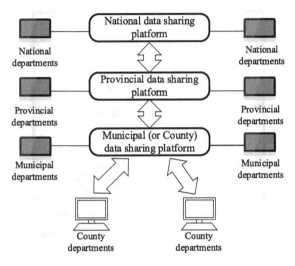

Figure 10.9   Architecture of a government big data open sharing platform.

Modeling Government Data Sharing System Based on Privacy-preserving Computing Techniques

The problem to be solved in this case is transferring data between government departments through government data sharing platforms. The transmission of government data poses a risk of privacy leakage. Therefore, to achieve business coordination between multiple departments, it is necessary to develop privacy protection schemes according to the architecture of different platforms. Government data sharing platforms follow the architecture of multilevel platforms and multilevel data sharing. The multilevel platforms include national, provincial, and municipal (or county) department platforms. The multilevel data sharing includes national, provincial, and municipal (or county) data sharing, as shown in Figure 10.9.

In the following, we introduce two privacy-preserving computing schemes according to the government data sharing architecture shown in Figure 10.9.

Government data sharing scheme based on local DP. Figure 10.10 shows the process of data sharing using local DP algorithms.

$$
B'_{ij} = \begin{cases} 1 & \text{with probability } \frac{f}{2}, \\ 0 & \text{with probability } \frac{f}{2}, \\ B_{ij} & \text{with probability } \frac{f}{2}, \end{cases} \tag{10.11}
$$

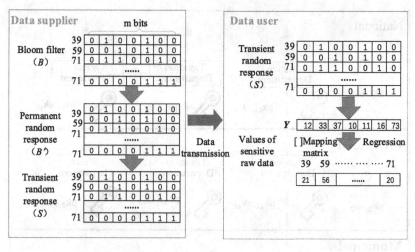

Figure 10.10 Process of sharing data based on local DP algorithms.

$$P(S_{ij} = 1) = \begin{cases} p & B'_{ij} = 0, \\ 0 & B'_{ij} = 1. \end{cases} \qquad (10.12)$$

The procedures for a data supplier are as follows:

- Use a Bloom filter to represent the value of a sensitive attribute a in each sharing record as a m-bit binary vector. All vectors are packed into a binary matrix B after the values of a in all records are processed.
- A new binary matrix B' is constructed by flipping each bit $B_{ij}(0 \le j \le m)$ of matrix B randomly with the equation specified in Eq. (10.11).
- For a given two-dimensional array $S_{n \times m}$, where n and m are the numbers of records and the length of a record, respectively, each bit is initialized to 0, and then S is flipped according to the rule defined in Eq. (10.12) to obtain a result set. Note that $p, q \in [0, 1]$.
- Send S the number of hash functions in the Bloom filter (k), the number of bits in the result set (m), and the candidate set composed of all possible values of the sensitive attribute (F) to the departments requesting the data.

The steps for a data user are as follow:

- Count the number of 1s in S and save it in a vector y.
- Input the candidate set F and parameters k and m to the Bloom filter and the MD5 algorithm to calculate a relation mapping matrix X.

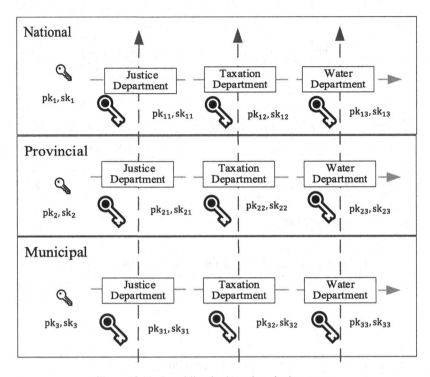

Figure 10.11   A multilevel privacy key sharing system.

- Input X and y to a regression algorithm such as Lasso to calculate the occurrence frequencies of attribute a's values.
- Output the statistics.

The privacy process is randomized by data owners and the background knowledge of the attackers is considered. Therefore, the scheme can resist attacks with any background knowledge and prevent potential intruders from knowing the precise information about the sensitive attributes of their targets so that citizens' privacy is well protected.

Government data sharing scheme based on multilevel privacy key systems. In some government platforms, the following requirements should be satisfied in data sharing:

- Data owned by different departments at the same level supports partial sharing.
- When sharing data owned by the same departments at different levels, the departments at a higher level have access to the data held by the departments at a lower level. The data transferred between multiple levels supports partial sharing.

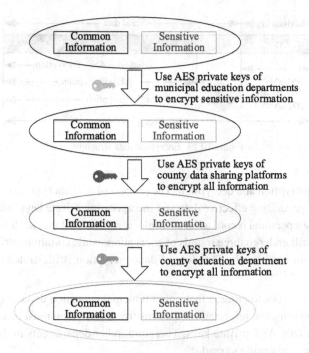

Figure 10.12 Flow of data encryption.

- Data owned by different departments at different levels supports partial sharing. It is necessary to transfer data between different departments securely and assign different data access privileges for different departments. Therefore, we need to develop a private key system with a high security level to meet the preceding requirements. Figure 10.11 shows a data sharing system based on multilevel private keys.

By setting department-level private keys, the requirement of sharing partial data between different departments and the same departments at different levels is satisfied. Platform-level private keys are primarily used to share data between departments at different levels. For some special cases such as sharing data between departments at different levels and types, two types of private keys can be used in combination. Furthermore, a multilevel private key sharing system follows two rules: the platform-level private keys are shared horizontally between the departments in the platform; the department-level private keys are shared from the bottom up inside the department. Meanwhile, adopting a combination of RSA and AES as the core encryption algorithm in such a system can solve the problem of high time consumption caused by using only

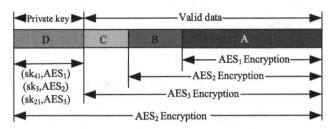

Figure 10.13 Encrypted data structure.

RSA for encryption and decryption. The process of data encryption is split into two parts: generating effective data and incorporating private keys into it. Take encrypting a personal record as an example: sensitive attributes such as account numbers will undergo three rounds of encryption, while common attributes are encrypted in two rounds. The flow of data encryption is illustrated in Figure 10.12.

- Step 1: In order to enforce that only municipal education departments have access to sensitive information, the sensitive information must be encrypted by their own AES private keys. Therefore, other departments in the county platforms are unable to read it.
- Step 2: All information is encrypted using the AES private keys of county platforms. Other county departments can obtain common information by decrypting the information with their platform-level private keys.
- Step 3: All information is encrypted using the AES private keys of county education departments.
- Step 4: The proportions incorporated with private keys include the AES private keys of municipal and county education departments encrypted by the corresponding RSA public keys and the AES private keys of county departments encrypted by the RSA private keys of county education departments, which are arranged in their decryption order. The encrypted data structure is displayed in Figure 10.13.

Effect of Different Schemes

Effect of Differential Privacy

As shown in Figure 10.14, raw data is different from the data processed by DP. However, the two types of data are consistent in their overall variation trends. Therefore, when a department needs to use the histogram data to aid in the decision-making for public services or performing regulatory obligations to study specific variation trends, a local DP technique can be adopted

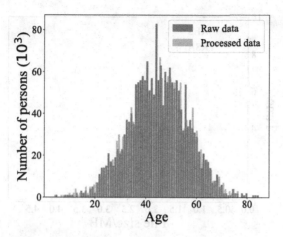

Figure 10.14 Histogram of local DP data and raw data.

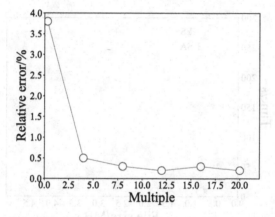

Figure 10.15 Variation of the relative error with different data scales.

to obtain data with high usability, although it bears accuracy loss. Meanwhile, the scheme is sensitive to data scale. As shown in Figure 10.15, the relative error decreases after executing privacy protection on sensitive data, revealing that data usability is determined by its scale in local DP.

Effect of Multilevel Private Keys

The multilevel private key scheme focuses on improving the effectiveness of government data sharing platforms. Figure 10.16 and Figure 10.17 show the results of comparing a hybrid encryption method based on RSA and AES with a singular encryption method based on RSA. The time spent on processing private keys is negligible because RSA is used only in the generation of

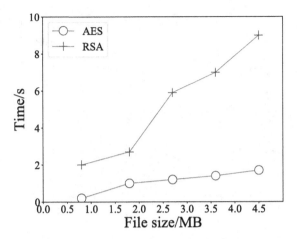

Figure 10.16 Encryption time with varying file sizes.

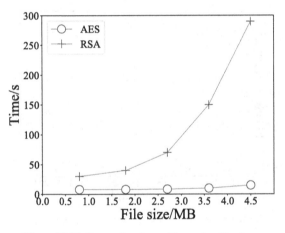

Figure 10.17 Decryption time with varying file sizes.

private keys in the hybrid encryption method and the effective information is significantly more than the private keys. Therefore, it is actually a comparison between AES and RSA. As shown in the figures, the efficiency of the hybrid encryption method is substantially higher than that of the singular one.

10.9 User Data Statistics

Large corporations such as Google, Apple, and Microsoft often need to understand how users behave on their devices. For example, Google and Apple, as the core developers of smartphone operating systems Android and iOS, need data regarding how users use their phones to optimize system performances. For example, applications that need to stay in memory (such as instant messaging) should be optimized in terms of memory cost. However, how users operate their devices often reveals private information about the users. It is thus important for large corporations to obtain accurate statistics on user behaviors while maintaining the data privacy of individual users. In this section, we study three examples by Google, Apple, and Microsoft to see how differential privacy is used in real-world applications of user statistics.

10.9.1 Google RAPPOR

Randomized Aggregatable Privacy-Preserving Ordinal Response, abbreviated RAPPOR (Erlingsson et al., 2014), is the system that Google uses to aggregate browser history and setups, and to perform statistical analysis. It is among the first deployments of DP by large corporations. The implementation of RAPPOR follows the same intuition as the Randomized Response, but with more delicate designs.

Without loss of generality, we consider a simplified problem similar to the randomized response. Suppose each user $i \in \{1, \ldots, n\}$ owns a private message $x_i \in \{0, 1\}$, and the task is to estimate the frequency of 1. This is a significantly simplified problem setting, and a few explanations would be needed to show that it is indeed general.

- First, $x_i \in \{0, 1\}$ works for binary statistics. As in the case of randomized response, $x_i = 1$ means cheating and vice versa.
- Second, any categorical statistics with C classes can be encoded using $\log C$ bits of x_i. Thus, by extending $x_i \in \{0, 1\}^k$, we can support arbitrary statistics with categorical answers.
- Finally, in practice, we can use hash functions to map arbitrary domains into 0-1 bits. For example, in RAPPOR, Bloom filters are used to transform strings into 0-1 bits. A Bloom filter can be viewed as a set of h independent hash functions, each of which maps a string to a 0-1 bit. Thus, we can map a string to $x_i \in \{0, 1\}^h$.

The problem seems already solved. Why not directly leverage the randomized response algorithm? The answer is that large corporations like Google do not stop after one query. Rather, the same queries may be repeated every day, or even every hour. Recall the composition theorem of DP: if a randomized response provides ε-LDP, then after 100 queries, the randomized response provides 100ε-LDP, which is often too big to claim any privacy protection. This should be intuitive: let $\varepsilon = \ln 3 \approx 1.1$, then 100ε-LDP means that $\forall D_1, D_2 \in \mathcal{X}$, $\Pr[\mathcal{A}(D_1) \in Y] \leq \exp(110) \Pr[\mathcal{A}(D_2) \in Y]$, and $\exp(110)$ is very large.

More concretely, let us consider the randomized response, with $\Pr[y_i = 1 | x_i = 1] = 3/4$. Suppose we repeat the query 100 times and find out that the student answers $y_i = 1$ 75 times. In this case, we are almost certain that $x_i = 1$, in that this would occur with probability 1.39×10^{-24} if $x_i = 0$. We thus conclude that randomized response alone cannot protect privacy under repetitive queries in the long term.

To address the issue, one naive way is to generate a randomized response only once and use the same randomized response for all future queries. Such a technique is referred to as *memoization*. By doing so, all future responses carry no additional information, and the only leakage happens in the first response. Again, the problem seems solved. However, this comes with two other issues. The first issue is that the mechanism is not foolproof, as the corporation can design new phrases for the same question that may elicit new randomized responses. The second issue is that, as responses from each user are fixed, the bit strings essentially become a quasi-identifier of users. To understand this issue, consider a randomized response with 128 bits, where it is extremely rare for different users to collide on the same response. Moreover, the strings never change. Thus, it is credible to identify users based on the fixed randomized response. This does not compromise differential privacy, but it may pose threats in certain real-world scenarios, e.g., bias and discrimination.

Based on these intuitions, Google designed RAPPOR, whose key idea is a bilevel randomized response. First, given $x_i \in \{0, 1\}^k$, a permanent randomized response $\hat{x}_i$ is generated by applying randomized response bit-wise, which is fixed afterwards. Then, whenever queried, the user returns an instant randomized response of $\hat{x}_i$. With the bilevel randomized response, we observe two advantages. First, it eliminates the "quasi-identifier" issue, as the response is different upon each query. Second, the instant randomized response strengthens the privacy guarantee when a limited number of queries are performed, while the permanent randomized response serves as a bottom line upon an infinite number of queries. An illustration of how RAPPOR works is shown in Figure 10.18.

One final step is needed. After the responses are collected, they should be interpreted back to meaningful user statistics. Here we omit the details of this step. Interested readers are referred to Erlingsson et al. (2014).

There is one case that cannot be handled by RAPPOR. Let us consider a case where x_i differs slightly with time, such as the user's exact age. In this case, we fail to obtain a permanent randomized response, and thus RAPPOR fails. We will discuss this issue in the application of Microsoft later.

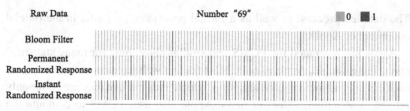

Raw Data   Number *"69"*   ■0 ■1

Bloom Filter

Permanent
Randomized Response

Instant
Randomized Response

Bits in the Bloom Filter

Figure 10.18 Illustration of RAPPOR with bilevel randomized responses. Figure adapted from Erlingsson et al. (2014).

Google performs user statistics extensively with RAPPOR. Characteristic examples include execution patterns of processes on Windows, default homepages of Chrome, and how many times default homepages are modified by malicious software. RAPPOR is open-sourced at https://github.com/google/rappor.

10.9.2 Differential Privacy in Apple

Apple is another major advocate of differential privacy. In this section, we introduce how Apple leverages DP to design algorithms for practical tasks.

Apple applies DP in scenarios similar to Google, i.e., analyzing the frequency of data, such as the frequency of users using emojis and browsing web pages. We introduce an algorithm used by Apple, called the *Private Count Mean Sketch (PCMS)*. Similar to the Bloom filter in RAPPOR, Count Mean Sketch can also be viewed as hash functions. We briefly illustrate the process of Private Count Mean Sketch as follows.

- Suppose a user visits a domain http://xyz.com. The client-side algorithm will sample a hash function h_j from a set of candidates $\{h_i\}_{i=1}^n$. Let $h_j(\text{http}://\text{xyz.com}) = 73$; then the visiting record is transformed into a one-hot vector $\mathbf{v} \in \{0, 1\}^m$ with $\mathbf{v}_{73} = 1$. Before sending $\mathbf{v}$ to the server, v is randomly flipped bit-wise (similar to a randomized response) to obtain $\tilde{\mathbf{v}}$ as an LDP version of $\mathbf{v}$.
- The server constructs a matrix $\mathbf{M} \in \mathbb{R}_+^{n \times m}$, with each row corresponding to a hash function, and each column corresponding to each bit of $\mathbf{v}$.
- The server adds $\tilde{\mathbf{v}}$ to $\mathbf{M}_j$, where j is the sampled hash function.
- After collecting sufficient data records, the server can obtain an unbiased estimate of the count of visiting http://xyz.com via

$$\frac{1}{n} \sum_{i=1}^{n} \mathbf{M}_{i,h_i(\text{http}://\text{xyz.com})}. \tag{10.13}$$

The detailed process, as well as a formal proof, can be found in the official document of Apple.[1]

Apple has leveraged the PCMS and similar algorithms for many statistical tasks. For example, Apple uses PCMS to detect web pages in Safari that cause high energy and memory consumption, which finds out that they are commonly related to shopping, video, or news. Apple also uses PCMS to compute the frequency of emojis used by users in different languages. The estimated emoji frequencies will be used to provide personalized emoji recommendations to devices from different locations (Apple, 2017).

10.9.3 Differential Privacy in Microsoft

Microsoft is the core developer of Windows, a PC operating system used by most people throughout the globe. Thus, Microsoft may also need to obtain statistics on user behaviors, such as the amount of time users spend on different softwares. Ding et al. (2017) describes a solution proposed by Microsoft.

We consider the problem of computing average under LDP. Suppose each user $i \in \{1, \ldots, n\}$ has a real number $x_i \in [0, m]$, we would like to compute $\mu = \frac{1}{n} \sum_{i=1}^{n} x_i$ while satisfying LDP. As this is a problem with continuous range, we can leverage the Laplace mechanism to solve the problem. Formally, since each piece of data has L_1-sensitivity m,

$$\hat{\mu} = \frac{1}{n} \sum_{i=1}^{n} (x_i + y_i), y_i \sim \text{Lap}(m/\varepsilon) \tag{10.14}$$

will lead to an ε-LDP estimate of μ. However, the downside of this method is that every $x_i + y_i$ requires $\Omega(\log m)$ bits to transfer, while in practice, with x_i denoting the amount of time a user spends on a software, most x_i should be very small. Thus, $\Omega(\log m)$ bits leads to low communication efficiency.

To address the problem, Ding et al. (2017) proposes a 1-bit communication method to solve the problem. Formally, each user only needs to transmit

$$z_i = \begin{cases} 1, \text{with probability } \frac{1}{\exp(\varepsilon)+1} + \frac{x_i}{m} \frac{\exp(\varepsilon)-1}{\exp(\varepsilon)+1}, \\ 0, \text{otherwise} \end{cases} \tag{10.15}$$

and the mean is estimated via

$$\hat{\mu} = \frac{m}{n} \sum_{i=1}^{n} \frac{z_i(\exp(\varepsilon) + 1) - 1}{\exp(\varepsilon) - 1}. \tag{10.16}$$

---

[1] https://tinyurl.com/2vjvbh5v.

Indeed, $\hat{\mu}$ is unbiased:

$$\mathbb{E}[\hat{\mu}] = \frac{m}{n} \sum_{i=1}^{n} \frac{\mathbb{E}[z_i](\exp(\varepsilon) + 1) - 1}{\exp(\varepsilon) - 1}$$

$$= \frac{m}{n} \sum_{i=1}^{n} \frac{\left(\frac{1}{\exp(\varepsilon)+1} + \frac{x_i}{m} \cdot \frac{\exp(\varepsilon)-1}{\exp(\varepsilon)+1}\right) \cdot (\exp(\varepsilon) + 1) - 1}{\exp(\varepsilon) - 1} \quad (10.17)$$

$$= \frac{1}{n} \sum_{i=1}^{n} x_i.$$

Also, $\hat{\mu}$ is ε-LDP. To show that, consider $x, x' \in [0, m]$:

$$\frac{\Pr[y_i = 1|x_i]}{\Pr[y' = 1|x']} = \frac{\frac{1}{\exp(\varepsilon)+1} + \frac{x_i}{m}\frac{\exp(\varepsilon)-1}{\exp(\varepsilon)+1}}{\frac{1}{\exp(\varepsilon)+1} + \frac{x'}{m}\frac{\exp(\varepsilon)-1}{\exp(\varepsilon)+1}}$$

$$= \frac{m + x_i(\exp(\varepsilon) - 1)}{m + x'(\exp(\varepsilon) - 1)} \quad (10.18)$$

$$\leq \frac{m + m\exp(\varepsilon) - m}{m}$$

$$= \exp(\varepsilon).$$

Consequently, the algorithm is communicationally efficient while being unbiased and ε-LDP.

Another contribution the paper makes is how to support memoization (i.e., permanent randomized response) in the case where x_i differs slightly upon each query, which is not supported by RAPPOR. Ding et al. (2017) propose a randomized rounding solution, such that memoization can also be used for slightly changing x_i. We will briefly discuss the method.

One intuitive solution is to divide the range $[0, m]$ into bins, and let each user report the bin centroid. Intuitively, each x_i should fall close to a bin centroid. In this way, if x_i changes slightly, it falls within the same bin with high probability, and thus we can reuse the memoization. However, it is hard to adequately discretize the range. If we divide too finely, we would change the memoization frequently. If we divide too coarsely, we would suffer from high error.

We explain how Ding et al. (2017) solve the problem using an instantiation. Before the process starts, each user i runs the 1-bit algorithm in Equation 10.15 for 0 and m and memoizes both values. We denote the values $A_i(0)$ and $A_i(m)$ respectively. It also samples $z_i \sim \text{Uniform}[0, m]$ as an offset. For following queries, if $x_i + z_i > m$, user i returns $A_i(m)$, and vice versa. Surprisingly though, Ding et al. (2017) show that this memoization method provides the same accuracy as the 1-bit algorithm in Equation 10.15 and does not degrade under repetitive queries.

From the three cases introduced in this section, we make the following observations:

- Differentially private algorithms can support a very wide range of tasks. Specifically, major corporations such as Google, Apple, and Microsoft have all adopted DP in collecting user statistics. The popularity of DP should be attributed to its flexibility and efficiency, which is especially important in large-scale real-world applications.
- Complex DP algorithms are all built upon fundamental building blocks such as the randomized response and the Laplace mechanism. Thus, when we analyze real-world DP algorithms, we should always start by decomposing the algorithm and identifying the fundamental building blocks.
- Practical challenges also arise when we apply DP to real-world, large-scale applications, such as repetitive querying in RAPPOR and unnecessary communication in Ding et al. (2017). Thus, the fundamental building blocks should be adequately leveraged and redesigned to address the practical challenges in real-world deployments.

11

Future of Privacy-preserving Computing

In this chapter, we discuss the application scenarios and research orientations of privacy-preserving computing. These are heterogeneous computing, security of computing, interpretability of computing algorithms, and so on.

As we all know, every significant advancement of computing technology, including the rapid development of AI, is inextricably linked to the support of the design of new algorithms, the power of deep learning and reinforcement learning, and the architecture of chips. Meanwhile, Big Data is another vital factor that we can never neglect. Without Big Data, AI would be stuck, like an automobile without fuel or batteries.

An important driving force behind privacy-preserving computing is data's IP right assessment and protection, that is, ensuring the fairness of data when it is treated as a production factor in our social lives. The topic about the fairness of digital society is itself an important issue to address because the human understanding of fairness is influenced by time and geography. Another concern about fairness is the availability and usability of data. If we cooperate with other people by sharing mutual data, we usually hope that the data can be used for global modeling while it remains private, that is, data's IP right can be assessed, as opposed to being reduced significantly after its first use.

Why is data's IP right assessment so important? Consider a scenario in which a person goes out for a whole day with his mobile phone at hand. The phone collects a large amount of data that seems to be useless to the person. However, it is valuable for a mobile phone company because it can be used to investigate people's interests to make further analysis and judgment. Therefore, data ownership becomes extremely crucial. While the blockchain technology can be of help, blockchain itself is not designed for modeling. Once data is sent out by copying, transferring, or utilizing, people lose all control over it. The major distinction between data and oil resources is that oil cannot be reproduced or duplicated. Nobody can make two barrels of oil out of one. However, one can easily make two copies of data out of one copy. Meanwhile, the users' privacy hidden in data imposes new constraints on the analysis and modeling of data, that is, data analysis and modeling must maximize data value under the constraint of protecting user privacy.

In the future, data trading will evolve into data value trading, triggering a new service called Data Exchange. In the past, when talking about data trading, we usually imagined a trader carrying a CD and exchanging it for cash. However, this kind of direct trading often violates the data privacy laws and cannot be carried out easily today. The current trend is to exchange data value and cooperation.

In the meantime, preserving a data market's fairness requires us to resist data's Matthew effect, which makes data-rich companies richer and data-poor companies poorer. As we all know, the most critical difference between small and big data is not their quantity but how much work they can do. Big data produces big models, and big models produce more effective services, which attract more people to join. The inclusion of more people subsequently produces more data. As a result, the Matthew effect of big data appears. Therefore, if the Matthew effect is not limited, small data will disappear and big data will monopolize a market, leading to an unhealthy digital society.

What can we do to counteract data's Matthew effect? From the perspective of legislation and politics, governments can promulgate digital antimonopoly laws. However, from the technology perspective, is it possible for us to design new technical models to defeat the Matthew effect? We believe that the anti-Matthew effect and anti-trust technologies form a Federated Ecology.

From the part of federated learning, data is distributed among different users in different locations and is heterogeneous. Is it feasible to effectively aggregate it into big data? The process has grown increasingly difficult due to legal limitations. For example, the regulations of European Union's General Data Protection Regulation (GDPR) are radical and stringent. Chinese laws about data security and privacy have also become more and more stringent. The restrictions and coverage of related laws will continue to expand in the future.

Since 1995, China's domestic laws and regulations about data have become more and more mature and comprehensive. A series of laws have been promulgated to protect people's privacy, such as Personal Information Security Specification, Data Security Law of the People's Republic of China (Draft), and Personal Information Protection Law of the People's Republic of China. The general direction of these laws, which is also the ultimate goal of privacy-preserving computing, is to protect the rights and interests of data owners and the legal usage of data.

There are three key directions in which privacy-preserving computing is developing. The first direction is secure multiparty computing, which has been developing since the 1970s. It is mathematically rigorous but inefficient in handling large models with thousands of billions of parameters. The second direction is solving problems by hardware, which is a mainstream in industry. Intel has its advantage in trusted execution environments such as secret warehouse. The third direction is federated learning, which is specifically proposed for distributed machine learning and designed for large-scale approximate computing. It is particularly suitable for the application scenarios of high concurrency and big data training and inferring.

Before 2018, theories represented by secure multiparty computing exerted great influence on the field of privacy-preserving computing in the academic world because they had complete theoretical systems. Since 2018, federated learning has entered people's vision and been integrated into real-world scenarios. Federated learning seeks cooperation between multiple data sources to build enhanced models and searches for optimal solutions while maintaining data security. Starting from federated learning techniques, a federated ecosystem has come into being. In 2019, the first open-source industrial federated learning framework in the world, namely FATE, was published, which has grown increasingly popular and has been applied in more than one thousand universities and enterprises.

There are two types of federated learning architectures. One is to partition data samples horizontally, which is suitable for one-to-many applications. For example, a big company can update the models stored in its tremendous edge terminals with a big server. The other is to foster collaboration between different institutions, also known as to-B. The communications between institutions can be encrypted to boost the growth of their local models so that the unified models can be put into practice. There exist some cross disciplines in the field of privacy-preserving computing. For example, the subject of how to achieve security compliance has close relation with legislation. Another subject is how to defend against attacks on data privacy. We cannot assume that every participant is a good man, half a good man, a bad man, or half of a bad man. A lot of research has been conducted on these subjects.

Privacy-preserving computing needs to set up a coalition mechanism for the cooperation of application and technology. The coalition mechanism refers to the design of a good economic model that allows different data owners (data islands) to profit by joining the coalition maximizing his profit through rational choices. As can be seen, an equitable coalition will grow in size while a selfish coalition will shrink, resulting in the formation of a market mechanism.

Suppose there are two institutions, each of which has its own privacy-preserving computing system. Can they cooperate to create a larger federated learning system? We can imagine a future digital society in a hierarchical form which includes the collaboration between small communities at the bottom and collaboration between communities at different levels. A number of research topics will emerge from the imagination, such as how to communicate between heterogeneous privacy-preserving computing systems.

On the problem of privacy-preserving computing on heterogeneous architecture, the AI groups of Fudata Technology and WeBank have realized the interconnection and communication between heterogeneous federated learning frameworks for the first time in 2021, which breaks the limitation of Privacy-preserving Computing on a single platform. Different enterprises can exchange their data based on common standards and the data pools available to each participant will be expanded, unleashing more data value and speeding up the digital upgrade of the industry. The Institute of Electrical and Electronics Engineers (IEEE) officially promulgated an international federated learning technology standard in March 2021, which is the first international federated learning standard that facilitates the communication between different federated learning systems.

How to combine humans and machines effectively is an essential topic in privacy-preserving computing. In the privacy-preserving computing network architecture, some entities are computers, others are robots that can be imagined as real persons. We can teach computers to learn the value preferences and instill human social values into machines (Hoffman et al., 2018).

A key direction in the future of privacy-preserving computing is automatic federated learning. Assume that a company or a person is unfamiliar with federated learning or machine learning. We can bestow automatic federated learning techniques on federated learning to form Auto FL (Bonawitz et al., 2019), resulting in the automatic learning and growing of federated learning mechanisms. In this manner, the shortage of federated learning engineers will no longer be a barrier to the advancement of federated learning techniques.

The security of privacy-preserving computing is an important topic. Privacy-preserving computing requires the involvement of multiple participants. Some of them may be semihonest, in the sense that they may snoop on the data they received or even poison it to affect the direction of global computation or global model training. For example, dishonest participants can gather the gradients transferred by other participants to guess their models and data. They can even deliberately upload incorrect model parameters in horizontal federated learning to damage the global computation. Detecting such behaviors and devising techniques to counteract them is an important topic in privacy-preserving computing.

The interpretability of privacy-preserving computing algorithms is another key direction. The reasoning process of privacy-preserving computing algorithms turns result retrieving into a black box. A question for each participant is: someone does not understand why they reach a conclusion. For example, a patient will often ask why he is diagnosed with a severe disease by an AI medical system. Similarly, in the scenario of privacy-preserving computing, a system has to automatically answer the question of how it arrives at a conclusion on the assumption of not disclosing patients' privacy. The problem is a critical research topic in the scenario of AI modeling at a single data center. In the future, we anticipate that it will also be an important topic in the scenario of multiple data centers.

In privacy-preserving computing, varying degrees of audit are required to track the effect of data usage, the contribution of collaboration, the assignment of incentives, and so on. The system should have various auditing functions such as transparency, untamperability and trackability. In this direction, the combination of privacy-preserving computing and blockchain may be a possible choice.

Finally, in practice, how to increase the efficiency of privacy-preserving computing will be a key challenge that determines the development speed of the industry and the modularization of secure data circulation. Privacy-preserving computing needs to incorporate different encryption algorithms and security protocols that demand massive computing powers (for computation and communication). For example, secure multiparty computation brings tremendous communication overhead, therefore runs one million times slower than plaintext computing. The fundamental techniques of federated learning (such as homomorphic encryption) also suffer from the problems of high computation and communication overhead. Therefore, the research on high-performance privacy-preserving computing, such as increasing transmission efficiency through network communication optimization and speeding up computation through the use of heterogeneous computing hardware and ASIC chips, will be an important direction in the future.

References

Abadi, Martin, Chu, Andy, Goodfellow, Ian et al. 2016. Deep learning with differential privacy. Pages 308–318 of *Proceedings of the 2016 ACM SIGSAC Conference on Computer and Communications Security.* Association for Computing Machinery.

Acar, Abbas, Aksu, Hidayet, Uluagac, A. Selcuk, and Conti, Mauro. 2018. A survey on homomorphic encryption schemes: theory and implementation. *ACM Comput. Surv.,* **51**(4).

Apple, Differential Privacy Team. 2017. *Learning with Privacy at Scale.* https:// machinelearning.apple.com/research/learning-with-privacy-at-scale.

Baidu. 2020a. *Federated Deep Learning in PaddlePaddle.* https://github.com/Paddle Paddle/PaddleFL.

Baidu. 2020b. *PaddlePaddle.* www.paddlepaddle.org.cn/.

Bailleu, Maurice, Thalheim, Jörg, Bhatotia, Pramod et al. 2019. SPEICHER: securing LSM-based key-value stores using shielded execution. Pages 173–190 of *17th USENIX Conference on File and Storage Technologies (FAST 19).* USENIX Association.

Beaver, Donald, Micali, Silvio, and Rogaway, Phillip. 1990. The round complexity of secure protocols. Pages 503–513 of *Proceedings of the Twenty-Second Annual ACM Symposium on Theory of Computing* edited by H. Ortiz. Association for Computing Machinery.

Beaver, Donald. 1991. Efficient multiparty protocols using circuit randomization. Pages 420–432 of *Annual International Cryptology Conference.* Lecture Notes in Computer Science, vol. 576. Springer.

Beaver, Donald. 1995. Precomputing oblivious transfer. Pages 97–109 of *Advances in Cryptology – CRYPTO' 95.* Lecture Notes in Computer Science, vol. 963. Springer.

Beimel, Amos. 2011. Secret-sharing schemes: a survey. Pages 11–46 of *International Conference on Coding and Cryptology.* Lecture Notes in Computer Science, vol. 6639. Springer.

Beimel, Amos, and Chor, Benny. 1994. Universally ideal secret-sharing schemes. *IEEE Transactions on Information Theory,* **40**(3), 786–794.

Bellare, Mihir, and Rogaway, Phillip. 2007. Robust computational secret sharing and a unified account of classical secret-sharing goals. Pages 172–184 of *Proceedings of the 14th ACM Conference on Computer and Communications Security.* Association for Computing Machinery.

Ben-David, Assaf, Nisan, Noam, and Pinkas, Benny. 2008. FairplayMP: a system for secure multi-party computation. Pages 257–266 of *Proceedings of the 15th ACM Conference on Computer and Communications Security.* Association for Computing Machinery.

Benaloh, Josh. 1994. Dense probabilistic encryption. Pages 120–128 of *Proceedings of the Workshop on Selected Areas of Cryptography,* edited by B. Preneel and S. Tavares. Association for Computing Machinery.

Benaloh, Josh, and Leichter, Jerry. 1988. Generalized secret sharing and monotone functions. Pages 27–35 of *Conference on the Theory and Application of Cryptography.* Lecture Notes in Computer Science, vol. 403. Springer.

Benaloh, Josh Cohen. 1986. Secret sharing homomorphisms: keeping shares of a secret secret. Pages 251–260 of *Conference on the Theory and Application of Cryptographic Techniques.* Lecture Notes in Computer Science, vol. 263. Springer.

Biondo, Andrea, Conti, Mauro, Davi, Lucas, Frassetto, Tommaso, and Sadeghi, Ahmad-Reza. 2018. The guard's dilemma: efficient code-reuse attacks against Intel SGX. Pages 1213–1227 of *27th USENIX Security Symposium (USENIX Security 18).* USENIX Association.

Blakley, George Robert. 1979. Safeguarding cryptographic keys. Pages 313–318 of *Managing Requirements Knowledge, International Workshop on Managing Requirements Knowledge (MARK).* IEEE Computer Society.

Blatt, Marcelo, Gusev, Alexander, Polyakov, Yuriy, Rohloff, Kurt, and Vaikuntanathan, Vinod. 2020a. Optimized homomorphic encryption solution for secure genome-wide association studies. *BMC Medical Genomics,* **13**(7), 1–13.

Blatt, Marcelo, Gusev, Alexander, Polyakov, Yuriy, and Goldwasser, Shafi. 2020b. Secure large-scale genome-wide association studies using homomorphic encryption. *Proceedings of the National Academy of Sciences,* **117**(21), 11608–11613.

Blundo, Carlo, De Santis, Alfredo, De Simone, Roberto, and Vaccaro, Ugo. 1997. Tight bounds on the information rate of secret sharing schemes. *Designs, Codes and Cryptography,* **11**(2), 107–110.

Blundo, Carlo, De Santis, Alfredo, and Vaccaro, Ugo. 1998. On secret sharing schemes. *Information Processing Letters,* **65**(1), 25–32.

Boemer, Fabian, Costache, Anamaria, Cammarota, Rosario, and Wierzynski, Casimir. 2019. nGraph-HE2: a high-throughput framework for neural network inference on encrypted data. Pages 45–56 of *Proceedings of the 7th ACM Workshop on Encrypted Computing & Applied Homomorphic Cryptography.* Association for Computing Machinery.

Bogdanov, Dan, Laur, Sven, and Willemson, Jan. 2008. Sharemind: a framework for fast privacy-preserving computations. Pages 192–206 of *Computer Security – ESORICS 2008.* Lecture Notes in Computer Science, vol. 5283. Springer.

Bonawitz, Keith, Eichner, Hubert, Grieskamp, Wolfgang et al. 2019. Towards federated learning at scale: system design. *Proceedings of Machine Learning and Systems,* **1**, 374–388.

Bonawitz, Keith, Ivanov, Vladimir, Kreuter, Ben et al. 2017. Practical secure aggregation for privacy-preserving machine learning. Pages 1175–1191 of *Proceedings of the 2017 ACM SIGSAC Conference on Computer and Communications Security,* edited by B. M. Thuraisingham, D. Evans, T. Malkin, and D. Xu. Association for Computing Machinery.

Boneh, Dan, Gentry, Craig, Halevi, Shai, Wang, Frank, and Wu, David J. 2013. Private database queries using somewhat homomorphic encryption. Pages 102–118 of *International Conference on Applied Cryptography and Network Security*. Lecture Notes in Computer Science, vol. 7954. Springer.

Boneh, Dan, Goh, Eu-Jin, and Nissim, Kobbi. 2005. Evaluating 2-DNF formulas on ciphertexts. Pages 325–341 of *Theory of Cryptography Conference*. Lecture Notes in Computer Science, vol. 3378. Springer.

Boura, Christina, Gama, Nicolas, Georgieva, Mariya, and Jetchev, Dimitar. 2018. *CHIMERA: Combining Ring-LWE-based Fully Homomorphic Encryption Schemes*. Cryptology ePrint Archive, Report 2018/758. https://eprint.iacr.org/2018/758.

Brakerski, Zvika, and Vaikuntanathan, Vinod. 2011. Fully homomorphic encryption from ring-LWE and security for key dependent messages. Pages 505–524 of *Annual Cryptology Conference*. Lecture Notes in Computer Science, vol. 6841. Springer.

Brakerski, Zvika, Gentry, Craig, and Vaikuntanathan, Vinod. 2014. (Leveled) fully homomorphic encryption without bootstrapping. *ACM Transactions on Computation Theory (TOCT)*, **6**(3), 1–36.

Breiman, Leo. 2001. Random forests. *Machine Learning*, **45**(1), 5–32.

Brisimi, Theodora S., Chen, Ruidi, Mela, Theofanie et al. 2018. Federated learning of predictive models from federated electronic health records. *International Journal of Medical Informatics*, **112**, 59–67.

Capocelli, Renato M., De Santis, Alfredo, Gargano, Luisa, and Vaccaro, Ugo. 1993. On the size of shares for secret sharing schemes. *Journal of Cryptology*, **6**(3), 157–167.

Catrina, Octavian, and De Hoogh, Sebastiaan. 2010. Improved primitives for secure multiparty integer computation. Pages 182–199 of *International Conference on Security and Cryptography for Networks*. Lecture Notes in Computer Science, vol. 6280. Springer.

Catrina, Octavian, and Saxena, Amitabh. 2010. Secure computation with fixed-point numbers. Pages 35–50 of *International Conference on Financial Cryptography and Data Security*. Lecture Notes in Computer Science, vol. 6052. Springer.

Chaudhuri, Kamalika, Monteleoni, Claire, and Sarwate, Anand D. 2011. Differentially private empirical risk minimization. *Journal of Machine Learning Research*, **12**(3), 1069–1109.

Chen, Hao, Dai, Wei, Kim, Miran, and Song, Yongsoo. 2019. Efficient multi-key homomorphic encryption with packed ciphertexts with application to oblivious neural network inference. Pages 395–412 of *Proceedings of the 2019 ACM SIGSAC Conference on Computer and Communications Security*. Association for Computing Machinery.

Chen, Hsinchun, Moore, Reagan, Zeng, Daniel D., and Leavitt, John (eds.). 2004. *Intelligence and Security Informatics*. Studies in Computational Intelligence, vol. 135. Springer.

Chen, Shaoqi, Xue, Dongyu, Chuai, Guohui, Yang, Qiang, and Liu, Qi. 2020. FL-QSAR: a federated learning-based QSAR prototype for collaborative drug discovery. *Bioinformatics*, **36**(22–23), 5492–5498.

Chen, Shaoqi, Xue, Dongyu, Chuai, Guohui, Yang, Qiang, and Liu, Qi. 2021. FL-QSAR: a federated learning-based QSAR prototype for collaborative drug discovery. *Bioinformatics*, **36**(22–23), 5492–5498.

Cheng, Kewei, Fan, Tao, Jin, Yilun et al. 2021a. Secureboost: a lossless federated learning framework. *IEEE Intelligent Systems*, 36(06), 87–98.

Cheng, Xiaodian, Lu, Wanhang, Huang, Xinyang, Hu, Shuihai, and Chen, Kai. 2021b. HAFLO: GPU-Based Acceleration for Federated Logistic Regression. *arXiv:2107.13797*.

Cheon, Jung Hee, Kim, Andrey, Kim, Miran, and Song, Yongsoo. 2017. Homomorphic encryption for arithmetic of approximate numbers. Pages 409–437 of *International Conference on the Theory and Application of Cryptology and Information Security*. Lecture Notes in Computer Science, vol. 10624. Springer.

Chien, Hung-Yu, Jan, Jinn-Ke, and Tseng, Yuh-Min. 2000. A practical (t, n) multi-secret sharing scheme. *IEICE Transactions on Fundamentals of Electronics, Communications and Computer Sciences*, **83**(12), 2762–2765.

Chillotti, Ilaria, Gama, Nicolas, Georgieva, Mariya, and Izabachène, Malika. 2020. TFHE: fast fully homomorphic encryption over the torus. *Journal of Cryptology*, **33**(1), 34–91.

Costan, Victor, and Devadas, Srinivas. 2016. Intel SGX explained. *IACR Cryptology ePrint Archive*, **2016**(86), 1–118.

Crawford, Jack L. H., Gentry, Craig, Halevi, Shai, Platt, Daniel, and Shoup, Victor. 2018. Doing real work with FHE: the case of logistic regression. Pages 1–12 of *Proceedings of the 6th Workshop on Encrypted Computing & Applied Homomorphic Cryptography*. Association for Computing Machinery.

CSAIL, MIT. 2011. *CryptDB*. http://css.csail.mit.edu/cryptdb/.

Damgård, Ivan, Pastro, Valerio, Smart, Nigel, and Zakarias, Sarah. 2012. Multiparty computation from somewhat homomorphic encryption. Pages 643–662 of *Annual Cryptology Conference*. Lecture Notes in Computer Science, vol. 7417. Springer.

Dayan, Ittai, Roth, Holger R., Zhong, Aoxiao et al. 2021. Federated learning for predicting clinical outcomes in patients with COVID-19. *Nature Medicine*, **27**(10), 1735–1743.

De Santis, Alfredo, Desmedt, Yvo, Frankel, Yair, and Yung, Moti. 1994. How to share a function securely. Pages 522–533 of *Proceedings of the Twenty-Sixth Annual ACM Symposium on Theory of Computing*. Association for Computing Machinery.

Demmler, Daniel, Schneider, Thomas, and Zohner, Michael. 2015a. ABY: a framework for efficient mixed-protocol secure two-party computation. Briefing paper presented February 7 at the 2015 Network and Distributed System Security (NDSS) Symposium, in San Diego, CA. www.ndss-symposium.org/ndss2015/ ndss-2015-programme/aby-framework-efficient-mixed-protocol-secure-two-party -computation/.

Deng, Jia, Dong, Wei, Socher, Richard et al. 2009. Imagenet: a large-scale hierarchical image database. Pages 248–255 of *2009 IEEE Conference on Computer Vision and Pattern Recognition*. Institute of Electrical and Electronics Engineers.

Diffie, Whitfield, and Hellman, Martin. 1976. New directions in cryptography. *IEEE Transactions on Information Theory*, **22**(6), 644–654.

Ding, Bolin, Kulkarni, Janardhan, and Yekhanin, Sergey. 2017. Collecting telemetry data privately. Paper presented at the 31st Conference on Neural Information Processing Systems (NIPS 2017), December 4–9, 2017, in Long Beach, CA, USA. *Advances in Neural Information Processing Systems*, **30**. www.microsoft.com/en-us/research/publication/collecting-telemetry-data-privately/.

Du, Wenliang, and Atallah, Mikhail J. 2001. Protocols for secure remote database access with approximate matching. Pages 87–111 of *E-Commerce Security and Privacy*. Advances in Information Security, vol. 2. Springer.

Du, Wenliang, Han, Yunghsiang, Sam Han, and Chen, Shigang. 2004. Privacy-preserving multivariate statistical analysis: linear regression and classification. Pages 222–233 of *Proceedings of the 2004 SIAM International Conference on Data Mining*. Society for Industrial and Applied Mathematics.

Duan, Huayi, Wang, Cong, Yuan, Xingliang et al. 2019. LightBox: full-stack protected stateful middlebox at lightning speed. Pages 2351–2367 of *Proceedings of the 2019 ACM SIGSAC Conference on Computer and Communications Security*. Association for Computing Machinery.

Ducas, Léo, and Micciancio, Daniele. 2015. FHEW: bootstrapping homomorphic encryption in less than a second. Pages 617–640 of *Annual International Conference on the Theory and Applications of Cryptographic Techniques*. Lecture Notes in Computer Science, vol. 9056. Springer.

Dwork, Cynthia. 2008. Differential privacy: a survey of results. Pages 1–19 of *International Conference on Theory and Applications of Models of Computation*. Lecture Notes in Computer Science, vol. 4978. Springer.

Dwork, Cynthia, McSherry, Frank, Nissim, Kobbi, and Smith, Adam. 2006. Calibrating noise to sensitivity in private data analysis. Pages 265–284 of *Theory of Cryptography Conference*. Lecture Notes in Computer Science, vol. 3876. Springer.

Dwork, Cynthia, Rothblum, Guy N., and Vadhan, Salil. 2010. Boosting and differential privacy. Pages 51–60 of *2010 IEEE 51st Annual Symposium on Foundations of Computer Science*. Institute of Electrical and Electronics Engineers.

Dwork, Cynthia, and Roth, Aaron. 2014. The algorithmic foundations of differential privacy. *Foundations and Trends in Theoretical Computer Science*, **9**(3–4), 211–407.

ElGamal, Taher. 1985. A public key cryptosystem and a signature scheme based on discrete logarithms. *IEEE Transactions on Information Theory*, **31**(4), 469–472.

Erlingsson, Úlfar, Pihur, Vasyl, and Korolova, Aleksandra. 2014. Rappor: Randomized Aggregatable Privacy-Preserving Ordinal Response. Pages 1054–1067 of *Proceedings of the 2014 ACM SIGSAC Conference on Computer and Communications Security*. Association for Computing Machinery.

Europe. 2019. *General Data Protection Regulation (GDPR) - Official Legal Text*. https://gdpr-info.eu/.

Evfimievski, Alexandre, Gehrke, Johannes, and Srikant, Ramakrishnan. 2003. Limiting privacy breaches in privacy preserving data mining. Pages 211–222 of *Proceedings of the Twenty-Second ACM SIGMOD-SIGACT-SIGART Symposium on Principles of Database Systems*. Association for Computing Machinery.

Fan, Junfeng, and Vercauteren, Frederik. 2012. Somewhat practical fully homomorphic encryption. *IACR Cryptology ePrint Archive*, **2012**, 144.

Feldman, Paul. 1987. A practical scheme for non-interactive verifiable secret sharing. Pages 427–438 of *28th Annual Symposium on Foundations of Computer Science (sfcs 1987)*. Institute of Electrical and Electronics Engineers.

Fellows, Michael, and Koblitz, Neal. 1994. Combinatorial cryptosystems galore! *Contemporary Mathematics*, **168**, 51–51.

Foundation, The Apache Software. 2020. *Apache Teaclave (Incubating)*. https://teaclave.apache.org/.

Friedman, Jerome H. 2001. Greedy function approximation: a gradient boosting machine. *Annals of Statistics*, **29**, 1189–1232.

Fu, Fangcheng, Shao, Yingxia, Yu, Lele et al. 2021. VF2Boost: very fast vertical federated gradient boosting for cross-enterprise learning. Pages 563–576 of *Proceedings of the 2021 International Conference on Management of Data*. Association for Computing Machinery.

Geiping, Jonas, Bauermeister, Hartmut, Dröge, Hannah, and Moeller, Michael. 2020. Inverting gradients – how easy is it to break privacy in federated learning? *Advances in Neural Information Processing Systems*, **33**, 16937–16947.

Gentry, Craig. 2009. Fully homomorphic encryption using ideal lattices. Pages 169–178 of *Proceedings of the Forty-First Annual ACM Symposium on Theory of Computing*. Association for Computing Machinery.

Gentry, Craig. 2010. Computing arbitrary functions of encrypted data. *Communications of the ACM*, **53**(3), 97–105.

Gentry, Craig, Sahai, Amit, and Waters, Brent. 2013. Homomorphic encryption from learning with errors: conceptually-simpler, asymptotically-faster, attribute-based. Pages 75–92 of *Advances in Cryptology – CRYPTO 2013*. Lecture Notes in Computer Science, vol. 8042. Springer.

Geyer, Robin C., Klein, Tassilo, and Nabi, Moin. 2017. Differentially private federated learning: a client level perspective. *arXiv:1712.07557*.

Gilad-Bachrach, Ran, Dowlin, Nathan, Laine, Kim et al. 2016. Cryptonets: applying neural networks to encrypted data with high throughput and accuracy. Pages 201–210 of *Proceedings of the 33rd International Conference on International Conference on Machine Learning*, vol. 48. Proceedings of Machine Learning Research.

Goldreich, Oded. 1998. Secure multi-party computation. *Manuscript. Preliminary version*, **78**, 110. https://www.wisdom.weizmann.ac.il/~oded/PSX/prot.pdf.

Goldwasser, Shafi, Micali, Silvio, and Tong, Po. 1982. Why and how to establish a private code on a public network. Pages 134–144 of *23rd Annual Symposium on Foundations of Computer Science (sfcs 1982)*. Institute of Electrical and Electronics Engineers.

Google. 2020. *Privacy-Preserving Smart Input with Gboard*. https://developers.google blog.com/2021/01/how-were-helping-developers-with-differential-privacy.html.

Guo, Guo-Ping, and Guo, Guang-Can. 2003. Quantum secret sharing without entanglement. *Physics Letters A*, **310**(4), 247–251.

Hard, Andrew, Rao, Kanishka, Mathews, Rajiv et al. 2018. Federated learning for mobile keyboard prediction. *arXiv:1811.03604*.

Hardt, Moritz, and Rothblum, Guy N. 2010. A multiplicative weights mechanism for privacy-preserving data analysis. Pages 61–70 of *2010 IEEE 51st Annual Symposium on Foundations of Computer Science*. Institute of Electrical and Electronics Engineers.

Hardy, Stephen, Henecka, Wilko, Ivey-Law, Hamish et al. 2017. Private federated learning on vertically partitioned data via entity resolution and additively homomorphic encryption. *arXiv:1711.10677*.

Harn, Lein, and Lin, Hung-Yu. 1992. An l-span generalized secret sharing scheme. Pages 558–565 of *Advances in Cryptology – CRYPTO' 92*. Lecture Notes in Computer Science, vol. 740. Springer.

Hart, John F. 1978. *Computer Approximations*. Krieger Publishing Co., Inc.

He, Kai, Yang, Liu, Hong, Jue et al. 2019. PrivC – a framework for efficient secure two-party computation. Pages 394–407 of *Security and Privacy in Communication Networks*. Lecture Notes of the Institute for Computer Sciences, Social Informatics and Telecommunications Engineering, vol. 305. Springer.

He, Kaiming, Zhang, Xiangyu, Ren, Shaoqing, and Sun, Jian. 2016. Deep residual learning for image recognition. Pages 770–778 of *Proceedings of the IEEE Conference on Computer Vision and Pattern Recognition*. Institute of Electrical and Electronics Engineers.

Hillery, Mark, Bužek, Vladimír, and Berthiaume, André. 1999. Quantum secret sharing. *Physical Review A*, **59**(3), 1829.

Hoffman, Robert R., Mueller, Shane T., Klein, Gary, and Litman, Jordan. 2018. Metrics for explainable AI: challenges and prospects. *arXiv:1812.04608*.

Hong, Junyuan, Zhu, Zhuangdi, Yu, Shuyang et al. 2021. Federated adversarial debiasing for fair and transferable representations. Pages 617–627 of *Proceedings of the 27th ACM SIGKDD Conference on Knowledge Discovery & Data Mining*. Association for Computing Machinery.

Hu, Rui, Guo, Yuanxiong, Li, Hongning, Pei, Qingqi, and Gong, Yanmin. 2020. Personalized federated learning with differential privacy. *IEEE Internet of Things Journal*, **7**(10), 9530–9539.

Hu, Yu Pu, Bai, Guoqiang, and Xiao, Guozhen. 2001. Generalized self-shrinking sequences on GF(q). *Journal of Xidian University*, **28**(1), 5–7.

Huang, Yangsibo, Song, Zhao, Li, Kai, and Arora, Sanjeev. 2020a. Instahide: instance-hiding schemes for private distributed learning. Pages 4507–4518 of *ICML'20: Proceedings of the 37th International Conference on Machine Learning*. Proceedings of Machine Learning Research.

Huang, Yangsibo, Song, Zhao, Chen, Danqi, Li, Kai, and Arora, Sanjeev. 2020b. Texthide: Tackling data privacy in language understanding tasks. *arXiv:2010.06053*.

Ishai, Yuval, and Paskin, Anat. 2007. Evaluating branching programs on encrypted data. Pages 575–594 of *Theory of Cryptography*. TCC 2007. Lecture Notes in Computer Science, vol. 4392. Springer.

Ishai, Yuval, Kilian, Joe, Nissim, Kobbi, and Petrank, Erez. 2003. Extending oblivious transfers efficiently. Pages 145–161 of *Advances in Cryptology – CRYPTO 2003*. Lecture Notes in Computer Science, vol. 2729. Springer.

Ito, M. 1987. Secret sharing scheme realizing general access structure. Pages 99–102 of *Proceedings of IEEE Globecom'87*. Institute of Electrical and Electronics Engineers.

Jain, Prateek, Kothari, Pravesh, and Thakurta, Abhradeep. 2012. Differentially private online learning. Pages 24.1–24.34 of *Conference on Learning Theory*. JMLR Workshop and Conference Proceedings.

Jiang, Di, Tan, Conghui, Peng, Jinhua et al. 2021. A GDPR-compliant ecosystem for speech recognition with transfer, federated, and evolutionary learning. *ACM Transactions on Intelligent Systems and Technology*, **12**(3).

Jie Lu, Wen, Huang, Zhicong, Hong, Cheng, Ma, Yiping, and Qu, Hunter. 2020. *PEGASUS: Bridging Polynomial and Non-polynomial Evaluations in Homomorphic Encryption*. Cryptology ePrint Archive, Report 2020/1606. https://eprint .iacr.org/2020/1606.

Jing, Qinghe, Wang, Weiyan, Zhang, Junxue, Tian, Han, and Chen, Kai. 2019. Quantifying the performance of federated transfer learning. *arXiv:1912.12795*.

Juvekar, Chiraag, Vaikuntanathan, Vinod, and Chandrakasan, Anantha. 2018. GAZELLE: a low latency framework for secure neural network inference. Pages 1651–1669 of *27th USENIX Security Symposium (USENIX Security 18)*. USENIX Association.

Kairouz, Peter, Oh, Sewoong, and Viswanath, Pramod. 2015. The composition theorem for differential privacy. Pages 1376–1385 of *International Conference on Machine Learning*. Proceedings of Machine Learning Research.

Kairouz, Peter, McMahan, H. Brendan, Avent, Brendan et al. 2019. Advances and open problems in federated learning. *arXiv:1912.04977*.

Kang, Yan, Liu, Yang, Wu, Yuezhou, Ma, Guoqiang, and Yang, Qiang. 2021. Privacy-preserving federated adversarial domain adaption over feature groups for interpretability. *arXiv:2111.10934*.

Karnin, Ehud, Greene, Jonathan, and Hellman, Martin. 1983. On secret sharing systems. *IEEE Transactions on Information Theory*, **29**(1), 35–41.

Khandaker, Mustakimur Rahman, Cheng, Yueqiang, Wang, Zhi, and Wei, Tao. 2020. COIN attacks: on insecurity of enclave untrusted interfaces in SGX. Pages 971–985 of *Proceedings of the Twenty-Fifth International Conference on Architectural Support for Programming Languages and Operating Systems*. Association for Computing Machinery.

Kilian, Joe. 1988. Founding Cryptography on Oblivious Transfer. Page 20–31 of *Proceedings of the Twentieth Annual ACM Symposium on Theory of Computing*. Association for Computing Machinery.

Kim, Miran, Song, Yongsoo, Wang, Shuang, Xia, Yuhou, and Jiang, Xiaoqian. 2018. Secure logistic regression based on homomorphic encryption: design and evaluation. *JMIR Medical Informatics*, **6**(2), e19.

Kim, Taehoon, Park, Joongun, Woo, Jaewook, Jeon, Seungheun, and Huh, Jaehyuk. 2019. Shieldstore: shielded in-memory key-value storage with SGX. Pages 1–15 of *Proceedings of the Fourteenth EuroSys Conference 2019*. Association for Computing Machinery.

Kim, Yejin, Sun, Jimeng, Yu, Hwanjo, and Jiang, Xiaoqian. 2017. Federated tensor factorization for computational phenotyping. Pages 887–895 of *Proceedings of the 23rd ACM SIGKDD International Conference on Knowledge Discovery and Data Mining*. Association for Computing Machinery.

Kissner, Lea, and Song, Dawn. 2005. Privacy-preserving set operations. Pages 241–257 of *Advances in Cryptology – CRYPTO 2005*. Lecture Notes in Computer Science, vol. 3621. Springer.

Kolesnikov, Vladimir, and Schneider, Thomas. 2008. Improved garbled circuit: free XOR gates and applications. Page 486–498 of *Automata, Languages and Programming*. Lecture Notes in Computer Science, vol. 5126. Springer.

Krizhevsky, Alex, Sutskever, Ilya, and Hinton, Geoffrey E. 2012. Imagenet classification with deep convolutional neural networks. *Advances in Neural Information Processing Systems*, **25**, 1097–1105.

Kunkel, Roland, Quoc, Do Le, Gregor, Franz et al. 2019. Tensorscone: a secure tensorflow framework using Intel SGX. *arXiv:1902.04413*.

Laih, Chi-Sung, Harn, Lein, Lee, Jau-Yien, and Hwang, Tzonelih. 1989. Dynamic threshold scheme based on the definition of cross-product in an n-dimensional linear space. Pages 286–298 of *Advances in Cryptology – CRYPTO' 89 Proceedings*. Lecture Notes in Computer Science, vol. 435. Springer.

Lalitha, Anusha, Kilinc, Osman Cihan, Javidi, Tara, and Koushanfar, Farinaz. 2019. Peer-to-peer federated learning on graphs. *arXiv:1901.11173*.

Lee, Dayeol, Kohlbrenner, David, Shinde, Shweta, Asanović, Krste, and Song, Dawn. 2020. Keystone: an open framework for architecting trusted execution environments. Pages 1–16 of *Proceedings of the Fifteenth European Conference on Computer Systems*. Association for Computing Machinery.

Lee, Jaehyuk, Jang, Jinsoo, Jang, Yeongjin, Kwak et al. 2017. Hacking in darkness: return-oriented programming against secure enclaves. Pages 523–539 of *26th USENIX Security Symposium (USENIX Security 17)*. USENIX Association.

Lee, Junghye, Sun, Jimeng, Wang, Fei et al. 2018. Privacy-preserving patient similarity learning in a federated environment: development and analysis. *JMIR Medical Informatics*, **6**(2), e7744.

Lee, Taegyeong, Lin, Zhiqi, Pushp, Saumay et al. 2019. Occlumency: privacy-preserving remote deep-learning inference using SGX. Pages 1–17 of *The 25th Annual International Conference on Mobile Computing and Networking*. Association for Computing Machinery.

Li, Baiyu, and Micciancio, Daniele. 2020. On the security of homomorphic encryption on approximate numbers. *IACR Cryptology ePrint Archive*. **2020**, 1533.

Li, Hao, Xu, Zheng, Taylor, Gavin, Studer, Christoph, and Goldstein, Tom. 2018a. Visualizing the loss landscape of neural nets. *Advances in Neural Information Processing Systems*, **31**.

Li, Wenqi, Milletarì, Fausto, Xu, Daguang et al. 2019. Privacy-preserving federated brain tumour segmentation. Pages 133–141 of *International Workshop on Machine Learning in Medical Imaging*. Lecture Notes in Computer Science, vol. 11861. Springer.

Li, Yi, Duan, Yitao, Yu, Yu, Zhao, Shuoyao, and Xu, Wei. 2018b. PrivPy: enabling scalable and general privacy-preserving machine learning. *arXiv:1801.10117*.

Liang, Gang, and Chawathe, Sudarshan S. 2004. Privacy-preserving inter-database operations. Pages 66–82 of *Intelligence and Security Informatics*. Lecture Notes in Computer Science, vol. 3073. Springer. doi: https://doi.org/10.1007/978-3-540-25952-7_6

Liang, Shiyu, Sun, Ruoyu, Li, Yixuan, and Srikant, Rayadurgam. 2018. Understanding the loss surface of neural networks for binary classification. Pages 2835–2843 of *Proceedings of the 35th International Conference on Machine Learning*. Proceedings of Machine Learning Research.

Liu, Chang, Wang, Xiao Shaun, Nayak, Kartik, Huang, Yan, and Shi, Elaine. 2015. ObliVM: a programming framework for secure computation. Pages 359–376 of *2015 IEEE Symposium on Security and Privacy*. Institute of Electrical and Electronics Engineers.

Liu, Yang, Kang, Yan, Xing, Chaoping, Chen, Tianjian, and Yang, Qiang. 2020. A secure federated transfer learning framework. *IEEE Intelligent Systems*, **35**(4), 70–82.

Loh, Wei-Yin. 2011. Classification and regression trees. *Wiley Interdisciplinary Reviews: Data Mining and Knowledge Discovery*, **1**(1), 14–23.

López-Alt, Adriana, Tromer, Eran, and Vaikuntanathan, Vinod. 2012. On-the-fly multiparty computation on the cloud via multikey fully homomorphic encryption. Pages 1219–1234 of *Proceedings of the Forty-Fourth Annual ACM Symposium on Theory of Computing*. Association for Computing Machinery.

Lyubashevsky, Vadim, Peikert, Chris, and Regev, Oded. 2010. On ideal lattices and learning with errors over rings. Pages 1–23 of *Annual International Conference on the Theory and Applications of Cryptographic Techniques*. Lecture Notes in Computer Science, vol. 6110. Springer.

Mahajan, Dhruv, Girshick, Ross, Ramanathan, Vignesh et al. 2018. Exploring the limits of weakly supervised pretraining. Pages 181–196 of *Proceedings of the European Conference on Computer Vision (ECCV)*. Association for Computing Machinery.

Martins, Paulo, Sousa, Leonel, and Mariano, Artur. 2017. A survey on fully homomorphic encryption: an engineering perspective. *ACM Computing Surveys*, **50**(6).

McMahan, Brendan, Moore, Eider, Ramage, Daniel, Hampson, Seth, and y Arcas, Blaise Aguera. 2017a. Communication-efficient learning of deep networks from decentralized data. Pages 1273–1282 of *Artificial Intelligence and Statistics*. Proceedings of Machine Learning Research.

McMahan, H. Brendan, Ramage, Daniel, Talwar, Kunal, and Zhang, Li. 2017b. Learning differentially private recurrent language models. *arXiv:1710.06963*.

McSherry, Frank 2009. Privacy integrated queries: an extensible platform for privacy-preserving data analysis. Pages 19–30 of *Proceedings of the 2009 ACM SIGMOD International Conference on Management of Data*. Association for Computing Machinery.

McSherry, Frank, and Talwar, Kunal. 2007. Mechanism design via differential privacy. Pages 94–103 of *48th Annual IEEE Symposium on Foundations of Computer Science (FOCS'07)*. Institute of Electrical and Electronics Engineers.

Microsoft. 2016. *Microsoft Always Encrypted*. www.microsoft.com/en-us/research/project/always-encrypted/.

Milutinovic, Mitar, He, Warren, Wu, Howard, and Kanwal, Maxinder. 2016. Proof of luck: an efficient blockchain consensus protocol. Pages 1–6 of *Proceedings of the 1st Workshop on System Software for Trusted Execution*. Association for Computing Machinery.

Mironov, Ilya. 2017. Rényi differential privacy. Pages 263–275 of *2017 IEEE 30th Computer Security Foundations Symposium (CSF)*. Institute of Electrical and Electronics Engineers.

Mohassel, Payman, and Rindal, Peter. 2018. ABY3: a mixed protocol framework for machine learning. Pages 35–52 of *Proceedings of the 2018 ACM SIGSAC Conference on Computer and Communications Security*. Association for Computing Machinery.

Mohassel, Payman, and Zhang, Yupeng. 2017. Secureml: a system for scalable privacy-preserving machine learning. Pages 19–38 of *2017 IEEE Symposium on Security and Privacy (SP)*. Institute of Electrical and Electronics Engineers.

Nandakumar, Karthik, Ratha, Nalini, Pankanti, Sharath, and Halevi, Shai. 2019. Towards deep neural network training on encrypted data. Pages 40–48 of *Proceedings of the IEEE/CVF Conference on Computer Vision and Pattern Recognition Workshops*. Institute of Electrical and Electronics Engineers.

Naor, Moni, and Pinkas, Benny. 1997. Visual authentication and identification. Pages 322–336 of *Annual International Cryptology Conference*. Lecture Notes in Computer Science, vol. 1294. Springer.

Naor, Moni, and Pinkas, Benny. 2001. Efficient oblivious transfer protocols. Pages 448–457 of *Proceedings of the Twelfth Annual ACM-SIAM Symposium on Discrete Algorithms*. Society for Industrial and Applied Mathematics.

Naor, Moni, and Shamir, Adi. 1994. Visual cryptography. Pages 1–12 of *Workshop on the Theory and Application of of Cryptographic Techniques*. Lecture Notes in Computer Science, vol. 950. Springer.

Nikolaenko, Valeria, Weinsberg, Udi, Ioannidis, Stratis, Joye, Marc, Boneh, Dan, and Taft, Nina. 2013. Privacy-preserving ridge regression on hundreds of millions of records. Pages 334–348 of *2013 IEEE Symposium on Security and Privacy*. Institute of Electrical and Electronics Engineers.

Ohrimenko, Olga, Schuster, Felix, Fournet, Cédric et al. 2016. Oblivious multi-party machine learning on trusted processors. Pages 619–636 of *25th USENIX Security Symposium (USENIX Security 16)*. USENIX Association.

Paillier, Pascal. 1999. Public-key cryptosystems based on composite degree residuosity classes. Pages 223–238 of *International Conference on the Theory and Applications of Cryptographic Techniques*. Lecture Notes in Computer Science, vol. 1592. Springer.

Pan, Sinno Jialin, and Yang, Qiang. 2009. A survey on transfer learning. *IEEE Transactions on Knowledge and Data Engineering*, **22**(10), 1345–1359.

Pang, Liao-Jun, and Wang, Yu-Min. 2005. A new (t, n) multi-secret sharing scheme based on Shamir's secret sharing. *Applied Mathematics and Computation*, **167**(2), 840–848.

Papernot, Nicolas, Abadi, Martín, Erlingsson, Ulfar, Goodfellow, Ian, and Talwar, Kunal. 2016. Semi-supervised knowledge transfer for deep learning from private training data. *arXiv:1610.05755*.

Peng, Xingchao, Huang, Zijun, Zhu, Yizhe, and Saenko, Kate. 2019. Federated adversarial domain adaptation. *arXiv:1911.02054*.

Pinto, Sandro, and Santos, Nuno. 2019. Demystifying Arm TrustZone: a comprehensive survey. *ACM Computing Surveys*, **51**(6).

Poddar, Rishabh, Lan, Chang, Popa, Raluca Ada, and Ratnasamy, Sylvia. 2018. Safebricks: shielding network functions in the cloud. Pages 201–216 of *15th USENIX Symposium on Networked Systems Design and Implementation (NSDI 18)*. Association for Computing Machinery.

Popa, Raluca Ada, Redfield, Catherine M. S., Zeldovich, Nickolai, and Balakrishnan, Hari. 2011. CryptDB: protecting confidentiality with encrypted query processing. Pages 85–100 of *Proceedings of the Twenty-Third ACM Symposium on Operating Systems Principles*. Association for Computing Machinery.

Priebe, Christian, Vaswani, Kapil, and Costa, Manuel. 2018. EnclaveDB: a secure database using SGX. Pages 264–278 of *2018 IEEE Symposium on Security and Privacy (SP)*. Institute of Electrical and Electronics Engineers.

Rabin, Michael O. 2005. *How to Exchange Secrets with Oblivious Transfer*. Cryptology ePrint Archive, Paper 2005/187. https://eprint.iacr.org/2005/187.

Ramaswamy, Swaroop, Mathews, Rajiv, Rao, Kanishka, and Beaufays, Françoise. 2019. Federated learning for emoji prediction in a mobile keyboard. *arXiv:1906.04329*.

Regev, Oded. 2009. On lattices, learning with errors, random linear codes, and cryptography. *Journal of the ACM (JACM)*, **56**(6), 1–40.

Rieke, Nicola, Hancox, Jonny, Li, Wenqi et al. 2020. The future of digital health with federated learning. *NPJ Digital Medicine*, **3**(1), 1–7.

Rivest, Ronald L, Shamir, Adi, and Adleman, Leonard. 1978a. A method for obtaining digital signatures and public-key cryptosystems. *Communications of the ACM*, **21**(2), 120–126.

Rivest, Ronald L., Adleman, Len, Dertouzos, Michael L. et al. 1978b. On data banks and privacy homomorphisms. *Foundations of Secure Computation*, **4**(11), 169–180.

Rong, Hui-Gui, Mo, Jin-Xia, Chang, Bing-Guo, Sun, Guang, and Long, Fei. 2015. Key distribution and recovery algorithm based on Shamir's secret sharing. *Journal on Communications*, **36**(3), 60–69.

Roy, Abhijit Guha, Siddiqui, Shayan, Pölsterl, Sebastian, Navab, Nassir, and Wachinger, Christian. 2019. Braintorrent: a peer-to-peer environment for decentralized federated learning. *arXiv:1905.06731*.

Sander, Tomas, Young, Adam, and Yung, Moti. 1999. Non-interactive cryptocomputing for NC/sup 1. Pages 554–566 of *40th Annual Symposium on Foundations of Computer Science (Cat. No. 99CB37039)*. Institute of Electrical and Electronics Engineers.

Scannapieco, Monica, Figotin, Ilya, Bertino, Elisa, and Elmagarmid, Ahmed K. 2007. Privacy preserving schema and data matching. Pages 653–664 of *Proceedings of the 2007 ACM SIGMOD International Conference on Management of Data*. Association for Computing Machinery.

Schwarz, Fabian, and Rossow, Christian. 2020. SENG, the SGX-Enforcing Network Gateway: authorizing communication from shielded clients. Pages 753–770 of *29th USENIX Security Symposium (USENIX Security 20)*. USENIX Association.

Shamir, Adi. 1979. How to share a secret. *Communications of the ACM*, **22**(11), 612–613.

Sheller, Micah J., Reina, G. Anthony, Edwards, Brandon, Martin, Jason, and Bakas, Spyridon. 2018. Multi-institutional deep learning modeling without sharing patient data: a feasibility study on brain tumor segmentation. Pages 92–104 of *International MICCAI Brainlesion Workshop*. Lecture Notes in Computer Science, vol. 11383. Springer.

Singh, Simon. 1999. *The Code Book: The Evolution of Secrecy from Mary, Queen of Scots, to Quantum Cryptography*. 1st ed. Doubleday.

Smart, Nigel P., and Vercauteren, Frederik. 2010. Fully homomorphic encryption with relatively small key and ciphertext sizes. Pages 420–443 of *International Workshop on Public Key Cryptography*. Lecture Notes in Computer Science, vol. 6056. Springer.

Song, Dawn Xiaoding, Wagner, David, and Perrig, Adrian. 2000. Practical techniques for searches on encrypted data. Pages 44–55 of *Proceedings of 2000 IEEE Symposium on Security and Privacy. S&P 2000*. Institute of Electrical and Electronics Engineers.

Su, Dong, Cao, Jianneng, Li, Ninghui, Bertino, Elisa, and Jin, Hongxia. 2016. Differentially private k-means clustering. Pages 26–37 of *Proceedings of the Sixth ACM Conference on Data and Application Security and Privacy*. Association for Computing Machinery.

Tang, Adrian, Sethumadhavan, Simha, and Stolfo, Salvatore. 2017. CLKSCREW: exposing the perils of security-oblivious energy management. Pages 1057–1074 of *26th USENIX Security Symposium (USENIX Security 17)*. USENIX Association.

Truex, Stacey, Baracaldo, Nathalie, Anwar, Ali et al. 2019. A hybrid approach to privacy-preserving federated learning. Pages 1–11 of *Proceedings of the 12th ACM Workshop on Artificial Intelligence and Security*. Association for Computing Machinery.

Van Bulck, Jo, Minkin, Marina, Weisse, Ofir et al. 2018. Foreshadow: extracting the keys to the Intel SGX kingdom with transient out-of-order execution. Pages 991–1008 of *27th USENIX Security Symposium (USENIX Security 18)*. USENIX Association.

Van Bulck, Jo, Oswald, David, Marin, Eduard et al. 2019. A tale of two worlds: assessing the vulnerability of enclave shielding runtimes. Pages 1741–1758 of *Proceedings of the 2019 ACM SIGSAC Conference on Computer and Communications Security*. Association for Computing Machinery.

Van Dijk, Marten, Gentry, Craig, Halevi, Shai, and Vaikuntanathan, Vinod. 2010. Fully homomorphic encryption over the integers. Pages 24–43 of *Annual International Conference on the Theory and Applications of Cryptographic Techniques*. Lecture Notes in Computer Science, vol. 6110. Springer.

Volgushev, Nikolaj, Schwarzkopf, Malte, Getchell, Ben et al. 2019. Conclave: secure multi-party computation on big data. Pages 1–18 of *Proceedings of the Fourteenth EuroSys Conference 2019*. Association for Computing Machinery.

Wang, Huibo, Sun, Mingshen, Feng, Qian et al. 2020. Towards memory safe Python enclave for security sensitive computation. *arXiv:2005.05996*.

Wang, Huibo, Wang, Pei, Ding, Yu et al. 2019. Towards memory safe enclave programming with Rust-SGX. Pages 2333–2350 of *Proceedings of the 2019 ACM SIGSAC Conference on Computer and Communications Security*. Association for Computing Machinery.

Wang, Shuang, Zhang, Yuchen, Dai, Wenrui et al. 2016. HEALER: Homomorphic computation of ExAct Logistic rEgRession for secure rare disease variants analysis in GWAS. *Bioinformatics*, **32**(2), 211–218.

Wang, Xiao, Ranellucci, Samuel, and Katz, Jonathan. 2017. *Global-Scale Secure Multiparty Computation*. Cryptology ePrint Archive, Report 2017/189. https://eprint.iacr.org/2017/189.

Warnat-Herresthal, Stefanie, Schultze, Hartmut, Shastry, Krishnaprasad Lingadahalli, Manamohan, Sathyanarayanan et al. 2021. Swarm Learning for decentralized and confidential clinical machine learning. *Nature*, **594**(7862), 265–270.

Warner, Stanley L. 1965. Randomized response: a survey technique for eliminating evasive answer bias. *Journal of the American Statistical Association*, **60**(309), 63–69.

WeBank. 2019. *Federated AI Ecosystem*. www.fedai.org/.

WeBank. 2021 (Dec). *WeBank Fintech*. https://webank.com/en/.

Wei, Kang, Li, Jun, Ding, Ming et al. 2020. Federated learning with differential privacy: algorithms and performance analysis. *IEEE Transactions on Information Forensics and Security*, **15**, 3454–3469. Institute of Electrical and Electronics Engineers.

Wu, Yuncheng, Cai, Shaofeng, Xiao, Xiaokui, Chen, Gang, and Ooi, Beng Chin. 2020. Privacy preserving vertical federated learning for tree-based models. *Proceedings of the VLDB Endowment*, **13**(11), 2090–2103.

Xia, Zhe, Schneider, Steve A., Heather, James, and Traoré, Jacques. 2008. Analysis, improvement, and simplification of prêt à voter with Paillier encryption. Pages 1–15 of *EVT'08 Proceedings of the Conference on Electronic Voting Technology*. Association for Computing Machinery.

XinhuaNet. 2021. *Data Security Law of the People's Republic of China*. www.xinhua net.com/2021-06/11/c_1127552204.htm.

Xu, Chun-Xiang, and Xiao, Guo-Zhen. 2004. A threshold multiple secret sharing scheme. *Acta Electronica Sinica*, **32**(10), 1688.

Xu, Depeng, Yuan, Shuhan, Wu, Xintao, and Phan, HaiNhat. 2018. DPNE: Differentially Private Network Embedding. Pages 235–246 of *Pacific-Asia Conference on Knowledge Discovery and Data Mining*. Lecture Notes in Computer Science, vol. 10938. Springer.

Xu, Runhua, Baracaldo, Nathalie, Zhou, Yi, Anwar, Ali, and Ludwig, Heiko. 2019. Hybridalpha: an efficient approach for privacy-preserving federated learning. Pages 13–23 of *Proceedings of the 12th ACM Workshop on Artificial Intelligence and Security*. Association for Computing Machinery.

Yang, Chou-Chen, Chang, Ting-Yi, and Hwang, Min-Shiang. 2004. A (t, n) multi-secret sharing scheme. *Applied Mathematics and Computation*, **151**(2), 483–490.

Yang, Qiang, Liu, Yang, Cheng, Yong et al. 2019a. Federated learning. *Synthesis Lectures on Artificial Intelligence and Machine Learning*, **13**(3), 1–207.

Yang, Qiang, Liu, Yang, Cheng, Yong et al. 2019b. Federated learning. *Synthesis Lectures on Artificial Intelligence and Machine Learning*, **13**(3), 1–207.

Yang, Qiang, Liu, Yang, Chen, Tianjian, and Tong, Yongxin. 2019c. Federated machine learning: concept and applications. *ACM Transactions on Intelligent Systems and Technology*, **10**(2), 1–19. _eprint: 1902.04885.

Yang, Qiang, Liu, Yang, Chen, Tianjian, and Tong, Yongxin. 2019d. Federated machine learning: concept and applications. *ACM Transactions on Intelligent Systems and Technology (TIST)*, **10**(2), 1–19.

Yang, Qiang, Zhang, Yu, Dai, Wenyuan, and Pan, Sinno Jialin. 2020a. *Transfer Learning*. Cambridge University Press.

Yang, Timothy, Andrew, Galen, Eichner, Hubert et al. 2018. Applied federated learning: improving Google keyboard query suggestions. *arXiv:1812.02903*.

Yang, Wensi, Zhang, Yuhang, Ye, Kejiang, Li, Li, and Xu, Cheng-Zhong. 2019e. FFD: a federated learning based method for credit card fraud detection. Pages 18–32 of *International Conference on Big Data*. Lecture Notes in Computer Science, vol. 11514. Springer.

Yang, Zhaoxiong, Hu, Shuihai, and Chen, Kai. 2020b. FPGA-based hardware accelerator of homomorphic encryption for efficient federated learning. *arXiv:2007 .10560*.

Yao, Andrew C. 1982. Protocols for secure computations. Pages 160–164 of *23rd Annual Symposium on Foundations of Computer Science (sfcs 1982)*. Institute of Electrical and Electronics Engineers.

Yao, Andrew Chi-Chih. 1986. How to generate and exchange secrets. Pages 162–167 of *27th Annual Symposium on Foundations of Computer Science (sfcs 1986)*. Institute of Electrical and Electronics Engineers.

Yu, Dan, and Li, Z. X. 2014. An overview of the development of secret sharing. *Natural Sciences Journal of Harbin Normal University*, **30**(1).

Zaharia, Matei, Chowdhury, Mosharaf, Das, Tathagata et al. 2012. Resilient distributed datasets: a fault-tolerant abstraction for in-memory cluster computing. Pages 15–28 of *9th USENIX Symposium on Networked Systems Design and Implementation (NSDI '12)*. Usenix Association.

Zahur, Samee, and Evans, David. 2015. Obliv-C: a language for extensible data-oblivious computation. *IACR Cryptology ePrint Archive*, **2015**, 1153.

Zhang, Cengguang, Zhang, Junxue, Chai, Di, and Chen, Kai. 2021. Aegis: a trusted, automatic and accurate verification framework for vertical federated learning. *arXiv:2108.06958*.

Zhang, Chengliang, Li, Suyi, Xia, Junzhe et al. 2020. Batchcrypt: efficient homomorphic encryption for cross-silo federated learning. Pages 493–506 of *2020 Usenix Annual Technical Conference (Usenix ATC 20)*. USENIX Association.

Zhao, Bo, Mopuri, Konda Reddy, and Bilen, Hakan. 2020. iDLG: improved deep leakage from gradients. *arXiv:2001.02610*.

Zheng, Wenbo, Yan, Lan, Gou, Chao, and Wang, Fei-Yue. 2020. Federated meta-learning for fraudulent credit card detection. Pages 4654–4660 of: *Proceedings of the Twenty-Ninth International Joint Conference on Artificial Intelligence Special Track on AI in FinTech*. International Joint Conferences on Artificial Intelligence.

Zhu, Ligeng, Liu, Zhijian, and Han, Song. 2019. Deep leakage from gradients. Pages 14774–14784 *of NIPS'19: Proceedings of the 33rd International Conference on Neural Information Processing Systems*. Association for Computing Machinery.

Index

Printed in the United States
by Baker & Taylor Publisher Services

Printed in the United States
by Baker & Taylor Publisher Services